GANGS IN GARDEN CITY

Gangs in Garden City

*How Immigration, Segregation, and Youth Violence
Are Changing America's Suburbs*

SARAH GARLAND

NATION
BOOKS

New York

Published by Nation Books, A Member of the Perseus Books Group
116 East 16th Street, 8th Floor
New York, NY 10003
Nation Books is a co-publishing venture of the Nation Institute and the
Perseus Books Group.

Books published by Nation Books are available at special discounts for
bulk purchases in the United States by corporations, institutions, and
other organizations. For more information, please contact the Special
Markets Department at the Perseus Books Group, 2300 Chestnut Street,
Suite 200, Philadelphia, PA 19103, or call (800) 255-1514, or e-mail
special.markets@perseusbooks.com.

Designed by Timm Bryson

Library of Congress Cataloging-in-Publication Data
Garland, Sarah, 1978–
  Gangs in Garden City : how immigration, segregation, and youth
violence are changing America's suburbs / by Sarah Garland.
      p. cm.
  Includes bibliographical references and index.
  ISBN 978-1-56858-404-1 (alk. paper)
  1. MS-13 (Gang) 2. Gangs—Central America. 3. Hispanic American
gangs—New York (State)—Garden City. 4. Gang members—New York
(State)—Garden City. 5. Central Americans—New York (State)—Garden
City. 6. Youth and violence—New York (State)—Garden City. I. Title.
  HV6439.U7G374 2009
  364.106'6089687280747245—dc22
                                    2009014094
10 9 8 7 6 5 4 3 2 1

To my grandmother, Dorsie Richmond

CONTENTS

Jessica, 1988–2001

Jaime and Daniel, 2000–2003

Julio, 2000–2005

Jessica, 2003–2007

Daniel, 2004–2008

PREFACE

The first time I visited Hempstead High School was in February 2004. As I walked through the halls to the principal's office, the scene was chaotic. Students screeched and jostled, while teachers and beefy security guards the size of nightclub bouncers yelled above the din. But the principal's office was an oasis of calm. Hempstead had been going through principals at a rate of about two a year, but the latest, Reginald Stroughn, who shared the same physique and tough glare of the security guards outside, had lasted longer than most. I found him behind a large desk in a room lined with bookshelves and carpet that muffled the noise outside. Slightly unnerved by his stern gaze, I explained why I had come.

The village of Hempstead, a Long Island suburb located at the heart of one of the richest counties in the nation, had been roiled by a series of gang murders, including the stabbing death of a fourteen-year-old boy on the steps of the Long Island Railroad station a year earlier. The town was surrounded by dormitory communities that housed the city's finance workers and its police and firefighters, making the fact that the murders were linked to a Central American gang with a growing reputation as the most ruthless on the continent all the more jarring. I wanted to find out how a war between the Mara Salvatrucha gang and its rival, 18th Street, which had originated in Los Angeles after the Salvadoran civil war, had spread to a suburban town nearly 3,000 miles away. The age of the victims had led me directly to the school.

Mr. Stroughn questioned me further about my credentials—I was a New York University graduate student at the time—and then agreed to let me meet with some of his students. I made my way to a freshman English as a Second Language class on the first floor and introduced myself to the teacher. The class was held in the art room, and student art in bold colors covered the paint-splattered surfaces. The classroom quickly quieted down as the teacher, a warm woman in her forties, began the lesson. Several boys walked in late, swaggering in low-slung jeans and slapping the hands of other students before slumping into seats in the back of the room. The teacher, ignoring them, explained that I wanted to interview the students individually about their experiences in Long Island. After I had spoken with a couple of other students, Daniel, one of the boys who walked in late, came and sat down.

The swaggering attitude quickly disappeared once we began talking. At first he was a little shy, but within a half hour he had opened up. He told me about his trip to New York from El Salvador, alone with a smuggler, and said he had been fighting with his mother since he had arrived three years before. Then he told me about joining the gang Salvadorans With Pride, which was loosely affiliated with the 18th Street gang. Most of its members were second-generation Central Americans, and he was proud that they had accepted him despite the fact that he was an immigrant and spoke little English. But the decision also haunted him. His first friend in New York, Jaime, had also joined a gang at around the same time, SWP's archrival, Mara Salvatrucha. Daniel's life had not been the same since.

After that initial conversation I returned to the school on a weekly basis until the end of the school year. On each occasion, Daniel spoke freely about his experiences in the gang. It struck me that he had probably had few conversations with adults about his traumatic life in Hempstead, that simply talking went some way toward alleviating the anxiety he kept pent up inside. He often talked about leaving his gang. By the time we said good-bye that spring, he told me that he had decided to leave the gang life behind, and I believed him. Two years later, as I began the research for this book, I tracked him down again through one of his friends. He had dropped out of school and told me again that he was planning on leaving the gang, but he was still having trouble breaking free.

Since my first meeting with Daniel at Hempstead High School, I had traveled to Central America to interview young gang members in prisons and had also met two other young people struggling with their gang pasts in Hempstead. Jessica was a member of Daniel's gang, but she was two years older. Like most of the members of Salvadorans With Pride, she was American-born. I met her when she was in a program started by a former gang member, Sergio Argueta, called Struggling To Reunite Our New Generation, or STRONG. She was trying to get out of the gang, too.

Sergio introduced us and left us in a room on the upper story of the ramshackle two-story house downtown that served as the STRONG headquarters. Jessica was calm and detached as I asked her to fill in the details of her life: the violence she had witnessed as a child, the sexual abuse, the drugs, the beatings she endured from her gang, the terror when she tried to leave the gang behind. As she told her stories, she often added analysis of her own past behavior and sometimes repeated mantras about the stupidity of gang life and how violence wasn't the answer, as if she were trying to shore up her resolve. Her teenage years had been so drug-addled that we often had to spend time going over the same stories over and over as she struggled to remember the order of events. It would slowly come back to her, and then we would move on.

I had met Julio in the Nassau County Jail several months earlier. His friends from a day-laborer advocacy group, the Workplace Project, and a documentary filmmaker, Daniel Flores y Ascencio, had told me about his deportation case. During our first meeting Julio fidgeted across a table in the jail's visiting room in his orange jumpsuit, his hair slicked back. He sketched a brief story of his journey to Long Island ten years before, mentioned his military service in the Salvadoran army during the civil war, and then talked excitedly about his passion: helping young Hempstead gang members pick up their lives and leave violence behind. I saw him again in an immigration court hearing in New Jersey, and then in San Salvador several years after he was deported. He was thrilled to have a visitor from the United States and showed me the sights of his childhood: the military base near his mother's house and the school where rebels took nine hundred children hostage, the neighborhood down the street from his home controlled by Mara Salvatrucha, the dumping grounds where bodies were thrown during the civil war.

Together, the stories of Daniel, Jessica, and Julio helped me to reconstruct how a pair of gangs reputed to be the most ruthless in the world made their way to the Long Island suburbs. This book is the result of hours of interviews with these three people and with many others who agreed to tell their stories and share their perspectives. They include the principal of Hempstead High School, Reginald Stroughn; the assistant principal, Henry Williams; Detective Richard Smith; Sergio Argueta; the former Hempstead police chief, James Russo; the current chief, Joseph Wing; the chief of the Freeport police, Michael Woodward; Pamela Corrente; Rosa Alvarenga; Clementina and Oscar Alguera; Julio's mother; Amory Sepulveda; Carlos Canales and Nadia Marin-Molina of Workplace Project; Bob Lepley; Edgar Ramirez, Silvia Beltran, and Alex Sanchez of Homies Unidos; and Jose Lino.

● ● ●

The names of Jessica, Daniel, and their families and friends have been changed to protect their safety. All other people who appear in the book are identified with their real names. The stories of the people depicted in the book are based on interviews with the subjects. Jaime Alvarenga's story was compiled primarily through interviews with Daniel and with his mother, Rosa. The information they provided about their lives was cross-checked whenever possible and supplemented with interviews of other people who took part in the events and with documents, including court records, police reports, and news articles.

Michael, 2008

CHAPTER 1

Michael

● ● ●

It was just after 3 PM on January 18, 2008, when Oscar Alguera stopped the family car in front of a honking snare of traffic blocking their cul-de-sac. Commuters jostled to outmaneuver the other cars clogging the road, their hostility toward the other drivers increasing the closer they got to home. Oscar, usually cautious and polite, nosed his car aggressively into the line of cars. He tried to calm down as they inched along, but the wailing of sirens a few blocks ahead seemed to echo the screaming in his head. Even the police cars were stuck. His wife, Clementina, frantically dialed her cell phone. She should have gone to pick up the boys as she always did, she muttered. Just this once, she had said okay, they could stay late at school. Play handball—why not? Snow had been forecast, but it was still mild outside. The boys had promised to be home before dark.

Oscar had been out in the shed arranging his tools and cleaning up the construction debris lying around the backyard when their son called. Oscar had just arrived home, and it had been a long day. He would probably have another long day tomorrow at work—a good thing, since construction jobs were hard to come by in the winter. Tired and covered with grime, he had been startled when Tina ran out from the kitchen with the phone in her hand. Oscar Jr., their middle child, had just called to say that Michael had been beaten up.

You go, he told her. He'll be fine. Boys always fight—hadn't the older boys gone through this at school? Michael was the youngest. He was pampered and protected by his two older brothers, but maybe it was time for him to stand up for himself. He was fifteen now, a high school freshman and about as tall as Oscar. He could fend for himself. It was part of growing up.

Oscar Jr. called back. He was crying and panicked. Michael had been stabbed. The men who did it ran away. They were on the handball court, waiting, and Michael was bleeding. Oscar dropped his tools and ran, following Tina to the car.

Unlike his strapping sons, Oscar was slight and wiry, with the leathery skin of a man who spent most of his days outdoors. His work clothes were dingy jeans and sleeveless T-shirts. On the weekends he donned his Mets jersey for family outings to the beach or the movies. He insisted that part of every weekend be set aside for family time, even as the boys got older. Steve, nineteen, was the eldest of the three boys: quiet, serious, and most like their mother. Oscar, seventeen, the middle child, was the gregarious troublemaker. Michael, fifteen, gentle and earnest, was most like his father. Oscar thought he looked like his youngest, too. He was proud of the resemblance, but he didn't want his boys to turn out like him. He wanted them to get jobs with decent hours and decent pay. He didn't want them coming home from work covered in filth and dust, with their backs aching and their hands calloused.

Oscar had grown up in a slum of San Jose, Costa Rica, and watched enviously as his older siblings left home one by one to move to the United States. His sister, Yadira, had wired money to the family in Costa Rica from jobs in Los Angeles, Miami, and finally Hempstead, a suburban town in Long Island, where she decided to stay. The money she sent home was enough to convince Oscar that Hempstead was the place for him, too. He left San Jose as soon as he turned eighteen in 1985 and headed directly to Yadira's doorstep in a quiet brick apartment complex at the end of a cul-de-sac called Villa Court, next door to an elementary school. Yadira found him a place to sleep in the crowded apartment and helped him find a part-time job in construction. She offered to help pay while he took classes to finish his education, but as soon as he received his first paycheck, Oscar decided he wasn't interested in school. He had never seen so much money. Why go to school when you could make more than $100 in your first week in the country?

He met Tina through Yadira. Tina was from Calí, Colombia, and came to the suburbs to work as a babysitter for a cousin. She arrived in the same year as Oscar and in the same way, crossing over the border by foot. Tina's cousin eventually returned to Colombia, but Tina didn't want to go back. There was little work there, and she loved the suburbs. The opportunities in Long Island seemed endless. Home was drudgery, poverty, and war. She found a job at a cosmetics factory and moved into a room in the apartment with Oscar and his sister. Not too long after, Oscar and Tina moved into their own apartment in Villa Court.

The boys came soon after. Both Oscar Jr. and Michael were diagnosed with severe asthma shortly after birth, and Tina quit her job to care for them. She drove the boys to school, picked them up every day, and oversaw their homework. Oscar set the rules: study first, no video games on school nights, and television only allowed after schoolwork is done. No staying out late or hanging out on the streets. Oscar also encouraged them to bring friends home on weekends to keep them out of trouble.

Not that Oscar detected any signs that the boys were involved in gangs. Steve and Oscar liked to go to parties and dance, but the boys were never defiant or rebellious. With Michael there was nothing to worry about. He preferred to spend his Saturdays at home, cooking pancakes and playing Nintendo. He made honor roll in his first semester in high school that year and told his parents he wanted to be a policeman.

The high school handball court was on the edge of Hempstead's busiest street, near the expressway entrance where traffic always backed up. Oscar pulled up behind the police cars. Ignoring the honking behind him, he braked, jumped out, and started running. Tina was close at his side, but as they ran across the trampled grass a policeman stuck out an arm to block them. No one was allowed down there. They needed to wait in the car. Oscar clenched his hands and stopped.

The courts sat at the bottom of a grass slope and were surrounded on three sides by woods. Through the trees was the main high school campus. Students weren't supposed to come to the rundown courts, which had been closed off after years of budget cuts, and the fences were locked. But they did anyway. A chain-link fence surrounded the crumbling handball wall, a magnet for graffiti, and the long-abandoned tennis courts, which were overgrown with weeds. It was easily scaled.

The ambulance pulled up. To Oscar, the paramedics seemed to be moving in slow motion as they gathered their equipment. Tina screamed at them to run. Oscar's heart sank when he saw one of the paramedics from among the mass of uniforms swarming around the court gesture for his colleagues to hurry.

What were they doing down there? Why didn't they take Michael to the hospital? How much time had passed—a half hour? Oscar strained to see and begged the police officer again to let them closer. You don't want to see your son like this, the officer said.

The police said they were deciding which hospital could receive him. Mercy was close by, but they might take him elsewhere. Wait in your car, the officer repeated. Oscar reluctantly turned back toward the car. Tina followed. They sat, staring out the windshield, and waited.

Oscar couldn't imagine who would want to attack Michael. The boy had so many friends. He was always smiling. The harried teachers in the Hempstead public schools adored him. They were used to troubled, disruptive students, and in comparison, Michael seemed like a gift. At the beginning of the year, Michael and his classmates described themselves on a worksheet handed out by their teacher. He wrote "intelligent," "hilarious," and "outgoing." For his favorite thing he listed handball. His least favorite was bullies. The worksheet asked him to list his favorite colors, and he responded with blue, black, white, and gold, the colors of each of the gangs that battled in his school. He liked them all.

Oscar was less worried about the bullies Michael complained about than Tina, who hated to hear about her sons being picked on, but he was concerned about the gangs. Four years earlier, on November 16, 2004, Olman Herrera, a friend of Steve's, was stabbed to death in the middle of the day down the street from the high school. Now, this.

When Oscar first moved to Hempstead, it appeared clean and safe, especially compared to San Jose. The neatly mown lawns and quaint village shops were the perfect place to raise a family. It was like a television sitcom. Oscar never imagined leaving. But lately, he was saving money to move the family to Florida. It was 2008, and in just one more year, Oscar thought he would have enough. They loved Florida, particularly Orlando. The family had gone every year for the last six years. The boys scorned Disney World because they said it was "for babies," but the family always spent a day at the Universal Studios and Islands of Adventure theme parks.

Oscar had hoped to move a year earlier, but the economy was worsening. Fewer calls came from suburbanites wanting to remodel their bathrooms and kitchens, his specialty, and gasoline prices were going up. He was determined to figure it out somehow. The violence was getting worse. It was time to leave Hempstead.

Tina got the call: Mercy Hospital. Oscar pulled back out into traffic, where the cars were still crawling at an infuriating snail's pace. He could see the hospital on the other side of the overpass. The ambulance was ahead of them with its siren wailing in vain as it idled in the sea of cars. Finally, after minutes passed, they broke free. Once inside the emergency room, Oscar explained who they were in his halting English. They were led into a waiting area. They still weren't allowed to see Michael. Oscar was on the verge of sobbing. He wanted to see him and to hold his hand. He wanted his son to know his mom and dad were near. No, came the firm answer. Wait.

They sat. The doctors and nurses filtered in and out. Finally, one came out and reached out to Oscar. He grasped the man's hand.

"I have five boys. I'm going to treat him like my own," the doctor said. "I'm going to do everything I can."

Michael arrived at the hospital without a pulse. His heart stopped in the ambulance. But they revived him. He needed extensive surgery and had lost a lot of blood. Oscar signed the stack of forms.

"He's very, very sick, but I'm going to do my best." The doctor turned and walked away.

Michael was alive. Oscar felt a wave of relief. He looked around the waiting room, which was filled with teachers from the school. Yadira and other family members crowded in. Even the principal, Reginald Stroughn, was there, and Henry Williams, the assistant principal, who knew most of the kids in the school by name. Mr. Williams had known Steve well and had met Michael a few times, although Michael hadn't been the sort to cross his path often.

Hours later, the doctor returned. The surgery had gone well, but on the way out, Michael's heart stopped again. They rushed him back into the operating room and revived him, but he wasn't doing as well as they hoped.

"Is he going to die?" Oscar asked.

"I don't know."

Michael might die. Oscar stared at the doctor in disbelief.

"Do you believe in God?" the doctor asked. "Pray."

At 4 AM, the doctor came back. They could come see Michael now. It had been thirteen hours since the attack. They stumbled after him into the intensive care room.

Oscar was afraid to ask, but he had to know if his son was dying. The doctor hesitated.

"I don't want to give you false hopes. Your son isn't going to make it," the doctor finally said. The nurses would tell the family when he was about to go. Until then, they could stand nearby. When it was time, they could hold his hands and touch him.

Oscar wanted to run away, or scream, or hit his head against the wall. But he stood still and waited. He felt as if he were dying, too. An hour passed. It was quiet, except for the steady beep of the heart monitor and the strained breathing of Oscar's other sons as they tried to hold back their sobbing. At 5 AM, the nurse called them over. The line ran flat, and the family yelled at him to resist and stay strong. They begged him not to go. Nurses gently pushed them out of the way to give him CPR. They tried for fifteen minutes. But Michael was gone. The single knife wound in the side of his torso had cut near his heart and punctured an artery. They had revived his heart twice, but he had lost too much blood.

Later, detectives told Oscar they knew who the killers were. They didn't know which individuals yet, but they knew MS-13 was behind this. Mara Salvatrucha. Oscar knew the name: MS-13, the gang that had painted the walls around town with graffiti. Hadn't they been involved in that other boy's stabbing at the school? He didn't know. He didn't care. He knew it had been the gang members who killed Michael, but he didn't only blame them.

Michael wasn't out late at night. He wasn't breaking any laws. He never joined a gang. He was at school, staying late on a Friday afternoon. This town had picket fences, backyards, and big-box stores, just like other suburbs. But elsewhere, parents didn't worry about their children's safety when they stayed late at school. Just the opposite. Something was terribly wrong, and a gang of young kids couldn't be the only ones responsible. There were more suspects in Michael's murder than Mara Salvatrucha alone, Oscar thought.

● ♦ ●

It was the quietest time of day at Hempstead High School, 3 PM on a Friday. Most of the students had been herded out of the building and off the campus an hour earlier. The only sounds were muffled singing and laughing in the cafeteria, where some students lingered to try out for the spring talent show. The phone rang every few minutes, and teachers wandered in and out of the office. Reginald Stroughn, the principal, sat at his desk and worked on paperwork. He was a little distracted. He had been nominated for the 2008 School Administrators Association of New York's Principal of the Year award, and that night he was being honored at a local dinner.

His achievements included raising the graduation rate from 40 percent to 65 percent in four years, but he was still reeling from the news that he had been chosen. He was being asked to attend dinners and meetings to talk about the school's progress. In the past, the school received attention only for scathing state education department reports about its lagging academics, which had been released at regular intervals for two decades. There was also the lingering disquiet that followed from the fatal stabbing of a student near school grounds four years earlier.

Stroughn was a stout former football player whose heavy square jaw seemed to pull his mouth down in a perpetual frown. Henry Williams, an assistant principal who had moved with Stroughn from the middle school when he took the principal job in 2003, was the good cop on their team, the one the students confided in and loved. Stroughn was the tough, no-nonsense disciplinarian. He instilled fear in most of the students, but he believed they had also come to respect him. He was born in the South Bronx, raised by a single mother, married at age sixteen, and a father of two by eighteen. He repeated the story often to his students. He knew what they were going through. It was hard, but they could follow his path and succeed if they tried. He believed they needed a firm hand to keep them straight, and it seemed to be working.

The walkie-talkie on his desk crackled and interrupted the calm. A student had been stabbed on the handball court. A security guard was already there, and Williams was on his way. Someone in the main office was calling 911. Stroughn jumped out from behind his desk. Students weren't supposed to be on the handball court. What were they doing down there? Stroughn walked quickly across the parking lot toward the gate leading to the courts. The school kept it locked. The students must have climbed over. He was frustrated, hoping that this student wasn't badly hurt. He was certainly going to be in big trouble.

He pushed through the woods and headed toward the voices. Williams was leaning over a boy lying on the ground. A security guard and two students, freshmen, stood nearby. Another boy sat on the concrete cradling the injured student's head in his lap. He clung tightly to him and pressed a T-shirt against the boy's side. Stroughn recognized him as Oscar Alguera. His little brother, Michael, must be the one who was hurt.

The younger boy's face was gray, and his eyes had rolled back in his head. His tongue was white. Williams shook his head at Stroughn. The security guard had already tried CPR. The boy's skin was icy. Stroughn didn't see blood on the ground. It must have collected inside his thick puffy jacket.

They waited for the ambulance to come and tried to calm the boys. A crowd was gathering. The other security guards arrived. Police officers climbed out of a squad car. The parents appeared, and an officer held them back. The paramedics pushed through and pulled Oscar away from his brother. The detectives began asking the boys questions as the paramedics went to work.

Michael and his friends had come to the court right after school to play handball. Someone had hit the ball past the wall, and one of the boys ran to get it. He bent, picked it up, and was turning when he noticed a group of men walking past on the sidewalk up by the road. He looked at them briefly and ran back behind the wall, out of sight.

Moments later the group of men, in bandanas and large coats, appeared on the court. They ordered the boys to put their hands against the wall. Michael and his friends obeyed. They stood still while the men rifled through their pockets and pulled out a cell phone, wallets, and an MP3 player. As the men turned to leave, one paused near Michael. He pulled out a knife and clicked it open. At the noise, Michael glanced over. Another of the men stopped and yelled for the man with the knife to come on. But before he turned to follow, he stabbed Michael in the side with the blade. The boys had apparently dragged Michael several feet away from the place where he fell before running for help.

After the paramedics loaded Michael into the ambulance, Stroughn turned to go back to his office. He had to call the superintendent to break the news. He stayed at his desk for several minutes after he hung up the phone. The school was silent. He thought back on his four years at the high school.

The school's progress had been real, but also—it was now clear—very fragile. This was the second student stabbed during his tenure. Most school principals didn't deal with that during their entire career. Stroughn sat and stared at his desk. The scene at the handball court played in his head. Then he remembered the dinner.

The ceremony went by in a blur. Later he wouldn't even remember who had hosted it. As soon as he could get away, he drove to the hospital.

The waiting room was filled with students and teachers. Michael's father approached Stroughn and asked if he wanted to see Michael. He followed him into the hospital room. Tubes snaked around the boy's body. Machines bleeped. Stroughn studied the numbers on the screens. The doctors had told the family little about his condition.

A white, heavyset doctor came in. Stroughn stood behind the parents as the doctor broke the news. He probably wasn't going to make it through the night.

Stroughn stayed a while longer and then went home. At 5:30 AM, his cell phone rang. It was Mrs. Alguera calling to tell him Michael had died.

Stroughn wondered how they could have prevented the murder. The school was short of security guards, but he didn't think a full roster of guards would have helped. They had worked so hard to turn the school around. He had believed the building was a safer place than when the last student, Olman Herrera, was stabbed. Students were better behaved. More of them thought about college. The gangs, or at least the outward signs of them, were banished from the school. He didn't know what else he could have done.

• ◆ ●

Sergio Argueta disembarked from the plane from London on Saturday, January 19, and checked his phone messages. The voicemail box was full. He rolled his eyes. He had left Hempstead for two days; couldn't people leave him in peace? The first message was from the police department. There was a student stabbed at Hempstead High School. It didn't look good. They needed his help. The second message came from a teacher at the middle school, an old friend of his. The stabbing, again. He should hurry to the hospital. She heard the boy was in bad shape, and he was only fifteen.

The third message was a young voice: Michael's cousin. He had participated in Sergio's gang prevention programs at Uniondale High School. His cousin had been stabbed. He died. Could Sergio come?

Sergio dropped off his suitcases at home. In England he had visited schools where a spike in gang violence—knife attacks in particular—had authorities in a panic. In early 2008, London was worried about twenty or so knifings across the whole city, a number that was set to triple that year. In the suburbs of Long Island, Sergio had attended a similar number of gang-related funerals in the past few years. In the office of Sergio's non-profit organization, STRONG Youth, a pile of cardboard gravestones he displayed at the annual peace demonstration was stacking up. The gravestones were meant to shock the community and the surrounding suburbs into recognizing the magnitude of the gang violence problem, but every year they had more names and more gravestones.

Before Sergio began organizing peace demonstrations, he was a gang member with a local clique, the Redondel Pride, in the early 1990s. He was outgoing and charismatic and became the leader by the time he was sixteen. That year, he also attended his first funeral when his close friend, Eduardo Arguello, was shot. Eduardo, who was nineteen, wasn't a gang member. But he associated with Sergio and his friends, and the shooters assumed Eduardo was one of them.

Sergio's gang bought a shotgun at the Kmart in Levittown to get revenge.[1] In a fight with the rival gang shortly afterward, the gun went off, and the bullet accidentally hit a Redondel member, Juan Carlos Fuentes. He died. After losing two friends in one year, Sergio began to have doubts about gang life. He retreated from the streets.

He graduated from high school and attended Nassau Community College. One evening in 2000, on his way back from a day at the Puerto Rican Day parade in the city, he met Eric Rivera. Eric was a friend of a friend and had just received his GED. They talked about school. Eric had also had encounters with gang life—he had dropped out of high school to avoid the violence—but he, too, was climbing his way out of the streets. At the train station in Hempstead, Sergio clapped hands with Eric and promised to see him again soon. Moments after they said good-bye, Eric was beaten to death in the street by a group of MS-13 members wielding baseball bats. They assumed Eric was in a gang.

Sergio was angry. He went to visit Eric's family and sat with them in their home as they cried. He thought about Eduardo and Juan Carlos. A few months later, he formed an organization, Struggling To Reunite Our New Generation, or STRONG Youth. He channeled his energy and his anger into antiviolence presentations in schools and prisons.

He organized his first peace demonstration to protest Eric's murder, a candlelit march through the streets. His speeches impressed preachers, and local officials called him inspirational. The Nassau County Youth Board offered him a job. He would be a gang intervention specialist, the first in the county, and his job description was to lure young teenagers away from gangs. In his spare time, he raised money for STRONG and found an office in the top story of an old farmhouse off of Main Street in downtown Hempstead. Over the course of four years, several former gang members graduated from an antiviolence program he dubbed STRONG University. But the gangs didn't go away. Peace was a hard message to get across in Hempstead.

Sergio knocked on the door at the Algueras' basement apartment in the Villa Court apartment building. It was Saturday afternoon, and he was still groggy from the flight. Michael's brothers opened the door. He recognized the two boys from the high school; they had attended his antigang presentations. They led him in. The house was full of people, but it was always obvious who the parents were in these situations. Oscar's eyes were red from sobbing. Tina's eyes were glassy and unfocused. They stayed close together. Sergio shook their hands. A fish tank burbled on a table in the dim living room, and a hamster shuffled the wood shavings in a tiny glass case. Sergio sat with the mourners. He would add the new gravestone to his collection soon.

●　●　●

Cops got the call on Friday, January 18, 2008, just after 3:30: male, fifteen, stabbed once to the torso. Location was the Hempstead High School handball court, at the corner of Peninsula Boulevard and Southern State Parkway. No security cameras in the vicinity. He was "likely"—shorthand for likely to die.

The three witnesses were all teenagers, two friends and a brother. They described the suspects as a group of seven to nine Hispanic males in their early twenties who fled eastbound on Peninsula after stealing a cell phone and an MP3 player. The boys said they were asked about their gang affiliation. Michael was the one who replied. "We're not related to no gang members," he told them.

Detective Ricky Smith was on the other side of town with members of the Hempstead Village gang task force—a detective from another police department and a federal agent. They were working another case but would have to drop it for now. This was big, a possible gang murder on school grounds. Not that Smith was surprised. The gangs had been in the schools for years. The administrators allowed police in to do gang presentations on occasion at the department's request and even allowed police presence at times. They had a better relationship with the new principal. But it wasn't enough, and sooner or later the school district was going to have to wake up. Too bad it had to take a murder on campus for anyone to notice. Smith felt sorry for the kid and his family, but not for the school board.

The police had locked up gang members for years, but the problem just kept spreading, especially in schools. Where else for eight hours a day can you recruit gang members? The police tried to get ahead of the gang—hadn't the Hempstead chief of police and the mayor brought in federal assistance before anyone else? And that was before September 11 turned "information sharing" into a hot law enforcement trend. Smith couldn't even count all the gang members convicted on federal racketeering charges and sent to prison thanks to their task force. But when it came to the schools, everyone seemed to look the other way.

Smith was born in Hempstead and joined the police department in the early eighties. Residency in the village was mandatory for new cops, but Smith kept his family there several years longer than required despite the growing violence and poverty in the village. He and his wife shopped in the burned-out business district downtown. Their two-year-old daughter pointed and giggled at the transvestite prostitutes gathered along the sidewalks. Tootsie, she called them, after the movie.

He and his partner considered themselves the first Long Island cops to take notice of the suburbs' fledgling gang problem in the early 1990s. With the support of their police chief, James Russo, they mapped out the territories of a handful of small posses banding together in the village's three main geographic regions, the Hill, the Heights, and Trackside. The Hill lay on the east side of the main road through town, Peninsula Boulevard. The Heights encompassed Bradley Park and the prewar apartment complexes in the north. Trackside cradled the Long Island Railroad route in the west.

At first, they were amateur gangs, nothing to get overly worried about. They spray-painted their names on walls and scuffled over the borders of their territory. The situation became more serious after the Redondel Pride murders. Then Salvadorans With Pride and MS-13 arrived on the scene in the mid-nineties and by 1998 had taken the violence to a new level. The Hempstead police cracked down. In 1999, they began using federal racketeering laws to send dozens of gang members away to prison. By 2006, they thought they had sent the gangs running scared. The gangs backed down for a while, but a year later they were back.

The detectives at the scene thought MS-13 was responsible. The student stabbed at the school didn't seem to be involved in a gang, though. Smith turned the undercover car around and headed away from the school, toward Main Street. They needed to talk to some gang members. The gangs were nothing if not creatures of habit. Always hanging out in the same spot, no matter how many times they got busted there. Mara Salvatrucha had a reputation for being dangerous and secretive, but Smith knew whom to talk to and how to talk to them. They weren't mysterious to him.

CHAPTER 2

"The World's Most Dangerous Gang"

●   ●   ●

Michael's murder was added to a growing list of crimes attributed to the Central American gang Mara Salvatrucha. In the course of a decade, the gang transformed from a group of ragtag war refugees in Los Angeles to one of the country's top public enemies. In 2008, the FBI ranked the gang's threat level as "high," and the Homeland Security secretary under President George W. Bush, Michael Chertoff, regularly listed MS-13 among the top threats to the country, along with Al Qaeda. Stories of its gruesome exploits burnished a reputation for savagery and fueled a spiraling national panic about the gang's rapid spread. Its main rival, 18th Street, another LA gang, was also described as particularly ruthless for a street gang. "This is not yet an ideological organization, but it is an organization which has the capability to do an enormous amount of damage," Chertoff said of the Central American gangs in an April 2008 speech about the nation's gravest security threats.[1]

In 2003, in Honduras, 18th Street killed three young women and left their decapitated bodies as warnings to the police. In Guatemala that year,

Mara Salvatrucha scrawled a note to the president, Oscar Berger, and pinned it on a naked corpse.[2] In 2004, members of Mara Salvatrucha in Honduras gunned down twenty-eight Christmas shoppers on a public bus to protest the government's crackdown against the gangs. In a message left on the bus windshield, the shooters said the attack was in response to a proposal to institute the death penalty.[3] In 2005, the gang fired an AK-47 at FBI agents in a Houston shootout that ended in the deaths of two of the gang members.[4] In 2006, the FBI warned that human smugglers were hiring Mara Salvatrucha members to assassinate border agents.[5] In 2007, in Newark, New Jersey, men linked to the gang shot a group of teenagers execution-style in a school playground.[6]

In 2008, the FBI estimated there were at least 10,000 members of Mara Salvatrucha.[7] In Central America, government officials put the number of members in both gangs at over 70,000.[8] The FBI, in a 2005 press release, compared them to the mob and accused them of running international drug and arms trafficking rings.[9] Other law enforcement officials often warned that the gangs had and could operate heavy artillery. The FBI and Homeland Security officials voiced concerns that the gangs would cultivate ties with Islamic terrorists.[10]

Yet it was the gruesome details of one murder in particular five years before Michael's death, in 2003, that played the largest role in focusing national attention on the gang. The death highlighted one of the most startling facts about the gang's presence in America—their choice of turf. The victim, a girl nicknamed "Smiley," was killed in the suburbs, and not just any suburb. She was murdered by a Mara Salvatrucha clique based in the wealthiest county in America, the home of many of the nation's top government officials and lobbyists: Fairfax, Virginia.[11]

Smiley, whose real name was Brenda Paz, was a seventeen-year-old Honduran immigrant who ran away from her family's home in Los Angeles. She followed her boyfriend, a member of MS-13, after he moved to the East Coast and soon joined the gang herself. She was among a growing number of girls joining gangs, according to the National Youth Gang

Center. Between 2000 and 2007, more than three hundred women were killed in gang-related murders. Gang-related killings of women rose 34 percent between 2001 and 2003. After a small decline, between 2006 and 2007 gang killings of women rose again—by 69 percent. The number of suburban girls under eighteen arrested for murder was also rising.[12]

Although she was sweet-faced and eager to please, Smiley was also more rebellious than other girls, who were often beaten into submission by the male-dominated gang. She was recruited to be an FBI informant when police picked her up while they were investigating a shooting by her boyfriend. She was quick to cooperate.[13] At first, she was happy to have a way out. She shared everything she knew about the gang, from secretive hand signs to drug trafficking. Her information was used in sixty cases against MS-13.[14] To keep her safe, the FBI put her in the federal witness protection program and moved her into a house in Silver Spring, Maryland, another DC suburb, and later to hotel rooms in Minnesota and Kansas City.[15] But isolated and lonely in witness protection, Brenda reached out again to her gang. She had left her family behind years earlier, and they were her only friends. Although she had turned against them, she didn't believe they would turn against her. She turned her new home into a party house and invited her old friends to hang out and drink with her there.[16] She realized she was putting herself in danger, but to Brenda, the loneliness was worse.

In the spring of 2003, she became pregnant.[17] She left the protection program for good and moved back in with her friends. They were staying at a Holiday Inn near the high-end Fair Oaks Mall in Fairfax.[18] On a summer day in 2003, several weeks after she returned to her old life, she followed along with the group as they piled into a white SUV in the mall parking lot.[19] They told Brenda they were going fishing in the Shenandoah River.

Rods in hand, they filed down to the riverbank, but they didn't cast their lines.[20] It only took a few minutes to kill Brenda. They stabbed her sixteen times in the chest while holding a rope around her throat, but avoided her swollen belly.[21] Then they climbed into the SUV and drove away. A fisherman found her mutilated body at the edge of the water.

Her murder became the touchstone for a new campaign against Mara Salvatrucha. The gang was already well-known in Los Angeles, along with dozens of other gangs, and they openly controlled swaths of Guatemalan backcountry, Salvadoran city slums, and Honduran farmland, but now they had executed a government witness in the suburbs of the nation's capitol. They were in America's backyard.

The media grabbed onto the story, and the murder became the center-piece of lengthy reports on the gang in magazines, newspapers, and television. A *Newsweek* article called them the "most dangerous gang in America," and a *National Geographic* documentary about Mara Salvatrucha went further with the title "World's Most Dangerous Gang."[22] In the documentary, the reporter traveled to El Salvador, where she filed online blog posts about dead bodies she saw piling up in the streets and described El Salvador as "utterly wild."[23] MS-13 was "ruthless ... ruthless," she wrote in one dispatch. In another she wrote that her interview subjects were "amazingly cool looking" and "bad ass."[24]

Nationally syndicated conservative columnist Michelle Malkin wrote that the murder proved a point she had been making for years: that this "violent illegal alien gang" was on its way to turning suburbs across the nation into a war zone.[25] "The peaceful suburbs of Washington, DC, are beginning to look and feel like East Los Angeles," she wrote in a column printed in the *Kansas City Star*. Malkin went on to warn suburban shoppers that they were no longer protected from the dangers of the inner city: "A spate of knifing attacks involving reputed MS-13 gangsters took place at a nearby Target store. Yes, Target—where the only fights that shoppers should have to worry about are the tug-of-war spats between soccer moms battling over Sonia Kashuk makeup bags on sale in Aisle 2."

After Paz's death, murders attributed to Central American gangs were reported in cities as far flung as Nashville and San Francisco.[26] But one of the most worrying destinations for these new gangs was another of the country's richest areas: the New York City suburbs on Long Island. In 2004 two bodies appeared in Old Westbury and Bethpage, two of the wealthiest, whitest towns in Nassau County. One was the tattooed body of sixteen-year-old Olivia Isabella Mendoza.[27] She was trying to leave her gang, her family said, and had planned to move out of state to get away.[28] Before she could, police said MS-13 members, who believed she was an informant, dragged her into the woods of Old Westbury and shot her in the head. A friend of hers, who the gang also believed was disloyal, was later found dead a few miles away.[29]

"This kind of stuff doesn't happen here," one resident told a newspaper reporter. "You're in paradise over here," another said.[30]

Politicians reacted to their constituents' concerns. In Virginia, a Republican candidate running for governor, Jerry Kilgore, staged a campaign press conference in 2005 near the Shenandoah River.[31] Against the backdrop of the riverbank where Brenda Paz died, he proposed a sweeping antigang plan encouraging the execution of gang leaders if they ordered their followers to murder.[32] The proposal came out of disappointment that Paz's killers hadn't been sentenced to death. Prosecutors called for the death penalty in the case, but the jury ordered life in prison for two of the defendants and acquitted an imprisoned gang leader accused of ordering his underlings to kill Paz.[33] The jury expressed hope in its verdict that the defendants would spend their sentences working to get others out of the gang.[34]

Kilgore lost the election, but others around the country were already pushing similar legislation at the state and federal level, and law enforcement agencies were taking action.

In 2004, the FBI announced the creation of a task force focused solely on Mara Salvatrucha.[35] The next year, the Department of Homeland Security started its own antigang task force, Operation Community Shield, that carried out immigration sweeps in search of Mara Salvatrucha gang members.[36] In 2006, the Justice Department sponsored a new National Gang Targeting, Enforcement, and Coordination Center, a multiagency effort that combined the efforts of the Bureau of Alcohol, Tobacco,

Firearms and Explosives, Federal Bureau of Prisons, Drug Enforcement Administration, FBI, United States Marshals, and Department of Homeland Security to fight Central American gangs.[37] The same year, the criminal division of the Justice Department formed a gang squad to coordinate federal prosecutions against Mara Salvatrucha.[38]

Local gang units were also being formed across the country, often with the help of federal resources. By 2003, 360 local police departments had gang units, the majority founded within the previous decade.[39] Starting in 2004, the Justice Department led its own violent crime teams on local raids to fight gangs.[40] It also launched the Comprehensive Anti-Gang Initiative, which began by giving $15 million to five cities and a region for antigang efforts—Los Angeles, Tampa, Cleveland, Dallas-Fort Worth, Milwaukee, and the Eastern District of Pennsylvania.[41] Half of the money went to prevention programs that offered social services to youth at risk of joining gangs, and the other half went to beefing up police efforts to track down gang members. Four other cities, Rochester, Oklahoma City, Indianapolis, and Raleigh-Durham, were later given $2.5 million each. The Bush administration launched Project Safe Neighborhoods in 2001 to tamp down gun crime, and in 2006, gangs were added to the program's mission. More than $2 billion was allocated to the program, mostly to hire more prosecutors to try gang cases. Other jurisdictions were also made eligible for millions of dollars in antigang federal funding under Violent Crime Reduction Partnership grants, which were aimed at facilitating the creation of more joint agency task forces and more gang prosecutions.

At the same time, federal funding for programs to prevent gangs and juvenile delinquency was cut by 67 percent between 2002 and 2005.[42] Some of it was restored in later years. In 2007, the Department of Justice dedicated $32 million of the Project Safe Neighborhoods money to prevention. But much of the Justice Department funding was spent on an in-school prevention program, Gang Resistance Education and Training (G.R.E.A.T.), which was modeled on D.A.R.E. (Drug Abuse Resistance

Education), a federally funded antidrug program, and had received mixed reviews by researchers studying its effectiveness.[43]

In 2005, as the federal government was beginning to spend billions on new gang units and prosecutions, Attorney General Alberto Gonzalez gave a speech to the fraternal order of police in New Orleans. Speaking less than a month before Hurricane Katrina hit the city, he warned about the "expanding danger of violent street gangs."[44] The gangs were becoming more sophisticated, regimented, and competitive, he told the officers, but, even "worse, our latest data indicates new trends in gang violence that we must anticipate and prepare for: The gangs that are migrating, spreading, and expanding are increasingly influenced by the California-style of gang culture." Some were using computer technology to expand their criminal enterprises, and the California culture spread by the gangs brought with it "more violent and targeted techniques for intimidation and control, as well as a flourishing subculture and network of communication," he told police. He evoked Paz's killing and in the next breath pointed to the "the quiet community of Hempstead on Long Island," where, he said, "we've seen drive-by shootings riddle neighborhoods and innocent bystanders with bullets."

Yet the more attention paid to them—and the more gang members swept up and sent back to Central America or to jail under the new federal initiatives—the more the gangs seemed to spread. In 2005, the FBI had tracked MS-13 to thirty-three states; by 2008, the agency said the gang was operating in forty-two. The breathless media and law enforcement reports that characterized Mara Salvatrucha and 18th Street as the largest, most dangerous gangs in the world had become a self-fulfilling prophecy.

"They wanna be the top gang, the top Hispanic gang. That's what they want," Brenda had been quoted as saying to her FBI handlers.

In short order, the feds and the media helped to grant them their wish.

• • •

When Alberto Gonzalez and others pointed to suburbs like Hempstead, a "quiet" town now riddled with bullets, they exhibited a fundamental misunderstanding about the nature of the gangs and the places that facilitated their spread. Gonzalez, grasping at an easily demonized target, blamed gangs, particularly Hispanic ones, for an infestation that was threatening American society and "our peaceful way of life." But the problem was not coming from the outside. Rather, the problem was the legacy of failed government policies and deeply rooted fault lines in American society. The spread of Central American gangs was just the symptom of a more insidious infection gnawing at the nation's core.

The reality was that Mara Salvatrucha and its shadow, 18th Street, gained their notoriety despite holes in the stories about their purported sophistication and strength. Pursuers of the gangs pointed to their frequent use of machetes, knives, and baseball bats as evidence of their unique savagery. A more logical conclusion from their use of these crude weapons might have been to question the savvy military expertise that was often ascribed to the gang. In the trial after Paz's murder, it had come out that the main source of revenue for her gang clique, the most powerful in Virginia, was begging from strangers at the mall.

The popular narrative of the gangs' spread—which posited that Mara Salvatrucha and 18th Street were sending out emissaries to purposefully expand their gangs' territory—was contradicted by, among others, the National Youth Gang Center, a subsidiary of Alberto Gonzalez's Justice Department. The center researchers cautioned that many of the new cliques sprouting up in far-flung cities and suburbs were copycats and that, "in most instances, there is little, if any, real connection between local groups with the same name other than the name itself." According to the center, the gangs were generally "homegrown," and the "factors which contribute to the emergence of gang activity in a community are not necessarily the same as those which contribute to its persistence." In other words, the gangs might have originated in Los Angeles and Central America, but they flourished in places like Fairfax and Nassau County because of specific local conditions there that facilitated the alienation and anger that gave rise to gangs.

The furor over the gangs also left out the inconvenient fact that violent crime, and gang crime with it, plummeted nationwide throughout the 1990s and into the next decade. Between 1991 and 2006, the violent crime rate dipped from 758 per 100,000 people to 474 per 100,000.[45] Reported crimes decreased 13 percent, even as the population of the United States swelled. Gang membership, along with gang crime, also appeared to be going down.[46] The number of youth in gangs fell by nearly 100,000 between 1996 and 2004, to 760,000 from 850,000.[47] In 1991, 1,748 gang homicides—the only relatively reliable gauge of gang crime—were reported in 408 of the country's largest cities compared with 1,492 in 1996.[48] The overall numbers hid increases in gang crime in about a third of the cities, but the increases were small. The vast majority of cities reported less than 10 gang-related homicides a year.[49]

The numbers continued to drop between 1996 and 1998. A few cities still saw some increases, among them Denver and Knoxville, but they reported fewer than 20 gang-related murders in total. Denver, for example, saw its gang homicides rise to 14 from 2 over three years. And of all the cities reporting gang homicides, 88 percent still reported fewer than 10 annually. In the historical trouble spots, New York, Los Angeles, and Chicago—where gang homicides had been in the hundreds—gang-related murders dropped precipitously.[50]

The reality on the ground was largely ignored. During the 1990s, as the gangs were just beginning to sprout in locations far from their roots in Los Angeles and El Salvador, the country was gripped with dual panics about a wave of youth violence and illegal immigration. When news of a Central American gang crisis hit in 2003, it ignited a nation well-primed to expect that violent immigrant gangs were on the verge of invading its cul-de-sacs.

The national panic fit a well-documented pattern. Research on fear about crime had found that usually the people who were most afraid of it were not the ones most likely to be victimized.[51] Gang members usually attacked other gang members, but women and the elderly tended to be just as fearful of being targeted. Often their anxiety had little to do with actual crime levels. Instead, it stemmed from perceptions that a community was changing from the way it used to be and usually—the fearful populace believed—for the worse.[52] Superficial signals of community deterioration, like graffiti and overflowing trash receptacles, added to the anxiety.[53] Neighborhoods with weak social networks were especially prone to fear of crime. Growing diversity—particularly the arrival of new immigrants—was one of the strongest contributors to worries about rising delinquency.[54]

In the nineties, those criteria were met on a national scale. The fear about an oncoming crime wave, particularly among youth, came as the country was experiencing an influx of new immigrants that matched the waves of Irish and Italians a century before.[55] The new influx was different, however. One in five people living in the United States would be immigrants by 2050, and most of the newcomers were Hispanic.[56] The Hispanic population was expected to triple in size by mid-century, rising to 29 percent of the American population—up from 14 percent in 2005. As they settled in, it became clear that their presence was about to transform the country as no other group of newcomers had done before: By mid-century, maybe sooner, census projections showed that the United States would no longer be majority white.[57]

The new arrivals landed in places that previous waves of immigrants had rarely ventured. They skipped urban centers and moved directly to the suburbs. By 2002, the majority of Latinos in the United States were living in residential rings beyond the inner cities that had long acted as the country's welcome mat. In the 1980s, the number of Latinos living in cities compared to the number in the suburbs was about the same, but after the 1990s suburban Latinos outnumbered their urban counterparts by 18 percent.[58] And while the suburbs of New York, Los Angeles, and Miami saw large increases in their already-large Hispanic populations, the growth was just as fast in places where previously only a handful of Hispanics had lived.[59] The suburbs of Washington, DC, and Atlanta were among a group of cities, many in the South and Midwest, that saw sudden and large arrivals of new Hispanic immigrants.[60]

The immigrants were following jobs, which proliferated in the booming economy of the '90s, and their presence helped to buoy the country's economic prosperity. They came to work, and the United States needed their labor. Some went to work in manufacturing and agricultural processing in new growth centers like North Carolina and Tennessee. Others were drawn to construction work as the housing industry exploded. Many had plans to stay, and those who came legally applied to become U.S. citizens in large numbers.[61] Besides helping the economy expand, the wave of Hispanic immigration coincided with the nationwide drop in crime. The new generation of immigrants was also arriving at a crucial moment—as the baby boomers were preparing to retire. The influx of immigrants meant there would be young workers to support the strained social security system.

But many Americans were alarmed at the rapid societal shifts around them. The backlash was harsh. By the end of the decade, states and the federal government passed some of the most severe criminal justice and immigration laws in the nation's history. Many new laws focused on street gangs—entities perfectly positioned at the confluence of the two issues, immigration and crime.

During the 1990s, children and teenagers were locked up in unprecedented numbers, while immigrants attempting to cross the border—many of them from Central American countries decimated by decades of conflict that had been funded by the United States—found the route increasingly difficult to navigate as the Border Patrol cracked down. At the same time, the money for gang and recidivism prevention programs in prisons and schools was slashed. Social services for immigrants were eradicated. The country enjoyed an economic boom, but it was reaching levels of income inequality not seen since the first half of the twentieth century.[62] Communities and schools across the country, especially suburban ones, were becoming more racially segregated. The racial achievement gap between the races, particularly for Hispanic students, was widening.

Meanwhile, Hempstead, like many of the other suburbs where the immigrants planted their hopes, was unrecognizable from the idyllic community the attorney general described in his New Orleans speech. Although all around it wealthy, white suburbs glimmered with bucolic charm and, just next door, Garden City's leafy streets and thriving malls offered suburban bliss, Hempstead's ranch houses and crooked picket fences hid another, unexpected reality, one that the public and policymakers either failed to see or willfully ignored. The village had once hosted a thriving middle class and excellent schools, but in the nineties poverty and desperation more commonly associated with the inner city had set in.

By 2006, fear of the immigrants and gangs gripped the suburbs after growing unease with the newcomers during the 1990s was exacerbated by a series of gang murders. The newest residents met a hostile reception, and the opportunities they came searching for were increasingly elusive. The first generation of Hispanic immigrants in Long Island, many with battle scars from wars back home, found their presence was not just unwelcome, but offensive and infuriating to many of their new neighbors. Some aggressively campaigned to send them back home. The immigrants' children attended schools and played in streets as segregated as the Jim Crow South.

Most of the newcomers did not join gangs. The majority of young people struggling under the weight of war, poverty, fear, and isolation steered clear of the gang life, despite the tempting promises of protection from the hostile outside world. But some couldn't resist. By 2006, crime was continuing to fall everywhere around the country, except in the South and in the suburbs, where it ticked very slightly upwards.[63] In June 2008, the National Conference of State Legislatures, an elected body that serves as a clearinghouse and think tank for state lawmakers, declared that gangs were still on the rise despite half a decade of concentrated law enforcement efforts and billions of dollars spent to bring them down. The gangs had now spread "from Boston to Los Angeles, across the Midwest and down to Georgia and Florida."[64] Citing FBI statistics, the group warned that, "while it was once only an inner-city problem, today gangs have spread nationwide to suburbs, small towns and Native American reservations."[65]

The conference suggested that gangs had more money and power than before and that their fancier cars and guns were luring more young people to join. But this analysis did not begin to tell the whole story. Their rise to power revealed not what the gangs offered to a new generation of immigrants and their children, but what America did not.

Julio, 1985–1995

CHAPTER 3

Garden Cities

● ● ●

In the 1800s, Hempstead Village was the central hamlet in the town of Hempstead, a loose conglomeration that encompassed Garden City and, later, Levittown. Hempstead was a hub for Long Island's rural residents, where potato farmers sent their children to high school and where small shops drew weekend visitors from other farming villages. After the turn of the twentieth century, as car ownership expanded along with a burgeoning American middle class, Hempstead began to draw more than just farmers. It became a magnet for New York City dwellers, a promised land where families seeking an escape from the gritty, jostling, and sometimes violent city could settle among like-minded people, safe behind the buffer of a green lawn and a garage. It was one of the nation's first suburbs.

The concept of the suburbs was not an American invention. The idea first caught on in Britain, where in 1898 a London court reporter with only a few years of schooling, Ebenezer Howard, proposed building a series of small towns on the outskirts of cities to replace the slums that had appeared during the Industrial Revolution. The towns would provide "healthier surroundings and more secure employment" for their residents.[1] They would be limited in population, the streets would be lined with trees, a glass-enclosed "Crystal Palace" would shelter shops and shoppers during inclement weather, and a "Central Park" would provide recreation. Each house would stand on its "own ample grounds," and the towns would be self-sufficient with a business district, a few factories, and a set of public schools. Howard called his little towns "Garden Cities."

The concept was praised in England as innovative. In America, the idea became a way of life.[2] Before long, suburban settlements like Hempstead were booming. The U.S. census first began to break out data on suburbs in 1910. By the 1940s, 17 percent of the country lived in the outer rings of cities.[3] In New York in particular, the population growth was explosive, with suburbs like Freeport, Glen Cove, and Hempstead swelling at a faster pace than the city.[4]

The newcomers were different from the original rural residents—they were middle-class parents shopping their way to the American dream. Hempstead was eager to meet their needs. Between 1870 and 1940, the population of Hempstead Village climbed from 2,316 to 20,856, and the local government promoted it as the island's "leading village" for both population and retail offerings.[5] To make room for all the people moving in and the shoppers flocking to town, the village embarked on several major public works projects.

In 1941, the village converted downtown Hempstead into a network of "parking fields" to ready the town for the automobile.[6] The village also pressed to eliminate "substandard housing" in an area of town known as the Hill.[7] Encouraged by the 1934 statewide Slum Clearance law that allowed New York City to raze so-called unsanitary housing, Hempstead initiated a makeover of poorer neighborhoods.[8] Police were sent to overcrowded buildings to "check-up on aliens, undesirables or persons wanted for crimes or for any other reasons." Some offending homes were torn down.[9] Owners of lodging houses were ordered to comply with building codes.[10] New apartments went up, including new "garden" apartments near Washington Street downtown in what would later be known as the Heights.[11]

In the early 1950s, the population of the Long Island suburbs surged again, boosted by the end of World War II. Unprecedented numbers of middle-class whites left the city with help from a new federal home loan system that had started in the 1930s and was expanded after the war.[12] Italians, Irish, and Germans—second- and third-generation immigrants—had moved up the economic ladder into better-paid municipal jobs and higher-end blue-collar professions. Some still lived in tightly packed urban enclaves that were being dismantled under the slum clearance initiatives of the city's parks commissioner, Robert Moses. Others lived in suburban-like neighborhoods in the outer boroughs that were being transformed as they filled with refugees from the tenements. The suburbs beckoned to them as the next step up in the American dream.[13]

Between 1950 and 1960, suburban growth outpaced the city at record speeds. New York City lost 1.4 percent of its populace, while the inner ring of suburbs, including Long Island's Nassau County, grew by more than a third. The outer ring of suburbs, which included Suffolk County, grew by more than half.[14]

During that time, Hempstead had made concerted efforts to expand by absorbing new neighborhoods on its outskirts into the village. One of the earliest Long Island Railroad lines terminated at a station in the heart of downtown, offering easy access to its shops, gabled churches, and quaint town square and advancing its position as one of the island's most important commercial centers. Hempstead secured its nickname, "The Hub," in 1952, after the arrival of an Abraham & Straus department store.[15] The store was the biggest in the A&S chain, and became a magnet for the young families setting up their new homes across the island. Many of the new towns that started out as bedroom communities for city workers had few local businesses they could tax to fund schools and other services. Hempstead, with its shopping center, was flush.[16]

Some worried about the mass, chaotic flight from the city. The suburban movement was the opposite of Moses's efforts to beautify and elevate the city through calculated, centralized planning, which was later criticized for its disregard of the character of local places and people. Ebenezer Howard's idea for the "Garden Cities" had called for careful regional planning. But in the American suburbs, growth was ungoverned by any central force. Instead, millions of people were making individual choices to carve out their own yards on measured lots, and there was no oversight or regional master plan.[17] The only agencies working on plans for suburban development on a regional level had no power to actually make policy; they could only make suggestions.[18]

Although there was no overarching plan for the region, there were specific and rigid rules at the micro-level.[19] Within each hamlet or village, preservation and character of local places and people was the focal point of government, not the casualty of it. The suburb's new attitude toward development grew out of a second, locally generated concept of the Garden City.[20]

A century earlier, in 1871, Alexander Tunney Stewart, a Scottish immigrant who made his fortune in dry goods, developed his own idea of a "Garden City" as a place that would never be marred by the blights of unsanitary housing conditions or the undesirables who lived in the city.[21] He emphasized exclusivity in his application to buy the acreage—an expanse of pristine, rolling prairie. The Town of Hempstead feared buyers might want to turn the land into a cemetery or a prison. But Stewart promised that his residential development would only admit the "desirable," not "the tenement houses and public charities of a like nature." Hempstead eagerly approved his application. To ensure that undesirables couldn't get in, Stewart refused to sell the houses, so that the renters could be screened to make certain they met his standards of "financial, family, religious, and social status." The plan failed—in the short term. Most of the houses stood unoccupied for many years.[22] Years later, however, Stewart's Garden City, with its tree-lined streets and large homes separated by wide yards, blossomed with prosperous residents as Hempstead declined into a slum.

Levittown, one of the first planned suburban developments designed to capitalize on the wave of new suburbanites after World War II, borrowed from both Garden City concepts. Each home was an island with a lawn and a garage that looked almost identical to its neighbor, while advertisements in the 1940s assured buyers that the town's newly constructed homes could not "be used or occupied by any person other than members of the Caucasian race."[23]

The suburbs were becoming starkly different from the cities to which they were attached. They represented a negation of the city, a place where the melting pot of New York City could not penetrate. New York City's median income dropped during the 1960s, while the average salaries in the suburbs skyrocketed, especially in Nassau County.[24] As whites departed for the suburbs, they were replaced with an influx of Puerto Ricans and African Americans, most of them poor.[25] By the 1960s, more than a million blacks lived in the city alongside about 600,000 Puerto Ricans— about a quarter of the city's total population.[26] But the flight from the city wasn't all white.

In fact, minorities were moving to the suburbs at a much faster rate than whites, if in smaller numbers. Between 1950 and 1960, the number of nonwhites in Suffolk County rose 166 percent, while nonwhites in Nassau County rose 137 percent.[27]

They confounded the expectations of some social scientists, who believed the suburbs to be invincible to the neighborhood life cycles in the city. In cities, new neighborhoods generally enjoyed a period of genteel, elite status before gradually eroding into working-class districts or slums.[28] But in the 1940s and '50s, it was hard to imagine such a fate for the brand-new, immaculate suburbs. The developments turned old potato farms into bucolic retreats and achieved an iconic status in the American imagination. But the suburbs weren't exempt from the rules of real estate and social status.[29]

Contrary to images of the suburbs as placid havens from the commotion of the city real estate, during the 1960s some neighborhoods saw their racial makeup transform almost overnight.[30] The open bans on blacks in places like Levittown in the 1940s were accompanied by subtler strategies that were just as effective in segregating minorities. Real estate brokers scared white homeowners away from neighborhoods when a minority family moved in with the specter of lowering property values, a tactic known as blockbusting. The system of redlining, which tied the value of a home to its proximity to people of color, also made it all but impossible for black families to find banks that would loan to them outside of majority black communities.[31] A 1961 state housing discrimination law was passed in an effort to curb the rampant problem, but had little effect on the suburbs, where a bunker mentality had set in when it came to protecting communities from outsiders.

When middle- and upper-class minority families were able to overcome discrimination and move in, many new white homeowners—panicked about the possibility of decreasing property values, or simply racist— moved on. They abandoned the aging Cape Cod and ranch homes of the first suburbs for newer, whiter subdivisions further east on Long Island, at a greater distance from the city.

Hempstead had begun as a nearly all-white village, but its old housing stock and its mix of apartment buildings and single-family homes opened it to economic and racial integration. In the 1960s, the main social frictions in the village were between gangs of Polish youth from opposite sides of town—the Hill and the Heights. But the town was changing.[32] As minorities moved in, white families moved out. In their place came more young black families attempting to follow the same path of upward mobility. By the 1980s, Hempstead's population was almost entirely black. Nearly all the whites had left, just as they had left New York City a half century earlier. In less than fifty years, Long Island became a densely settled black and white patchwork—the most segregated suburban region in the country.[33]

At the same time, Hempstead's once-booming retail businesses buckled under competition from modern new shopping centers, among them the Roosevelt Field Mall in Garden City.[34] The A&S—once the pride of Hempstead—closed its doors and moved to Garden City in 1991.[35] Stores were left vacant, and weeds sprouted in the "parking fields," which now sat half empty. Some businesses burned when landlords saw more profit in their insurance policies than the trickle of customers willing to brave the village's increasingly mean streets.[36] Hempstead's tax base, once the envy of other towns, dwindled. Public education in the village, once the island's pride, faltered. Hempstead was no longer the "Hub" of commerce. Isolated and fast deteriorating, as household incomes and the tax revenue plummeted, it was becoming a hub of crime.

To a village police detective, James Russo—who was born and raised in Hempstead during its heyday—Hempstead was starting to resemble the pictures of the South Bronx he saw broadcast on the news. He had dodged brawls between the Polish gangs in the 1960s, but during the '70s and '80s, the department had started to confront a more lethal problem. Drugs filled the vacuum businesses left, and the crack trade thrived.

In 1989, Russo was named the chief of the village police department, which was about 90 percent white despite the drastic demographic changes in the town. Soon after he took the helm, the national crack epidemic ended, to his relief. But his detectives noticed a new problem: graffiti. The drug dealers always tried to be discreet. Vandalism wasn't their thing—it alerted the police to their presence. Russo wasn't sure what to make of the new trend yet, but he was paying attention.

A new phenomenon was poised to transform the town. The newest immigrants to the United States were moving directly to the suburbs to meet a growing demand for labor.[37] America's shift to a service economy meant there were plenty of restaurant and retail jobs in the outer rings of metropolitan areas. The mini-mansions in the newly sprouting exurbs—the suburbs of the suburbs—needed roofing, pruning, and vacuuming.

For the first time ever, the rate of growth of suburban Hispanic residents exceeded urban Hispanics. Most of the growth was fueled by single men.[38] In Long Island, there was an 80 percent jump in Hispanic residents between 1990 and 2000.[39] Between 2000 and 2005, the number of Central

Americans in Long Island grew to 103,658 from 60,915, making them the largest Hispanic group in Nassau County and the second largest in Suffolk after Puerto Ricans.[40]

Few of the locals noticed them at first. The first Salvadorans arrived in the 1970s, and were believed to have come from Poloros, a town in southeast El Salvador, the epicenter of the civil war.[41] Soon, more followed. Some shared houses or downtown apartments in white towns like the upscale Port Washington, where the jobs scrubbing their neighbors' yachts were within walking distance.[42] But many others found it easier to afford homes in the black suburbs.

As their numbers grew, the island took notice. One *Newsday* reporter followed an immigrant home to his ranch house on a block of "two-car garages and modestly landscaped front lawns," only to shock the reader with the revelation that "the classic suburban scene" was "an illusion."[43] The home masquerading as that of a middle-class white family was chopped up inside to hold a family and several other boarders, also immigrants, all living in squalor. It wasn't a "symbol of success," the reporter wrote, but a "false front." The neighbors had no clue.

The news report was sympathetic, depicting the sadness of newcomers who missed their homes and families. It described the difficulties they faced working grueling jobs and surviving in a place where they didn't speak the language. But as whites realized they were losing ground in the towns intended exclusively for them, many responded virulently. In the early 1990s, several village governments began the first attempts to pass ordinances that banned gatherings of day laborers and limited the number of people who could share a rented home.[44] It was the beginning of a backlash by the majority white population. The bunker-down mentality was reemerging in full force.

Chief Russo felt differently than many of his neighbors. The immigrants seemed to be reviving suburbs like Hempstead. Some of the new arrivals branched out from construction and house-cleaning jobs and started their own businesses. Soon, Hempstead and other struggling older villages were bustling again, although now shoppers flocked to Spanish tax preparation services, Western Unions, and *pupuserias* selling the meat and bean pancakes craved by homesick newcomers. A Home Depot opened in the vacant building where A&S once stood, drawing contractors and homeowners, and convincing a handful of other retailers to return to Hempstead despite its troubled reputation. Although the thriving businesses did not bring back all the white customers with their larger pocketbooks, for the first time in a decade it seemed like Hempstead's decay might be reversible. Perhaps these new strivers could help Hempstead pick itself up out of the ashes.

Still, Russo was worried. These immigrants had a right to live here, just like his own ancestors. He was happy to see Hempstead's downtown revitalized and the drug trade die, but the graffiti nagged at him that something wasn't right.

CHAPTER 4

Soldier

● ● ●

In the winter of 1986, Julio sat on the side of the mountain and stared into the darkness. He gripped his AK-47. Despite his exhaustion, his eyes were wide open. The cold mountain air kept him alert. Thinking about the ticks burrowing in his hair and the snakes rustling nearby helped, too. For good measure, he discreetly popped a Sin-Sueño pill as the other soldiers in his troop settled into their sleeping bags nearby, hoping the jolt of powdered caffeine would keep him from nodding off. But fear alone was enough to keep him awake as he stood lookout.

Not that he could see the enemy before they came. A month after his troop arrived at this mountain post in eastern El Salvador, they were sleeping when a guerilla bullet flashed through the woods and killed one of his friends. Julio had been lying only a few feet away. They were often jolted awake by the crack of gunfire in the distance and bombs landing nearby. More had died since then. Some were carried away on stretchers for burial. But in other cases, they could only retrieve a few body parts, or nothing. Later, those would be classified as missing in action. It was the memory of that first dead body that stuck with Julio, though. It played over in his head on nights like this.

His watch would last two hours, and then he could sleep. As soon as the responsibility of the lookout position was lifted from his shoulders, he knew he would pass out immediately. The day had been indistinguishable from the nineteen days that preceded it. Walking, walking, more walking. Remembering the rhythm—slow, steady, repetitive—was enough to lull his eyes closed. The cold canned food he wolfed down earlier had settled heavily in his stomach. He fought the wooziness. The time alone each night, struggling to keep awake, was time to think. He had been thinking a lot lately.

Just the other day, his lieutenant caught him taking one of the caffeine pills and yelled at him. If Julio became addicted to the pills, they would all be in trouble, the officer warned: the day he ran out of them, he would fall asleep on watch. Then they could all be dead. The scolding cut deeply. The lieutenant usually singled Julio out as one of the best soldiers in the unit. Julio thought it was partly because he was a city boy, and slightly more sophisticated and educated than the other soldiers, who mostly came from small farming towns, where the army did most of its recruiting. He was also a favorite because he had extra training and could work the pack radios. The lieutenant sometimes called Julio his son. Julio basked in the affection, and the lieutenant's displeasure troubled him more deeply because of it.

One of the sergeants had also recently singled him out, and not for the usual praise. Julio had become a chain smoker in the army. He loved cigarettes. He used his $30 monthly paycheck to buy up cartons in the army canteens when they came back to the barracks, stowing them in his pack when they set off on their forays into the mountains. The sergeant made fun of him for smoking so much.

"You're too young to smoke," the officer had sneered at him. "I'm going to teach you a lesson."

The officer poured water into a bowl and took a handful of cigarettes. Then, methodically, he began crushing the cigarettes into the water, stirring it into a thick brown soup.

"Drink it," the officer said. It was an order. Julio had no choice. He drank the whole thing and quickly vomited. If he had learned anything in the army, though, it was that the more pain you endured, the more respect you earned. Follow directions, and act tough. After a few months in the Salvadoran government forces, he had it down pat.

It was not what he had imagined when he first joined up in 1985. He had been fourteen. It was the middle of the war, and the army was desperate for front-line troops. It had plenty of money from the Americans to recruit more soldiers. The recruiters found him on his way home from the local school, walking along a dirt street in his neighborhood. He was wearing his school uniform. The idea of trading it for one of the Rambo-style camouflage outfits intrigued him. When the recruiters ordered him to come with them, he followed. There was no point in arguing with men carrying M-16s. He wouldn't mind looking like them and having that kind of power. He went along.

He didn't think his family would be worried about him. Julio was the second youngest of five siblings and had been the black sheep of the family almost since he could walk. As a toddler, he climbed to the roof of a nearby house and fell through onto a pile of debris. His mother sat by his side for two days in the hospital waiting for him to regain full consciousness. When he recovered, he was as feisty as ever—a troublemaker who, beneath it all, craved discipline and order. In kindergarten, he stole crayons and coins from the other children, hiding his loot in his socks. His mother usually discovered it at the end of the school day, and always forced him to take the stolen goods back to their owners. He relented, shame-faced. But it was never long until he was in trouble again.

He made friends quickly, his aggressive sociability and winning smile hard to resist. But he also had a temper. As he got older, he often got into fights with the other boys at school and gained as many enemies as he did friends.

Since the time he was little, Julio's mother cared for him by herself. His father had started another family across town and rarely visited. His grandparents had left for the United States at the beginning of the war. His older brothers soon followed, and his grandparents sent for his younger sister as the worst of the violence set in.

His mother cooked at a nursing home in the city and wasn't home often. Her wages paid for a small plot of land on a hill overlooking San Salvador, in a neighborhood known as San Jacinto. They didn't have running water, electricity, or a sewer line. Most of the time, Julio and his remaining younger brother were left to fend for themselves.

They ran wild, and his mother worried Julio was destined for the streets. Eventually, his father agreed to help pay for him to go to a military boarding school in Apopa, a city about thirty minutes away. His parents hoped the structure would keep him out of trouble. Julio took well to the hierarchy and strict rules at the school, and excelled at the trumpet. After a while, his parents allowed him to return home and reenroll in the neighborhood school. But when the army found him at age fourteen, he had already been molded into a perfect recruit, with the rituals and discipline of war instilled in him.

To Julio, life in the army wasn't too different from his life before. His base was only a few blocks from his home, closer than the boarding school. But his mother was horrified when she learned he had been recruited. Emergency provisions passed by the government had lowered the legal fighting age to sixteen, although the law was often ignored.[1] But to protest the decision could mean death: The disappearances of people who pushed back against the government's war effort had begun nearly a decade before, and there were stories of mothers who were killed for asking the army to release their sons.[2]

Still, she went to the barracks to beg the officers to release Julio. It took her six months to convince them. By that time, Julio had already established himself as a favorite among the officers. He had seen American Green Berets—macho heroes who struck him with awe. He had also learned by heart a motto often spoken around the base: "The life of a soldier is worth the lives of three civilians." They let him go, but he knew he would return.

The army waited a year before they picked up Julio again, this time in San Miguel while he was visiting an uncle. His mother couldn't protest this time. He had just turned sixteen, so he was legal. Julio was sent almost immediately to the front lines. He helped pinpoint where the guerrillas were camped for the artillery and air units. Occasionally, the army made use of his young face and friendly disposition to send him into farming villages in civilian clothes. On those missions, his job was to mix with the locals and learn whether they supported the rebel forces. It was the job he liked least, the one that made him feel the dirtiest.

Julio looked up to the officers and had believed the lieutenant when he had said he loved him like a son. But a few months later, he was starting to doubt their sincerity. They had turned on him in a flash, and for little reason. His status as the favorite hadn't lasted long. His doubts about the officers led him to ponder the war in general. At first he believed that they were going to save the country and that the Communists wanted to tear it apart. Then in the villages he had seen the faces of the old farmers, hollow-eyed and dressed in rags. There had been children and pregnant women, too. As he sat shivering on the mountainside hugging his machine gun, he felt betrayed. He missed home, and he was tired. The pride he once felt in his uniform now felt foolish and naïve.

They had lied to him. The villagers were not the enemy. The enemy was sleeping around him. In 1987, a year after he joined, Julio was given a ten-day leave from the army to visit his family. He never went back.

CHAPTER 5

The War

● ● ●

The Salvadoran conflict officially began in 1980, but its roots reached back to an incident known simply as La Matanza, or The Massacre, fifty years earlier. Thirty thousand Pipil Indians, once the major indigenous group in El Salvador, were slaughtered after officials discovered that left- ist groups were planning a communist uprising to overthrow the reign- ing military junta.[1] Only 10 percent of those killed had actually been involved in planning the revolution. The country's indigenous popula- tion was all but wiped out.[2] The massacre fulfilled its mission, though, and the army went on to rule the country for the next fifty-three years.[3] But the brutality was never forgotten.

The military government did not bring stability. El Salvador churned through coups and violent confrontations between the military and left- ist student and peasant groups until 1979.[4] By that year, the dramatic in- come gaps between the rich and poor had worsened, and a small group of elite families controlled most of the tiny country's land.[5] Out of all arable land, 78 percent belonged to 10 percent of the country's landowners, and anyone who questioned this balance of resources was labeled a Communist.

In 1979, a group of moderate reformers supported by a group of young military officers overthrew the reigning military government in another coup. The new leaders promised land and social reforms to appease disgruntled peasants, church leaders, and university students.[7] But the coalition quickly disintegrated, as it became clear the military leaders would not loosen their grip on the country's government. The reforms envisioned by the civilian leaders never materialized. Meanwhile, leftist groups continued to organize. Disgruntled members of the elite and the military coalesced in new, shadowy paramilitary groups and lashed out violently against their opponents on the left.[8] Thousands of peasants who were supposed to take over new plots under the land reforms were scared off or forcibly evicted by ex-landlords and the military, which soon reassumed its traditional role of backing the oligarchy.[9]

The repression only had the effect of making the leftist groups bolder in their organizing, and in 1980 they united in one central organization, the Farabundo Marti National Liberation Front (FMLN), a militia named in honor of one of the peasant leaders killed in La Matanza.[10] By then, the killing had begun in earnest. The country quickly tumbled into an all-out civil war.

The violent climax of the war came early. Between 1980 and 1982, tens of thousands were killed by death squad hunts and indiscriminate massacres.[11] The countryside hosted a patchwork of dumping grounds for the remains of the disappeared. Most Salvadorans could conjure up the image of at least one dead body glimpsed on the way to school or work. Some were missing their heads. Many had suffered tortures before death that left them slashed or burned beyond recognition.[12] Other attacks targeted whole villages. In one case, the Salvadoran army teamed up with the Honduran military to trap Salvadoran civilians believed to be sympathetic to the rebels as they tried to flee across the country's northern border.[13] Hundreds were slaughtered.[14] In 1980, the army occupied the national university, in the process killing twenty-two people and tearing apart the campus. Later, eighty-one more scholars were killed, including the university rector.[15]

In 1981, the army perpetrated a massacre that echoed the horror and viciousness of La Matanza in 1932.[16] Soldiers descended on the rural town of El Mozote in the course of a major offensive to take back swaths of land in the eastern province of Morazan.[17] Although most of the surrounding villages emptied upon the news that the army was coming, the people of El Mozote stayed and even took in some of the displaced villagers from elsewhere.[18] The town was neutral. The army had never bothered them before.[19] But not this time. First the army tortured and killed the men. Then they separated the mothers from their children, whom they locked in a nearby convent. Then they tortured the women and killed them within earshot of their children. Finally they sprayed the children with their machine guns and left.[20] About 480 people were killed in all.[21] More than half of them were children.[22]

The soldiers who participated in El Mozote had likely been trained by Americans.[23] The war might have ended years earlier, but the United States, concerned that another country in its backyard would fall to communism, as Nicaragua had in 1979, poured billions of dollars into El Salvador to fund the military and prop up the government. Between the Carter and Reagan administrations, more than $6 billion in economic and military aid, along with direct American training, was given to El Salvador during the 1970s and '80s. The money pouring into El Salvador from its northern benefactor was only stopped once, in 1977, and only when the Salvadorans rejected money from the Carter administration rather than submit to human rights requirements.[24] During the most vicious era of Salvadoran government repression in the early '80s, the aid flowed unhindered by concerns about human rights abuses.

When four American churchwomen were found buried in a shallow mass grave, naked from the waist down, raped and murdered in December 1979, the investigation into the Salvadoran soldiers responsible seemed to go nowhere.[25] But the stalling in the high-profile case had little effect on the continued flow of American cash into El Salvador's war coffers. Even after the shooting deaths of two Americans and the head of El Salvador's land reform effort in a hotel in January 1981, Washington didn't halt support.[26] The Salvadoran government ignored American pleas—and a personal phone call from President Reagan—begging for the killers to be brought to justice.[27] The American money continued to arrive.[28]

The paramilitary death squads were the most ruthless of the murderers that ran rampant in El Salvador during the war. Shadowy groups run by the far right that operated mostly with impunity, they were deployed to assassinate left-leaning civilians and clergy, and any government officials who seemed to get in the way of the rightists' determination to keep the country's oligarchy in power. In the beginning, active military personnel openly controlled the death squads.[29] But when they were banned in 1979, the connections between the military and the death squads were simply covered over. The U.S. government, which had CIA intelligence about the death squad's continued role in assassinations and repression, looked the other way.[30]

The most notorious death squad leader, Robert D'Aubuisson, a former Salvadoran National Guard member, participated in the assassination of Archbishop Oscar Romero.[31] As the civil war heated up, the archbishop had become an increasingly vocal advocate for the poor, a position that was tantamount to treason and communist sympathy in the minds of the Salvadoran elite. He was shot in the chest on March 24, 1980, in the chapel of the Hospital of Divine Providence as he was saying Mass.[32] His death came at the beginning of El Salvador's descent into a decade of hellish chaos, and as if to make the point that the country's people had been abandoned even by God, assassins attacked Romero's funeral procession, too. The assassins killed as many as forty churchgoers and injured two hundred.[33]

Two months later, D'Aubuisson was arrested with documents that implicated him in the planning of Romero's assassination.[34] He denied the allegations and was eventually released from prison. Two years after

Romero's death, he became the president of El Salvador's National Assembly as the founder of a far-right party called the Nationalist Republican Alliance (ARENA).[35] Still, American money flowed in. ARENA, with its slogan, "El Salvador will be the tomb of the reds," would become the political party that ruled the country for the next seventeen years following the war's end in 1992.[36]

By the time Julio joined the army, the worst of the war was over. The death squad killings and civilian massacres started to slow, although beheadings and bombs were still a part of everyday life. One of the most harrowing realities of the war was that the fighting and killing was mostly carried out by child soldiers, some as young as seven. But this children's army was not something widely acknowledged during, or even after, the war. The army was more reluctant to admit it than the rebels, but both blatantly ignored the law prohibiting them from recruiting soldiers younger than sixteen. A World Bank study conducted after the war found that 80 percent of government soldiers were younger than eighteen. Fewer than half of the government's young soldiers had joined voluntarily. Many deserted within a year or two. Once they were out, they were often left with few options in life. Among those surveyed for the study, less than a third of government soldiers were literate, and none had completed middle or high school.[37]

Julio was among the lucky ones. He reached seventh grade. For several months after he deserted, he laid low in San Jacinto. He had returned to his mother's house, only a few blocks from the army base, but the soldiers didn't bother looking for him and rarely ventured up the hill to the maze of ramshackle homes where he lived. On March 26, 1987, he was spending the morning flirting with an admirer at his old elementary school, a sprawling colonial building with large barred windows that took up almost an entire city block. His experience as a soldier, even though he was a deserter, had made him popular among the young girls in the neighborhood. As he stood under the window of the classroom whispering up to her, he noticed a man and a woman heading into the school. They were carrying flour sacks. As they got closer, they pulled out two rifles. Julio ran.

Within seconds, the couple was shouting that they had guns and were taking the school hostage. Soon, the park was filled with sobbing mothers, including Julio's own. Police and soldiers from the nearby barracks flooded the area. But Julio couldn't pull himself away. The school held more than nine hundred children. Just an hour earlier, rebel forces had ambushed a group of police officers in downtown San Salvador, killing two and injuring three. The police arrived, expecting the worst. A military swat team trained by American soldiers climbed the roof ready to launch an assault— apparently with the children inside—if negotiations fell through. Officials and the archbishop of San Salvador filed in and out of the school for six hours trying to make a deal with the pair. Some children crawled out of the building's large windows, while most of the rest were released over the course of several hours until there were thirty left.[38]

One of the hostage takers was an army deserter named Juna Francisco Medrano. Like Julio, he had worked in communications. Three days before his siege on the elementary school, Medrano had stolen two rifles from an army unit. A day later, he had participated in an attack against one of the paramilitary death squads. The woman who joined him for the assault on the school was an eighteen-year-old rebel soldier who was identified only as Gloria.[39]

Finally, a deal was reached. Police escorted the hostage takers out of the building. The rest of the children were released.[40] But the ordeal wasn't over for Julio. He had spent the day waiting anxiously alongside his neighbors in the park. After the school was cleared, the police began sweeping the area. They arrested Julio, loaded him in a van, covered his head in a hood, and drove away, ignoring his mother's screams that he was innocent. He was held for eight days as his mother frantically searched the city for him. She was sure that her child had disappeared forever.

Julio knew nothing about the hostage plan. He had begun to feel sympathetic toward the rebels during his last days in the army, but he wasn't a part of their movement. The guerrillas had also denied having anything to do with the San Jacinto school incident. The police finally let him go. But Julio returned home even more terrified: He was certain now that he would be recaptured and sent back to the front lines. His mother was worried, too. One of his brothers began cobbling together money to pay for Julio to leave the country. His plan was to travel to Guadalajara, in Mexico, where he could stay with family friends for a while. He was on a bus out of San Salvador by the next month.

A friend his age from the neighborhood was his only company on the long trip. In Guatemala, they switched from the bus to a freight train. But they were caught by Mexican immigration agents at the border and sent back. His friend went home, but Julio tried again. This time he made it. Along the way, he begged for food in the villages where the train stopped. In a town in Chiapas, he came across a semitruck hauling bananas north from Central America and hopped on. He burrowed inside the bananas for two days. But the bananas were green, and he had nothing to eat, so he finally had to climb out from his hiding place in search of food. He made it to Guadalajara and was taken in by his parents' friends. But Julio was unhappy and ached for home. As soon as he figured it was safe, he boarded a bus headed south. Within six months, he was back in his old neighborhood.

Julio was seventeen. He looked for work, but there was little to do with the war still raging. He found a job volunteering as a lifeguard with the Red Cross, although the organization only paid for meals and travel. But he hoped an extra benefit would be protection from the army and death squads, and he spent whole days in the Red Cross compound near the city's center.

In 1989, for the first time during the war, the FMLN rebels attacked San Salvador.[41] They had hidden caches of arms in the city's residential neighborhoods with the help of sympathizers.[42] That fall, as negotiations with the new right-wing government teetered toward collapse, the FMLN went ahead with the operation to take over the capitol. They moved quickly and took the government by surprise, but the government responded to the attack by bombing working-class and poor neighborhoods.[43] In the midst of the mayhem, the army also took the opportunity to attack the city's Jesuit university, where the rector and several priests were killed.[44] Some of the bombs hit houses on the other side of the hill from where Julio and his mother lived.

The government's ruthless response against its own citizens cemented Julio's sense of betrayal. The army and the government it controlled clearly cared nothing about the people or the country. He could see that now. They only cared about protecting their wealth. To them, his life and those of his family and neighbors were expendable. By the end, in 1992, an estimated 75,000 people had died since 1979, mostly civilians.[45]

Even with the war coming to a close, Julio was overcome with a feeling that death squads were after him. His desertion from the army and his association with the hostage incident at the school convinced him he had been targeted for death. Strangers who entered the neighborhood made him nervous. One day, as he was walking on a street near his home, two men coming the other direction suddenly attacked him. One of them sank a knife into his shoulder before Julio could wrestle free. He made it home, stumbling away with blood streaming down his arm. Julio was convinced they had been sent to assassinate him, although his mother dismissed the attack as one of the many random acts of violence that were replacing the war's more organized bloodshed. Still, she agreed he should leave.

At the time, Julio's girlfriend was pregnant with a boy. He had planned on naming the baby Cesar, his middle name. But the baby was not enough to convince him to stay. He decided to head north again. In El Salvador, the treaty signed in Mexico by the government and rebel forces that promised political reforms and an end to the military's grip on power brought little peace, and there were still no jobs. In the United States, he might be able to find work to send money home and support his son. This time, he would stay more than a few months.

He took the same route he had taken earlier—a bus to Guatemala and then freight trains all the way north. He skipped Guadalajara this time and kept going. In Baja California, he called his oldest brother, who had become a success in the decade he had lived in Los Angeles, working his way up to become the owner of four McDonald's franchises. He said he would send a friend to pick him up; all Julio had to do was figure out how to get across the border.

Julio hitched a ride up the highway to Los Angeles to the border fence. It was tall, but Julio was still fit from his years training in the army. He walked alongside the fence until he came across two Mexicans who were clinging to the top of the wall and scanning the view on the other side. He scrambled up alongside them. Below lay a parking lot. A border patrol agent was cruising slowly through the parked cars with his door ajar. They waited silently. There was no time to hear the stories that had brought the other two to this point. Julio assumed that, like him, it was desperation. The agent cruised past and began to turn.

Julio jumped. He landed in a crouch, briefly bending to kiss the ground before he began his sprint toward the lights of the highway. Across it sat the McDonald's where he was supposed to meet the woman his brother had sent to pick him up. But the border agent had heard the smack of his sneakers hitting the pavement and was out of his car in an instant, bolting through the parked cars toward him. Julio was faster. He reached the highway, waiting for a break in the cars. Then he shot across the lanes, weaving in and out of the cars as they picked up speed out of the border checkpoint. As he reached the McDonald's parking lot, his brother's friend signaled to him. She was holding two bags of hamburgers. He began laughing as he jumped into the car, and they screeched onto the highway. The hamburgers tasted as delicious as he had imagined they would.

CHAPTER 6

Los Angeles

● ● ●

In fleeing to Los Angeles, Julio was joining a mass of nearly half a million refugees from the Salvadoran and Guatemalan civil wars.[1] That didn't count Hondurans and Nicaraguans leaving behind their own country's problems. By 2000, there were more than a million Salvadorans and Guatemalans and more than 200,000 each from Honduras and Nicaragua living in the United States.[2] But only a handful of these were granted asylum at the beginning, about 2 percent of applications in the first five years of the Salvadoran conflict.[3] The other requests were deemed "frivolous."[4] Accepting the claims of refugees that they faced an abusive government back home meant admitting the U.S. government had funded a killing machine that targeted innocent civilians.

Many immigrants had managed to avoid the fighting, but just as many were ex-combatants like Julio. They carried with them their training and trauma from the battlefield. Others, like his sister, who had spent the war living with his grandparents in California, were sent out of harm's way by their parents to stay with relatives they had never met. Arriving in Los

Angeles, the refugees discovered a city being pulled apart by another kind of warfare—street gangs battling each other over drugs and territory.

At first Julio lived with his brother in his house in Inglewood, a mostly black neighborhood in western Los Angeles. His brother gave him a job cleaning one of the McDonald's franchises. The town was becoming increasingly Latino, but Julio felt uncomfortable there. He missed home, and he was chafing at the rules set down by his older brother. Julio was nineteen, and he felt like a man now. He had lived through the war, something his family in America, who had left him behind, didn't understand. He didn't want to depend on their handouts or live by their rules.

Two months after he arrived, he moved out. He wandered around Los Angeles and eventually made his way to Hollywood, where he found others, like himself, who had fled the war and were looking for work. At a homeless shelter for immigrants, he even found a friend, Carlos, who was also from San Jacinto. The two spent their days on the corners looking for work as day laborers. He picked up his first English phrase hanging out with the guys on the corner: "Hey, you looking for somebody to work?" For a while, they worked for a florist arranging flowers together. After a month at the shelter, they moved into an apartment that they shared with three other men. Julio enjoyed day labor. But he was restless.

He began exploring the city again and one day discovered MacArthur Park in downtown Los Angeles. The century-old park had a view of the city center framed by tall palm trees. Stucco and tiled homes lined the surrounding streets.[5] Vendors sold Salvadoran food. The Rampart neighborhood around the park had one of the highest concentrations of Latinos in California, and most were newcomers like him.[6] It was the closest he could come to home, so he decided to stay.

The park was also one of the main centers of drug activity in Los Angeles. Crack addicts and heroin-addled homeless men prowled around the picnic tables where the dealers held court, keeping their eyes open for the Rampart police patrol. As a central battlefield for one of the city's most rapidly growing gangs, Mara Salvatrucha, and one of the largest and most deeply entrenched,18th Street, the park had also become one of the city's murder hubs.[7]

One side of the park was controlled by 18th Street, a gang formed by Chicano kids in East LA in the 1960s.[8] Its style and structure came from a gang tradition that went back much further, to the Chicano street cliques of the 1920s. The groups had formed when Mexicans fleeing the Mexican Revolution were flooding Los Angeles and making homes in migrant farm worker camps and shantytowns around the city.[9] As the city developed, older Chicano residents were also being pushed out of downtown and into the same areas.[10]

The gangs formed by young boys raised in these isolated communities were a product of poverty, segregation, and boredom, but the styles and attitude they adopted were the opposite. They were dandies who wore colorful zoot suits borrowed from black culture. They danced to big band music and spoke caló, a form of street slang derived from the language of the Spanish Gypsies.[11] Proud and bold, they rose above the grime and dirt of their surroundings. In their first incarnation, they were known as pachucos, a word that in Spanish meant "overripe."

But their aggressively ostentatious style was soon equated with gangsterism in white mainstream society, and newspapers began to sound warnings about out-of-control youth violence.[12] The fears culminated in the Zoot Suit riots in 1942. American servicemen on leave clashed with a group of zoot suiters during a night of drunken barhopping.[13] For a week following the fight, American soldiers prowled the streets beating up Mexican youth. They were egged on by the press, who blamed the pachucos for the violence, labeling them as hoodlums. Eventually, the violence and riots eased, but the concerns about Hispanic youth, and their supposedly violent tendencies, lingered and would rise again.[14]

The pachucos' descendants, including 18th Street, were fiercely territorial groups that battled each other but also staked their identity on their Chicanoness. Their language and slang were a mix of Spanish and English. They were proud Catholics. One of the first Chicano street gangs, the

White Fence, was created by faithful churchgoing boys who gathered to protect the neighborhood's younger children as they walked to school.[15] The groups were also sentimental and be-bopped to 1950s and '60s love songs.[16] Like the zoot suiters, they took pride in their sharp dressing, wearing crisp khakis and white T-shirts and shaving their heads in a look that came to be known as *cholo,* a Spanish word for half-breed. They were as American as they were Mexican, and their culture and identity were an inseparable blend of the two. But they had also taken lessons from the riots: They were insular and proud, and prized loyalty to the group above all else. Their creed was to defend each other from outsiders to the death.

In a 1988 magazine-length article in the *Los Angeles Times,* the reporter contrasted the Chicano gangs with their black counterparts by noting that the Chicanos were "caught up in something more profound, a web of rivalries so old that past sins assume a mythical quality." The police were also finding that the Chicano gang members were the toughest criminal suspects to crack.[17] The code against snitching was so ingrained that few would give up a fellow gang member, even a rival, to the larger enemy, the police.[18] By the late 1980s and early 1990s, as black gangs like the Bloods and Crips gained notoriety, a few news articles pointed out that the Chicano gangs were much bigger. In 1992, police estimates put the number of Chicano gang members controlling small squares of turf across Los Angeles County at 60,000, nearly double the number of black gang members.[19]

But also by the 1990s, a new Latino subculture was challenging the Chicano gangs' traditions—along with their power and control over LA's streets. The groups called themselves "stoners." Besides their obsession with marijuana, the LA stoners cared passionately about heavy metal. They wore Iron Maiden shirts and let their hair grow long, the better to head-bang at sweaty, angry rock shows. They were Hispanic, but their look, activities, and attitude were contrary in almost every way to the old Chicano gangs. On the surface, they had more in common with white suburban teenagers who had made the punk, heavy metal trend popular.

They were sloppy and slovenly. In the beginning, they didn't require beating initiations or demand lifelong loyalty. They claimed turf almost half-heartedly.[20] And they didn't seem to have the same strong ties to national heritage—to the dismay of some in the community, who saw that Chicano gangs as partly positive because of their cultural pride. Some were even into Satanism. In 1984, one group of stoners was caught desecrating a cemetery.[21]

Mara Salvatrucha started out as any other group of stoners. They first appeared in 1984, in the Pico Union neighborhood of Los Angeles just south of MacArthur Park, not long after the first exodus of Salvadorans from the war had begun.[22] It was a densely populated, low-income neighborhood that received many of the civil war refugees. At first MS was a scrappy group of boys in ripped Levis 501 jeans, combat boots, and black concert T-shirts, barely noticed by the larger gangs in the neighborhood.[23] The other stoner gangs were known for pickpocketing and stealing cars, but initially Mara Salvatrucha members were more controlled. They cared more about listening to rock music and smoking pot.[24] But by 1990, Mara Salvatrucha had grown from a few dozen to five hundred members, and their reputation was changing.[25]

While the origins of their name eventually would become as mythical as the old Chicano rivalries, it was most often interpreted to mean "Beware of the Salvadoran Swarm." The word *mara* was used in Central America to refer to a swarm of red ants and had also been applied to youth gangs. The word *trucha* was slang for "beware." The *Salva* derived from the home country of most of the gang's members, El Salvador, but it also tied the gang to the Spanish word for savage—*salvaje*, which transformed the name to Beware of the Savage Swarm.

At first the gang didn't living up to its grandiose title, but by the early 1990s, its name had become more apt—according to the telling of its exploits by police and other city officials. They frequently fought with the other Chicanos groups whose neighborhoods they shared, and some members became involved in the drug trade. By then, some had been arrested and sent to jail.[26] In jail, they hardened and returned to the streets angrier and tougher.

By 1992, Mara Salvatrucha became one of the largest of the 450 Hispanic gangs grappling for space in LA. It rivaled 18th Street in size.[27] Both gangs absorbed many of the Central American war veterans to bolster their numbers. As they competed for turf and members, the two gangs became sworn rivals. Mara Salvatrucha expanded to the dilapidated neighborhoods west of downtown LA and to Hollywood. In the process, they abandoned the carefree "stoner" ways. The baggage of prison and the war transformed the gang into a more serious, and dangerous, operation. They began marking their chests and arms with tattoos to show their loyalty to the gang and graduated from drug users to dealers, as the crack trade thrived in Los Angeles.[28] By the early 1990s, they had been implicated in more than five murders.[29] In the United States, MS-13 was still confined to LA, but by the mid-1990s deportations had planted the seeds for the gang to grow in Central America. Social workers and police who came into contact with their members said they were even more intractable and mysterious than the notoriously secretive Chicano groups.[30] They were depicted as shadowy and ominous, always moving and changing shape, a little like an urban guerrilla force.

The police and the media were quick to note the potential links between the rapidly expanding Central American gangs and the experience of their members in the wars back home. A police official told the *Los Angeles Times* in 1990 that the emerging Mara members, as compared to the more established Chicano and black gang members, were quicker to use violent tactics because they were "used to bombs and decapitated bodies."[31] The official, Manuel Velasquez, a spokesman for the city's Community Youth Gang Services agency, said the new Central American gang members "laugh at drive-by shootings."

He didn't offer any evidence that the gang members used grenades and war-grade weapons. Instead, it appeared the gangs were learning from the more established Los Angeles gang members. El Salvador had its share of street toughs before and during the war, but they were nothing like the serious, structured gangs that controlled swaths of Los Angeles and ruled the city's drug trade in the nineties. In Los Angeles, unlike El Salvador, gangs had a hierarchy that extended even beyond the cliques, with powerful gangs like La Eme assigning territories and organizing smaller groups to distribute heroin around the city during the eighties and early nineties.[32] In El Salvador during the war, people were dragged away by shadowy paramilitary groups in the night. In Los Angeles, violence was characterized by the brazen violence of a drive-by shooting. In El Salvador, it had been the military and the police people feared. In Los Angeles, people feared the gangs. This was the city of Hollywood, and the gangsters were glamorous with their color-coded costumes and elaborate tattoos. For the newcomers, this image of the gangster was seductive and new, something to aspire to, although, contrary to the warnings being spread in the media, the Hispanic gang members mostly used fists and occasionally bats and pistols to battle their rivals. They were also involved in increasing numbers of drive-by shootings.[33]

It was true that many of the young people arriving were deeply traumatized from the war. For Julio, nightmares woke him in a sweat, and his suspicious temperament always kept him on the move. He was a human grenade—during the war anger at his family, the army, and the government had built up in him and was always simmering just below the surface, waiting to explode. Even for those who didn't directly participate as army or rebel combatants, it had been impossible to avoid the gratuitous and sadistic violence that saturated El Salvador. And as the war drew to a close, the government made little effort to reach out to help the ex-combatants flooding back into society. The World Bank study of child soldiers found that only a third of child soldiers in El Salvador were offered outside help as they tried to readjust to society after the war's end.[34] Many, like Julio, headed north.

The miracle was that more didn't give up and succumb to the nihilistic gang lifestyle that surrounded them. A study of Central American refugee students in Los Angeles by anthropologist Marcelo Suárez-Orozco during the 1980s found that most young people who had either survived the war or fled as refugees were coping fairly well.[35] They were dealing with a mixture of guilt, anxiety, and posttraumatic stress as they were thrust into LA's troubled inner-city public school system, but most passed their classes. A number went on to college and graduated with a degree. But for those like Julio, alone and nineteen—too old to go back to school— integration into society was far harder.

Julio never received any therapy or attended any sort of program to help him recover from his stint in the military. He didn't take any classes to make up for the years of education he lost when the army pulled him out of school. Instead, he fended for himself, dealing with the guilt, bitterness, anxiety, and paranoia by trying to ignore it. The only signs that something was wrong were the nightmares, his shortened temper, and the endless, restless roaming in search of a place to set down roots.

In his first moments in MacArthur Park, he thought he had found the place. The scenery and the smells made him feel as if he had stumbled back into San Salvador. He arrived on the Mara Salvatrucha side of MacArthur Park, although he didn't realize it at the time, and made friends almost immediately. A few blocks farther west, MS tags covered the decrepit stucco buildings, but the blocks that Julio discovered on the edge of the park were controlled by one of the city's many lesser Hispanic cliques, a motley little group called the Wanderers. Like 18th Street, they had begun as a Mexican gang but gradually accepted Guatemalans and Salvadorans into their ranks as the number of refugees in the city grew. They had also made the tactical decision to align themselves with the biggest gang on their side of town, Mara Salvatrucha, to help them fend off the 18th Street members roaming the park nearby.

Most of the Wanderers lived in an abandoned house on the edge of the park near the corner of Grandview and West Seventh streets. Julio liked the lifestyle. Occasionally they made fun of him for being green, teasing him about his lack of English. To prove himself, he got his first tattoo: the name of the gang splayed across his back. Originally, the group had been called the Huaraches, a Spanish word for sandals. As scrubby, half-homeless squatters, most of the members couldn't afford the white sneakers worn by other gangs. Later, to improve their image, they took on the Wanderers name—after the New York gang featured in the 1970s movie and the Richard Price novel. They hoped their rivals would be intimidated by the connection with the glamour, machismo, and grit depicted in the movie. But to Julio, hearing the name always made him hum the 1961 song "The Wanderer": "Well I roam from town to town / I go through life without a care / And I'm as happy as a clown / With my two fists of iron / but I'm going nowhere."

Julio moved into the gang's crash house, leaving the apartment he shared with Carlos. The rules and hierarchy were strict, but he didn't mind. He respected the leaders of this group more than his family, who had abandoned him, and the requirement of loyalty to the group above all else was one already ingrained in him by the Salvadoran army. It was better than the stifling life he had led at his brother's house. He could take off any time he wanted. He didn't plan on being in the United States long anyway, which is why he didn't follow his brothers' efforts to get political asylum. As soon as it was safe, he would go home. He continued his day laborer work, although the gang members mostly depended on the brisk drug trade in MacArthur Park to earn money.

A few months after he joined the Wanderers, he was arrested. His quick temper had led him into a fight with a drug addict in the park, but when the man's friends showed up, Julio took off running toward the safety of the Wanderers' territory. Several blocks away, he stopped at the sight of one of his fellow gang members. As he stood catching his breath, a police siren bleeped behind him.

His friend ran away as the car pulled to a halt, but Julio didn't move. The officers flashed a beam in his face and then began methodically searching the area. They soon found what they were looking for, a small crack vial not too far away from Julio's feet. It was close enough for him to have tossed away before the officers climbed out of their car. In seconds, the handcuffs were out. He insisted the drugs weren't his, arguing that they had been planted there or dropped by someone else. But they didn't listen.

He wasn't surprised when a major corruption scandal erupted in the police unit that arrested him. The officers, part of the Rampart gang unit, known as Community Resources Against Street Hoodlums, or CRASH, were accused of planting guns and drugs on suspects, filing false reports, and randomly beating gang members in and around MacArthur Park.[36] CRASH had become its own sort of gang: insular and isolated, single-minded about defending its territory, valuing loyalty above all else—a macho brotherhood that eventually stooped to participating in the crime it was assigned to fight.[37] As in a street gang, the crimes committed by the officers helped strengthen the bond between them, and no snitching was their rule.[38]

More than fifty officers were investigated.[39] Many of the suspects they had targeted were from the fledgling Central American and Mexican gangs. In one case, they shot an unarmed 18th Street member. After they realized he had no weapon, they planted one on him as he lay bleeding.[40] The gang unit acted with impunity until one of its officers was caught stealing cocaine from a police evidence locker.[41] The gang members who had run-ins with the unit had never come forward, certain their word wouldn't be believed over that of the officers. Most pleaded guilty.

So did Julio. He was sentenced to three months in jail, slipping through the cracks of the federal immigration agency like thousands of other immigrants who committed crimes in the nineties.

The civil war in El Salvador had toughened and aged Julio. But it hadn't prepared him for jail in California. On one of his first days, he sat down at a long cafeteria table to the right of a withered little man, a repeat offender known as Pinto. The nickname seemed to be derived from the Spanish word for painted, *pintado*. The man was covered in tattoos from head to toe. A water pitcher sat in the middle of the table, to the old man's left. Julio emptied his cup and then reached for it, brushing his elbow over the man's plate. The old man suddenly lunged. Julio was nearly thrown to the floor as Pinto grabbed for Julio, yelling that he was a dead man. Taken by surprise, Julio was sent flailing as another man grabbed Pinto from behind and tried to calm him down. He explained that Julio was new, that he didn't know any better. Other inmates pulled Julio aside.

"Yo, man, don't do that again. Don't disrespect anybody in here," they murmured.

Good table manners weren't the only life-or-death rules he had to master. He learned that the brutal struggle over turf in MacArthur Park between Mara Salvatrucha and 18th Street meant little inside. In the jails and prisons, each race stuck by its own. Sur 13, an affiliate of Mara Salvatrucha, ruled the Hispanics, and his association with the Wanderers opened the door for him into the prison gang's ranks. When two white guys sidled up to him and offered to help him with his English, a Sur 13 leader quickly reprimanded him for associating with them. "What's wrong with you?" he demanded. "If you have a problem, are they going to help you out?"

The answer, Julio learned, was no. Regular fights between the black and Latino gangs broke the monotony of the days. Julio was often pulled into the struggle. By the end of his sentence, his fellow members could no longer mock his innocence. Instead, they rewarded him when he got out. One of the Wanderers had a plane ticket to New York, but decided to stay in LA. When he offered it to Julio, Julio didn't ask questions; he just took it.

During his time in jail, no one in his family had come to visit him, although his brothers, sister, and grandparents had all known where he was. As far as he was concerned, there was nothing tying him to Los Angeles. It was still too dangerous in El Salvador to venture back home. The war had officially ended two years earlier, but Julio had heard that the death squads were still operating. New York promised a new adventure.

On January 16, 1994, he left the West Coast, flying east. The next morning, Los Angeles was torn apart by a huge earthquake. Half the city seemed to have crumbled, and the airport was closed down. Julio thought briefly about turning back. Then he thought better of it. His family had made it clear they didn't need him. He concentrated on his new destination. Maybe in New York he could finally find peace.

CHAPTER 7

New York

● ● ●

Julio's plane landed in Newark airport. After wandering around the desolate New Jersey city looking for work for a few hours, he decided to move on. This was no place for him. Here, the locals could barely make ends meet. The problems were the same as MacArthur Park, but without the view and the thriving Hispanic culture. He asked people on the streets where he might find some other Salvadorans. Someone pointed him to Queens and told him where he could find a train headed east.

It took him a day to cross the two rivers standing in his way. He slept in the subway stations and moved on when police nudged him awake. Finally he boarded a subway train that carried him out of Manhattan's dark tunnels and into the sunshine of Queens. Descending from the elevated platform to the bustling street level, he thought he had found what he was looking for. On Roosevelt Avenue, the faces caught in the sunlight that slipped through the train tracks above were brown like his. Salsa and merengue music blared from shops. He couldn't find Salvadoran *pupusas*, the bean- and meat-filled pancakes that were a Salvadoran street food staple, but cheese-filled Colombian corn *arepas* would be an adequate substitute.[1]

Almost immediately he began using his favorite English phrase, "Hey, you looking for someone to work?" He approached a group of men leaning against a wall under the tracks. At every passing van, the men surged toward the curb in a wave, receding as the van moved on with one or two men from the crowd crammed in the back. The other workers welcomed him in. He spent several days at the curb with them, vying for the construction and landscaping jobs the vans offered. Then he found a job cleaning fish at a market owned by a Korean woman who spoke almost flawless Spanish.

There were three other workers, two Koreans and a Mexican man. Julio didn't like the way one of the Korean workers bullied him, though. He suspected the man of skimming off the tip jar, and Julio let his irritation with him be known. The bad blood quickly led to a knife fight in the basement. When the owner caught them, Julio was the one kicked out. He shrugged and moved on. There was always work at the curb.

But he had yet to find a community of Salvadorans, and his optimism was wearing thin. He missed home. He lived in a crowded Queens apartment and enjoyed the company of the Ecuadorians, Colombians, and Mexicans, but it wasn't the same camaraderie he had enjoyed with the Central American war veterans in the Wanderers, or even among the jail inmates back in LA. He started asking around again for where he might find the Salvadorans.

The suburbs, he was told. It was only a half hour away by train. He hadn't realized he was so close. Within hours he was on his way to the Long Island Railroad station in Jamaica, Queens, pushing his way into a train full of white commuters in business suits.

Hempstead was at the end of a train line. Most of the men in suits got off at the earlier stops. At the last stop, the people around him were once again mostly brown faces. As he stepped out of the station and onto the street, he paused to take it in. There was a wide parking lot full of public buses, a few grimy bodegas, and a line of plain brick apartment buildings. A hulking windowless courthouse overshadowed the shops along the town's Main Street. A white steeple cut into the low sky to the east. The air tasted slightly salty. This wasn't how he had pictured the suburbs. Then he saw it: the blue and white flag flapping in the breeze. It was a Salvadoran restaurant.

He hurried in. Seated in the dim dining room, he ordered before the waitress could set the menu down: a pile of *pupusas*, please. He dug in, savoring the taste of home. If he closed his eyes, he could picture the glaring sun baking San Salvador's dusty streets. In almost no time, he charmed the owner into giving him a job. The restaurant converted to a disco at night, and she told him to show up after closing time to clean up. She also agreed to rent him a room in her building. For the first time in a while, he felt content.

Energetic and talkative, Julio quickly became a fixture in the Hempstead streets. He was looking for another job to add to his salary. It wasn't difficult to find one. It was the late 1990s, and the suburban economy was booming. At a pool hall downtown near the train station, he played billiards and networked with the other men. One of them found him a job working security at the discos. He left his cleaning job and supplemented his salary with day labor. Occasionally, he was able to save enough to send some money home to his son—about $100 every few months. He moved in and out of apartments, sometimes moving to other towns farther out on the island, nearer the work. But he always came back to Hempstead.

Most of the men he spent time with on his days at the curb and his nights in the discos were from El Salvador, and many had fought in the civil war, too. Sometimes they talked about the days back in the mountains: the cold nights; the days marching through jungles, dodging land mines; the politics of the war they didn't understand then. They could spend hours arguing about it now. The banter was something like therapy. Unlike his Colombian and Ecuadorian buddies along the curb, these men had braced AK-47s to their shoulders and followed orders to fire into the shadowy woods. They probably had the same nightmares he did, phantom bullets jolting them awake in their sleep.

Julio had found friends, but Hempstead wasn't the sanctuary he first imagined. Some of his new friends recounted stories of being attacked as they walked near the Terrace, still a black stronghold even as the rest of the town was gradually giving way to Central Americans. Besides the black gangs, Julio's extroverted and occasionally hotheaded personality had won him some enemies among his countrymen, too.

In one fight, he insulted his boss at the security firm that worked in the discos. Julio was fired, and the two became bitter enemies. Julio suspected his former boss was connected to the Hempstead police, and believed he had asked his friends in the department to harass Julio. Officers always seemed to be eyeing him as he drove around town or as he stood on the corners waiting with the day laborers. On one occasion he was stopped when he was driving the car of a new employer—with permission—and questioned. He immediately suspected he had been framed. In his mind, the police, the death squads, and the army seemed indistinguishable. They had always betrayed him. He did not trust them.

His new friends from the pool hall were there for him. Most worked day jobs, but they had taken to calling themselves a gang, mainly to scare off the other Hispanic and black gangs that often picked on them. To add to their street credibility, Julio's friends adopted the name Mara Salvatrucha. They liked the nationalist pride the name invoked and were already hearing stories from Los Angeles and, more recently, El Salvador, about the gang's exploits.

After the war ended in El Salvador, street gangs had rapidly filled the vacuum left when the army and rebels disbanded. The peace accords, signed in Chapultepec, Mexico, in 1992, set up a program to disarm the combatants from both sides. But it didn't work. AK-47s, grenades, and other war-grade weapons were ubiquitous. So were ex-combatants. The end of the war also meant the end of the guerilla army, and the government forces were cut in half. Thousands more soldiers had deserted in

previous years. About 40,000 men and boys were cut loose with little education, few job prospects, and expertise in killing.[2]

Then, in 1996, the U.S. Congress passed a law requiring the deportation
of immigrants convicted of crimes with a prison sentence of a year or
more.[3] Between the years 1996 and 2002, the INS deported 30,696 criminal aliens to Central America. Of those, 12,098 went to El Salvador, a
country the size of Massachusetts with a population of around 6.5 million
and a police force of 20,000.[4] There, the veterans of American jails struck
awe in their younger brothers and neighbors. They brought *cholo* style
and Spanglish to their old neighborhoods. It was only a matter of months
before new cliques of 18th Street and Mara Salvatrucha created by Los
Angeles transplants were flourishing. The same phenomenon was happening in Guatemala and Honduras. Young men drawn into the gangs in
Los Angeles were arrested and deported back home. By the end of the
decade, the gangs would number in the tens of thousands across the region. Journalists and politicians fed the gangs' notoriety, calling them the
most murderous gangs in the Americas.[5]

At first, Julio chuckled at the idea that this ragtag group of ex-soldiers
in a Hempstead pool hall would claim a connection to the hardened gangsters he had known in Rampart. They looked a little more like the earlier
incarnations of the Wanderers—back when they had been known as the
Huaraches. Few of the members of the newly formed Mara Salvatrucha in
Hempstead besides Julio came directly from Los Angeles. Most had made
their way from Central America during or just after the war. So they modeled their gang on stories passed along from relatives and from the ex-
amples set by the black and Caribbean gangs already established in
Hempstead.

Julio told them stories about his own gang encounters back in LA. They
were impressed. He was already one of them, but soon they were urging
him to make it official: Jump in; prove your loyalty. They promised him
protection and support if he had problems with the police or other rivals
in town. He agreed. He was officially inducted in 1995, enduring the blows

of six of his new friends for thirteen seconds before they declared him a member. He tattooed an MS sign over the Wanderers on his back. They etched another five-inch-high "MS" on his stomach for good measure. He was in for life, they told him. He put a final tattoo on his right wrist: three dots in a triangle.

The dots symbolized the three places where a gang member ended up: the hospital, the cemetery, or prison. He had already cheated death and survived prison. He had little to lose.

He believed he had something to gain, though. Many of these guys had gone through the war, been lied to and used, just as he had. They had been cannon fodder, and they had survived. If he could trust anyone to watch his back and not to betray him, it was these men.

Jessica, 1988–2001

CHAPTER 8

Jumping In

In September 2000, Jessica stood in a clearing in the woods strewn with used condoms and broken bottles. Cicadas hummed in the country club grounds edging the campus of the high school, a brick fortress with narrow windows and a weedy green lawn. Beyond the trees that separated the high school from the golf course, commuters from Eastern Long Island zipped along the expressway on their way to work in the city. Jessica was hot and out of breath after running all the way from her middle school a mile away.

She was thirteen, and it was her first week of seventh grade. Earlier that morning she stood in front of her school, basking in the status of a new-found group of friends, and debated whether to go to class. Standing with them, she felt superior to the other kids watching from the school buses. She imagined herself through their eyes and savored the thrill. They had picked on her in elementary school. Now, with a look, she dared them to try it and swigged from a bottle of malt liquor before passing it to the older boys beside her. They wore black and white, the colors of Salvadorans With Pride.

Her euphoria crumbled when she saw her uncle and his girlfriend walking toward them. He was wearing blue and white, the colors of Mara Salvatrucha. The gang had expanded since Julio first joined five years earlier. New cliques had sprouted across the island in other aging suburbs. The Hempstead MS-13 clique controlled swaths of the town, and SWP had taken on the role 18th Street played in Los Angeles as its archrival. A war over the village's winding suburban streets had been raging between the two gangs for three years.

At first he didn't see her in the crowd, and she debated what to do—she couldn't run. She didn't want him to see her fear. But she couldn't help feeling terrified every time she saw him. Her mind always leaped to the image of him standing in her bedroom doorway, and then to his body on hers. Her muscles tensed. He spotted her hanging back from the others and shot her a withering look. She had never told her family what he had done to her, and all at once, she seethed with rage, at him and at them. Her family had never protected her. She raised her fingers, twisting them into the symbol she had learned from her friends, and waved them at him in defiance.

One of her friends threw a beer bottle. Her friends recognized him as a rival, and the couple was instantly surrounded. Jessica jumped into the fray, but she couldn't bring herself to touch her uncle. She took out her rage on his girlfriend, aiming her punches at the light blue bandana covering the girl's mouth. She jabbed and kicked. She took everything out on this girl, who eventually fell to the ground, her uncle struggling nearby against the onslaught of teenagers.

When they heard sirens, they ran. Someone grabbed Jessica by the hand, and she ran, too.

Now, sheltered in the woods, she felt panicky. Her mother would know soon enough, and her uncle would be furious. The others were laughing and replaying the fight, but then everyone turned quiet. They were watching her. Jessica's anxiety transformed into a nervous excitement. One of the older boys pulled out a black-and-white marbled notebook from his backpack and handed it to her. Scrawled inside it were all the gang's secrets: its handshakes, history, and symbols, and even some photographs of its teenage enemies. She was instructed to memorize it. She had fifteen minutes, and then she would be quizzed. If she passed, she would move on to the beating.

Jessica held the notebook carefully and began turning the pages. She would have needed much more than fifteen minutes to memorize the information—she had drifted through elementary school without ever learning to read. But she'd been hanging out with members of the gang for months, and several had already confided some of its secrets to her.

She answered every question correctly and was even able to recite the gang's prayer in her rusty Spanish before she was pushed into the middle of the circle.

One of the boys looked at his watch and gave the signal. Two boys and three girls lunged at her, kicking and punching. A couple swung sticks. She fought back. She was supposed to. Jessica was small, but she was tough. She wore bandanas across her forehead and chains around her neck, baggy pants and shirts that made her look much bigger than she actually was. Her hair was pulled into tight cornrows on her scalp, which led people to mistake her for a boy. A row of fake diamond studs arced up her earlobes, and she didn't wear makeup. A deep dimple in her chin gave her a look of innocence, but she was a skinny bundle of muscles and rage. Her body was a burden that had betrayed her, attracting her uncle to her bedroom while her mother was passed out on the couch downstairs. As she succumbed to the beating, she felt an odd sense of release. She curled into a ball on the ground as their sneakers and fists rained down on her. At the end of fifteen seconds, she felt baptized and clean.

They picked her up gently. One of her attackers put his arm around her and lifted her into his car. Mercy Hospital was a few blocks away. They dropped her off at the door, bleeding and limping, and sped away.

After the nurses had bandaged her cuts, they left her lying in the emergency room bed alone. She struggled up out of bed, ignoring the pain shooting through her spine, and strolled out trying to look nonchalant. No one noticed her. Soon she was across the street at a phone booth. Her decision to join the gang was supposed to have severed her ties with her family, but the only person she could think of to call was her mother. She dialed, and her mom answered. She already knew what had happened.

"Call a taxi," her mother said. Jessica walked home.

● ● ●

Jessica told people to call her Jay, although she tattooed her full name across the back of her right hand in flowery black letters. Her second tattoo was a barely visible trio of dots arranged in a triangle that looked like freckles at first glance. She'd had it done just after she joined Salvadorans With Pride as a gesture of defiance against MS-13—Mara Salvatrucha members usually put the tattoo on their left hand, on the flesh between the thumb and index fingers. It was considered sacrilegious to put the tattoo on the opposite side and in the wrong place, as she had done.

She intentionally corrupted the symbol; she accepted its grim prediction as her future: the hospital, prison, or the grave.

Hempstead was all she had ever known except for occasional weekend trips to New York City and one trip to Honduras when she was twelve. The town sat just beyond the city's limits. In winter, the slow season for lawn and construction work, idle men leaned against the smeared brown windows of bodegas along Main Street. Seagulls faced off with pigeons in the acres of potholed parking lots and auto-body shops that took up much of the real estate downtown. Women of nearly every age and color but white hurried past each other, pushing baby strollers and shopping carts.

Until middle school, Jessica had lived in a house that stuck out from the rest of the bland suburban architecture with its red paint, white trim, and blue door. Neighbors dubbed it the "crack house" for its often drug-addled residents and visitors. The house was near the edge of town in a residential pocket locked between a strip of auto garages and the railroad tracks. The tracks led to Garden City, a suburban utopia of tall trees, man-icured lawns, clothing boutiques, and gourmet sandwich shops, but Jessica rarely traveled the few blocks to glimpse in the windows. To her, Garden City was another world.

Jessica's mother, Ana, had moved to the United States from Honduras in the mid-1980s in search of work. She had been born into a big family of brothers in a tiny village where there were few prospects for jobs. Ana could have looked for work in San Pedro Sula, the nearby city, but it was a rough town—not a place to raise a family. Several of her brothers had left for the United States, so she followed.

Her first stop was Texas, where she married a Honduran man she met there, Raul. They had a baby, Jessica's brother, but their relationship was troubled. Raul had a criminal record and a temper. Ana drank. They fought often. Eventually, she convinced him to move nearer her family, who had settled in the Long Island suburbs. Her brothers said there was work and a growing community of Central Americans. The family could live in a house with a yard. Her brothers were in Hempstead, and from what they described it sounded like a promised land, so they moved. The small fam-ily first found a place to live in East Meadow, a town down the road. Ana became pregnant again, this time with Jessica. She and Raul hadn't planned for another baby. Their fights got worse. He left after Jessica was born.

Ana's only choice was to move to Hempstead, to the red house. They squeezed into a room upstairs. Her brothers helped with money. It wasn't how she had pictured the suburbs. The men worked twelve-hour days to send money back to Honduras and support themselves. Their wages were meager, and the work was backbreaking. At the end of the day, they feared being robbed by the gangs that ruled the town. A couple of her brothers had gotten involved with a group of tough guys who hung out in the downtown pool hall. They came home drunk and rowdy, and nights often ended with them sprawled on the living room couches. Soon the house was a central meeting place for their fledgling new gang, Mara Salvatrucha. But Ana and the babies stayed. They had nowhere else to go.

CHAPTER 9

The Red House

● ● ●

At age six, Jessica liked to stand behind the screen door of the red house on afternoons when she wasn't in school, staring out into a world rendered gray and hazy by the crisscrossing wires pressed against her nose. From there, she could watch the men come and go from the sagging Victorians across the street and hear the trains pulling into the Long Island Railroad station behind a fence covered in tangled vines at the end of the dead-end block. The trees of Garden City lined the horizon. Sometimes she imagined her father might appear at the end of the street, coming back to rescue her.

He had moved out when she was born, but returned occasionally to visit until she was two or three. Jessica adored her father, but she was wary of her mother, who was less affectionate. When he disappeared completely, Jessica was devastated. He returned to Texas, the scene of happier times for their family, but she later heard rumors that he was arrested and sent to prison for an unknown crime. She was left with her older brother, her mother, and her uncles. While one uncle tried to step into the role of a father figure, it wasn't the same. Her other uncles were a group of tattooed, gruff men who drank heavily and brought home friends who scared her. Her mother was gone most days, cleaning houses or selling jewelry door-to-door to pay for the white bread and peanut butter sandwiches that Jessica and her brother lived on. They didn't have a television until Jessica was eight years old, and she had few toys, so she played out in the streets, which sometimes seemed safer than being indoors. On rainy days, though, Jessica waited by the door, scurrying out of the way when her uncles passed through on their way to work and the bars downtown.

One of those days, she was standing with her forehead against the screen when one of her uncles appeared at the end of the street. A man limped along beside him. By this time, Jessica had learned that the symbols on her uncles' arms and backs represented their membership in another family: Mara Salvatrucha. The gang had cemented into a serious operation since its days as a loose conglomeration of war veterans, and her uncles were now among its leaders. The group had been connected to murders and dabbled in the drug trade. Hempstead's Main Street, MS-13 turf, was impassable for members of SWP.

As she watched, her uncle pulled the man, one of his rivals, toward the front porch. Rain drizzled beyond the awning, which made the neighborhood look grayer and more dismal than usual. He pulled out a razor. The man looked badly beaten, and Jessica froze as her uncle lifted the blade. Then he began slicing. His arm moved rhythmically as he sawed into the man's face, ignoring the sudden screams and the blood oozing across his hands. Jessica was transfixed by fear and fascination. Then her uncle let the man drop, and Jessica darted away from the screen.

She hid in her room, cowering in fear that he would come for her next. He didn't, but she was too afraid to tell Ana what had happened when she arrived home from work that night. She kept it to herself. But the image of the man's hacked-up face stayed with her.

In first grade she was placed in an English as a Second Language class, even though she spoke English fluently. Her mother was furious when she found out, but that wasn't until the end of the year. Ana didn't speak English, and most of the report cards and notes home didn't get read. The next year Jessica was moved to an English-only class. She sat in the back and stayed inconspicuous by keeping her head down on her desk. She quickly fell behind. The school began shuttling her to a remedial reading class during her lunch period. Her mother only got involved at school when Jessica was suspended for fighting. The other ESL kids nicknamed her *La Diabla*. Some days she couldn't restrain the sudden fits of fury that would grab her. She would pick a fight with the nearest person. She was skinny and short, but her classmates stayed clear of her. She had a reputation for throwing chairs.

Her teachers shook their heads and sent more notes to her mother. After one fight, she sat back down in her chair and tried to collect herself. As her teacher came and stood over her, Jessica could no longer hold back the tears. She looked up and met her teacher's eyes. The defiance was gone. She was silently pleading as tears started rolling down her face, but she didn't know what for, and the teacher just looked at her irritably before walking away.

Her depression deepened as she entered fifth grade. She hardly ate and became more catatonic in class, except for her occasional tantrums. Her family moved from the red house to a new apartment building, and then to another. The buildings were all within walking distance of downtown Hempstead. Jessica also shuttled between the village's decrepit elementary schools several times. The harried teachers and guidance counselors had little time or resources to deal with a problem child like her. Two of the schools were eventually closed because the buildings, plagued by water leaks, structural hazards, mold, and rodents, were declared too dangerous to house students.[1]

In July 1999, Jessica turned eleven. Her mother promised her a birthday party in Bradley Park, down the street from their new house. Ana had just given birth to twin boys, and the party would partly be a celebration for them, but Jessica was excited anyway. In the fall, she would be going to middle school, and she was consumed by giddy fear, but also hope that her new school would be different. She was already going through puberty, and people said she was pretty. Although her personality still vacillated between extreme shyness and all-consuming rages, the sense that her life was about to change energized her. At the party, she felt confident and happy, surrounded by her mother's friends and her uncles. Soon they were drunk, and Jessica herself was tipsy after sneaking a beer. They laughed and danced on the scraggly brown grass of the park. The sun slipped from the sky, but they stayed on. Jessica didn't feel sleepy. Her brother called for her from behind some shrubs, where he was sitting with some of his high school friends. She skipped over and sat down. When they passed her a joint, she took a drag, coughing, then laughing at herself and coughing more. Jessica gleefully took another drag. She felt happy.

The glow of the party lasted only a few days. One afternoon soon after, Jessica was at home in her room when her uncle slipped through the door. It was the uncle who often appeared in her dreams, razor in hand. Jessica always kept her distance from him. He scared her, but as he approached her bed, a new sort of terror welled up and paralyzed her. She closed her eyes.

The abuse lasted for several months. Jessica did not tell anyone that it was happening. By the time she started at Alverta B. Gray Schultz Middle School, her expectations for a new start had withered. But for the first time in sixth grade, two teachers paid attention to her—a rookie social studies teacher from Brooklyn with tattoos and a sweet-natured, older English teacher. The social studies teacher was tough on her, and she basked in the mothering style of her English teacher. For a while she tried to finish her homework. She had struggled with reading in elementary school but was slowly starting to catch up.

But Alverta B. Gray was just as troubled as the village's elementary schools and lagged far behind schools in other nearby towns when it came to academics. After Jessica was promoted to the next grade, she lost contact with the two teachers and made some new friends. A few she met through her brother, who sometimes let her tag along with him. Most were in high school and came around in the afternoons to the middle school parking lot to hang out. They were members of Salvadorans With Pride, and she liked their tough swagger. She also felt safer around them. When the other kids saw her with the high school boys, they didn't bother her or call her slow. They left her alone. For the first time ever, she felt like someone was on her side.

CHAPTER 10

The Rivals

● ● ●

Many of the Hispanic immigrants who arrived in Hempstead in the 1990s, including Jessica's family, found themselves in neighborhoods like the Hills and the Heights. There, drug dealers had replaced the Polish gangs. Later, the Bloods and the Crips took over. The newcomers were easy targets for the gangs; many were undocumented immigrants and did not have bank accounts, so they carried cash in their pockets on payday. When they were robbed, they were usually too scared of deportation to call police. To defend themselves, the men banded together. One group chose a name that borrowed the English of their aggressors: the Redondel Pride. They grew quickly.

The group was more than a gang. It also functioned as a support organization for the men, most of them day laborers. They raised a pot of money for members to draw from if they fell behind in rent or got sick, and they helped each other find work. As the group evolved, the leaders came up with a new idea. Worried that they would create even more problems for themselves if police perceived them as a gang, they decided they should transform themselves into a community organization. The plan was to promote themselves as a self-help group and to make it clear that they disdained violence. They envisioned a center where Salvadoran workers could come for job training and take computer and English classes.[1] In keeping with its positive ambitions, the group broke away from the Redondel Pride and named themselves Salvadorans With Pride. They formed a board and marched in the Central American parade.[2] They even called a meeting with the village police to discuss their goals.

Chief Russo agreed to the meeting, but he was skeptical. He had watched the graffiti evolve and could decipher the tags that identified which neighborhoods belonged to which gang. His detectives had recently arrested fifty members of the Redondel Pride, SWP's predecessor, for dealing guns and cocaine.[3] Some SWP members had also been arrested for fighting.[4] Nevertheless, along with some other village leaders, he showed up at the appointed time to listen to the men's proposal. They explained their goals and made their plea for police recognition.[5] In the end, he didn't buy it. Russo and other officials saw little difference between SWP members and other gangs.[6]

SWP chose white as the color of their bandana, meant to symbolize a flag of surrender and their neutrality in Hempstead's gang conflicts. They called their parties "fundraisers." Alcohol flowed freely, and money was collected and held in reserve for the group. But as new members joined, their good intentions began to unravel.

Along Main Street, Mara Salvatrucha was not professing the same positive goals as SWP. MS-13 had grown, too, and mostly concerned themselves with drinking and fighting with their black and Hispanic rivals. The two diverged as SWP tried to work with police and MS-13 became more involved in drugs and violence. Personality clashes, including enmity between Julio and one of SWP's founders, a friend from his early days in Hempstead who he believed had betrayed him and was collaborating with police, widened the divide. Still, for a while the two groups got along. Mara Salvatrucha members even stopped by SWP parties occasionally. But it was at one of those joint parties in the late nineties that SWP's higher-minded goals collapsed entirely.

MS-13 members from Hempstead arrived late in the evening at an SWP house in Uniondale, near the border with Hempstead. Most of the SWP members were already staggering drunk. MS-13 members pushed their way in and grabbed bottles. The music boomed, and a few couples swayed to the rhythm in the center of the room. The MS-13 members stood on one side, getting rowdier and more aggressive. All it took was a remark about one of the women. A bottle flew across the room, and the party erupted into a brawl. A gun was drawn and brandished at the MS members, who fled into the night. The two gangs—some in SWP were beginning to embrace the term—became bitter enemies.

A bloody series of assaults followed over the next several weeks. Then, on March 29, 1998, MS-13 members shot dead a member of Salvadorans With Pride in front of a church in the nearby town of Mineola.[7] Chief Russo was dealing with an escalating gang war, not just graffiti. It was what he had feared all along.

At the same time, murder, and crime in general, was plummeting. By the mid-1990s, the crime rate in Nassau County was hitting its lowest point since officials started keeping track in 1975.[8] Hempstead still had a larger share of the murders and other crime than other places in the county, but in 1996, there were only twenty-two murders compared to fifty-five in 1984. Despite the fighting between the gangs, the village was slowly rising out of the ashes.

But it didn't feel that way to the police as they watched the two groups flex their muscles. Although they favored baseball bats and fists—more like the Polish gangs than the storied Bloods and Crips—the newcomers somehow seemed more threatening.

Chief Russo called the school and asked them if he could post an officer or two—he was convinced the gangs would appear there if they hadn't already—but school officials rebuffed him. They did not want to talk about gangs.[9] School was a place of learning, not a jail. Frustrated, Russo assigned a group of officers to focus on the graffiti. They formed a quick response team and bought buckets of paint to erase any vandalism as soon as it appeared. Russo also started keeping a list of gang members in a binder, along with photos and symbols deciphered from the graffiti. Any boys who fulfilled at least three characteristics of a gang member—tattoos, wearing colors, friendships with known gang members—were added. It was an idea Russo had borrowed from California, and the binder quickly grew fat.

He took trips around the country studying different police departments' gang units, including Boston's innovative gang prevention program. The city sent "street workers" on nightly patrols to meet face-to-face with gang members and mediate conflicts. Police, together with community organizations, also visited the gangs in their neighborhoods and promised to crack down hard if the gangs kept up their fighting and to ease up if the violence stopped. Russo convinced the school board to let him bring in a new national gang prevention strategy supported by the Justice Department based on the principles of the D.A.R.E. drug program. The program, known as G.R.E.A.T., taught students to repeat the same mantra they learned in D.A.R.E., "just say no."[10] The program's effectiveness received mixed reviews, but for now, it was all Hempstead had.[11]

In Long Island, Russo felt as if his police department were the only one willing to acknowledge the gangs. The feds, on the other hand, were talking about youth gangs as a nationwide problem. He and the village mayor made some calls. The Drug Enforcement Administration, the Bureau of Alcohol, Tobacco, and Firearms, and the U.S. district attorney's office quickly agreed to assign agents to help fight the Hempstead Village gangs. The Nassau County police and district attorney also sent representatives. Russo now had a federal gang task force. He assigned some of his veteran narcotics detectives to the team, among them Detective Ricky Smith.

In 1999, as the gang unit took shape, a white college student, Damian Corrente, was murdered in Freeport, a racially mixed suburb a few miles south of Hempstead. His killers were members of Mara Salvatrucha. The suburbs were stunned.

Damian was from a nice, middle-class family. His maternal grandparents, the offspring of Irish immigrants, had been some of the first homeowners in Levittown. His father's side of the family was Italian, and he grew up in New Jersey. His parents met in an Italian club on Long Island, where Damian's father played in a band that took requests for Italian folk songs. The couple raised four children in Freeport, in a nice house, in a nice neighborhood.[12]

The Correntes didn't notice the new wave of Hispanics in town. The men who gathered in front of the Home Depot downtown didn't bother them, and the new Hispanic-owned shops downtown seemed to be keeping the town viable as it recovered from a slump during the '80s and '90s. In 1988, Pamela, Damian's mother, wrote a letter to the editor defending her village after a newspaper story was published about the spread of the crack epidemic in Freeport. She didn't see it. Years earlier, she had chosen the suburban town as the perfect spot for her own four children to replicate the idyllic middle-class childhood she had in Levittown. There were problem pockets, but the people who lined up at the town's soup kitchen were mostly working people struggling to pay their bills, and they came from elsewhere, she wrote in her letter—the rest of town was as lovely as it had ever been with its picturesque waterfront and ice skating rink that was "the envy of many towns."[13]

She felt the same a decade later. Like most white suburban mothers, what she knew of gangsters came from movies—although she may have known a bit more than most. Her casting business found jobs for her son's strapping Italian and Irish friends in mafia films, including *Goodfellas* and *A Bronx Tale*. Damian himself played parts in *Law and Order*, *NYPD Blue*, and the film *Hurricane Streets*, about young street hoodlums in New York City.[14] He put his acting career on hold, however, to become a premed student at the State University of New York in Stonybrook, upstate.[15]

On the morning of January 14, 1999, Pamela sent Damian, who helped out with the family business whenever he was in town, on an errand to the bank. On the way, Damian got a phone call. It was Harold, one of his friends from elementary school and a troublemaker whom Pamela never liked. He wanted a ride, and Damian agreed. He didn't know about the fight Harold was in two days earlier with a group of Salvadoran gang members.[16]

Harold was headed to a pool hall in a strip mall, and as they pulled into the parking lot, a trio of men jumped out from behind some parked cars and ran up to the car. Harold got out to confront them, but Damian stayed where he was. The men shouted in Spanish as they pulled out guns. Harold was shot once as he turned to run. Damian was shot five times: twice in the head, twice in the chest, and once in the side.[17]

At around 3:30 that afternoon, Pamela drove home from work past the pool hall. She glanced over at the parking lot filled with ambulances and police cars, and kept driving. She assumed the sirens were sounding the notes of someone else's tragedy. A few minutes later, she got a message. A friend had heard something happened to Damian. She called the police, but they told her nothing. She called around to emergency rooms and finally found the one where Damian was taken. When she arrived, he was already gone.

The next day, she felt as if she were seeing her town for the first time. The beatific place she had described in her letter ten years earlier now seemed like an urban hell. Overnight, the town appeared to have been scrawled in ominous graffiti—warnings in neon bubble letters she had failed to heed before, at her family's peril. A dazzling rainbow of T-shirt colors worn by local teenagers was a code she didn't understand but knew it meant danger. The new faces she once ignored in the supermarkets seemed to leer knowingly at her. She went to community meetings held in the wake of the murder. There she scolded the other parents and pointed her finger at the illegal immigrants. But much of her anger was directed at the police.

She went to a meeting with Freeport's police chief, Michael Woodward, but became impatient when he began to outline in meticulous detail the history of the gangs, starting with Los Angeles.

"You motherfucker, my son dropped dead right in front of your doorstep," she screamed at him before storming out. "We don't want to hear about Los Angeles, and fucking 17th Street or whatever it is."

She wanted the killers in jail, or better: dead.

Chief Woodward did some research and created a pamphlet about the gangs, which he dedicated to Damian. The Veterans of the Vietnam War paid to print it, and the front page listed eight American wars. "Our veterans did not fight, sacrifice their future or die in these wars to protect other nations and for this country's own freedom to have it decay from within as a result of Gangs in America robbing our youth and country of a future," it read. On the inside, the pamphlet listed ways of identifying gang members and announced the Freeport police's new home visit program, in which police would go to the homes of youth reported to be in gangs to meet with them and their families. Woodward met again with Pamela, and the two eventually joined forces.[18] They created a television public service announcement, and Woodward started giving presentations about gangs in the local schools. Later, Woodward and Russo joined the same organization, Fight Crime: Invest In Kids, a group of state police chiefs that issued a series of reports calling for more gang intervention programs in their towns.

Damian's murder, along with the rising media attention to gangs around the nation, reverberated elsewhere on the island. The county was on high alert as officials and the media sounded an alarm about a new crisis lapping at the edge of its green suburban lawns. Reports of grisly gang-related murders multiplied, even as the actual tally of murders and violent crime dropped again in 1999. In 1998, two months before Damian's murder, the *Times* ran a long article about Long Island's rising gang problem. A slew of other articles soon followed.

The *Times* story, which included the subtitle "The Invasion: From Big Cities to Your Town," warned that gangs like Mara Salvatrucha came equipped with knowledge of "heavy weaponry."[19] The Hispanic gangs had "no respect for law or family" because of their experience in the civil war back home, one expert suggested. Others stated that the gangs were a product of alienation, poverty, "lack of education," and "lack of family discipline."[20] Woodward was quoted, too. He argued that ending gang violence in the suburbs wouldn't be a "quick fix" but would "need a tremendous amount of resources."[21] Police couldn't do it all, he said. Yet as concern swelled to a panic after Damian's death, the only fix that gained traction was more policing.

In Hempstead, the gang task force got to work. As the crime rate continued to drop, the Hempstead Village Police and the federal agents constructed a case against what was now Nassau County's most feared gang, SWP. It wouldn't be just any indictment. The mission was to cut off the head of the defunct social service organization, put away its members for life, and scare off wannabe gang members. Their strategy was to use RICO.

The Racketeer Influenced and Corrupt Organizations (RICO) law passed in 1970, at a moment when federal officials were fretting over the Italian mafia's potential threat. In a major federal report on crime commissioned by President Lyndon B. Johnson, issued by the Katzenbach Commission, officials worried that the mob—which the report said worked "within structures as complex as those of any large corporation, subject to laws more rigidly enforced than those of legitimate governments"—was getting involved in white collar crime.[22] Congress followed up with a law it hoped would keep the mob from using dirty money or violent intimidation to muscle its way into the legitimate economy and would protect "legitimate" businessmen from the competition of the Sicilian-led syndicate. The creators of RICO never imagined that the statute would eventually be stretched into the "crime of being a criminal."[23]

The law prohibited using dirty money to buy an interest in a legitimate enterprise, extortion, loan-sharking, and running an enterprise using those methods. Most important for the effort against gangs later on, it prohibited individuals from engaging in conspiracies to do any of the above. Vague terms like "enterprise" and "corruption" made the law open to wider usage beyond the lawmakers' original intentions.[24] In the law, a racketeering activity was defined as any two or more crimes, one of which could simply be membership in the "enterprise." The law also allowed for harsher prison sentences including the death penalty, even in states that didn't have capital punishment.

Although it took a few years, federal prosecutors eventually caught on to the fact that Congress had handed them a weapon of unprecedented legal power. Armed with this broad new law, U.S. attorneys now had the power to try traditionally local crimes like murder and robbery.[25] Any set of crimes committed in a series by a group of people were potential targets for a RICO case. The second crime didn't even have to be with the same group of people.[26]

Some legal experts worried the law undermined protections against double jeopardy.[27] They argued that juries shouldn't be allowed to consider other crimes when deciding whether to convict a defendant. But RICO withstood the scrutiny of the Supreme Court. It was set to stay.[28]

While the law brought down some corrupt government officials and white-collar fraudsters, it became known for breaking the Italian mafia. Then, in the eighties and nineties, as street gangs like the Bloods, Crips, and Latin Kings appeared to be going national, prosecutors used RICO against them, too. The federal investigation into SWP, which started around the time Damian was murdered, was completed within a year. In December 2000, they made the arrests. Eight men were hauled in, including one of SWP's founders.[29] Four were charged with murder, the rest with assaults and robberies.[30]

With the indictments, the members of gang task force clapped themselves on the back. There was more work to be done, they told newspapers, but they had lopped off the head of the beast. The younger members were already getting word of the indictments, and the police were certain the gang would be crippled, if not crushed completely.[31]

CHAPTER 11

Blood Out

● ● ●

Jessica's family expected her to join Mara Salvatrucha in the way others assumed their children would follow in their footsteps to become doctors or lawyers. Her uncles had stayed deeply involved, and her cousins often repeated a mantra passed along to the next generation: "*sangre por sangre*, blood in, blood out. You were born into MS; you're gonna be in MS."

But on the day she watched her uncle beaten by the gang in seventh grade, she thought she had found a way out. Her SWP friends had done more to protect her than her real family ever had. She heard about the SWP members arrested a year earlier, but she was undeterred. SWP promised to be her true family, and she believed them.

She had only a vague idea of MS-13's global reach or SWP's designation as one of the most dangerous gangs on Long Island. Her patchy knowledge of gang life in Central America came from the news on Spanish-language television and stories told by relatives. One of her aunts described the screams she heard when Mara Salvatrucha members boarded a bus in Honduras at Christmastime and fired on the passengers. One of her uncles was said to have bribed his way out of a Honduran prison with a pair of Nikes and some American dollars one week before a gang riot broke out and the prison burned down.

In Long Island, the two gangs borrowed their styles from their black counterparts. Gang members in Central America tattooed their faces— not in Hempstead. Salvadorans With Pride accepted a handful of 18th Street members who trickled into town from Los Angeles, but most of their members were drawn from the halls of the middle school and high school. They were first-generation Americans, born to the original wave of Central American immigrants. MS-13 was made up mostly of new arrivals. Some were familiar with the gang in their countries, but they wore the oversized blue T-shirts, baggy pants, and protective hoodies that were the uniform of American gangs.

To Jessica, the gang was simply her social circle. She knew little about the world beyond the Laundromat parking lot where she hung out with her local posse. She spent most of her time there drinking, smoking marijuana, and snorting cocaine in the green glow of the neon outlining the Laundry Palace's domed towers. She went to school less and less, but no one seemed to notice.

Although traditions and rituals that communicated gang affiliation in Long Island, such as clothing colors, sneaker brands, and belt lengths, meant nothing to gang members in Central America, who differentiated their friends and foes by tattoos, other aspects were universal. Respect was earned by the amount of pain one was able to inflict and endure, and enduring pain was something Jessica was good at.

Being a girl in the gang automatically reduced her status, since the common route to becoming a girl gang member was frequent sex with the boy members. Jessica was determined not to fit the stereotype. She cultivated her androgynous look, abandoning girly attire and hiding her growing body in baggy pants and loose T-shirts. She got into fights to prove herself whenever she could. When she couldn't participate, she would stand to the side like a boxing coach and direct other members' punches, telling them to slam a rival's head against the cement or on a car hood. She would throw rocks and bricks, and when she did jump into the fray, she was out for blood. She was living out the violent scenes she had watched from the red house's front door.

By the time she was fourteen, life at home was worse. Her mother remained furious that Jessica had joined the gang, but she also needed Jessica to help her with the twin toddlers. Sometimes they forged delicate truces. During one of these periods, Ana took Jessica to a family gathering at the home of an aunt, Angela, who was dating a Mara Salvatrucha member. Jessica had once been close to Angela, who was only slightly older than she was, but they hadn't spoken since she joined SWP. In an act of teenage defiance, Jessica wore a white flag, her gang's symbol, draped around her neck to the party. A stupid mistake, she realized, as she looked around the smoky living room. The room was full of empty beer cans, and the boyfriend's gang member friends were mostly hulking men with prominent Mara Salvatrucha tattoos. Ana's presence was all that protected her.

She stuck to her mother's side the whole evening. But Ana was drinking again, and soon was swaying out the door home. Jessica was right behind her, but her aunt blocked the way. Jessica should stay here, spend some time with her cousins, Angela sweetly suggested. Ana nodded distractedly. Then she walked out. After watching her go, Jessica slipped into a side room to watch television with a younger cousin. Angela appeared at the door.

At first she was friendly, asking Jessica about school and boys. Then she changed the subject, and her tone turned menacing. She had heard Jessica joined SWP, and MS-13 had it out for a few of Jessica's new friends, she hissed. Jessica better watch her own back, too. Jessica tried to contain her anger. She wouldn't have a chance in this house full of drunken MS-13 members. But she had never been good at controlling herself. Jessica jumped off the couch and snatched the cigarette from her aunt's hand, jamming the burning end against Angela's skin. Angela grabbed at her, but

Jessica was too quick. She ran out the door before anyone could catch her. She walked the mile back home, hugging the walls of buildings and ducking into the shadows. For the next few weeks she glanced over her shoulder every few seconds.

She tried to be careful, but Hempstead was a small town. One afternoon she was walking to the salon alone to get her nails done—one of the feminine weaknesses she allowed herself—when a blue van pulled up next to her. Her aunt and three of her friends from the party jumped out. There was a fat one, two short ones, and Angela. The fat one held a box cutter. Jessica steadied herself—if she was good at anything, it was fighting. She went for the big one first, jabbing her fist into the woman's face.

But soon they overpowered her. Two of them forced her to kneel on the ground, her arms splayed, while her aunt kicked her in the back, her weak spot. It had never fully recovered from the beating she got the day she was jumped into the gang. Another kicked her in the face and slapped her. Angela walked around in front and took the box cutter from her friend. She stood there, glaring down at Jessica for what seemed like minutes. Jessica pictured her uncle, razor in hand. She braced herself for the pain. But Angela went easy on her. She lifted Jessica's limp hand in hers, the cigarette burn still blistering on the back, and sliced three times. Then the women let her drop to the ground, climbed back into the van, and took off.

Jessica lay on the street, waiting for the ambulance that would take her back to Mercy.

Jaime and Daniel, 2000–2003

CHAPTER 12

Border Crossing

● ● ●

In the winter of 2001, Daniel followed his aunt into the crowded bus terminal in San Miguel, a smoggy colonial city in El Salvador. A few elderly people dragged cheap suitcases and oversized plastic bags filled with clothing, but most were young and traveled lightly. They craned their necks anxiously in lines snaking away from the ticket booths, as children played around them on the grimy floor. He gripped his aunt's hand as she steered him around clusters of families clinging to each other in teary farewells. The monotone of an announcer reading through lists of destinations drowned out their hurried footsteps. Off to the side of the jostling mass, a man and two wide-eyed younger children stood waiting. They stopped there. The children stared at Daniel, who was short for a twelve-year-old, with a round face that made him look even younger. He smiled, hoping it would force him to feel as brave as he looked. His aunt spoke softly to the man. Then she turned to say good-bye with a quick hug, and walked away.

The stranger, a coyote contracted by his mother to guide him across the three borders that lay between him and his mother, didn't talk much.

Daniel followed him onto a bus marked "Guatemala." He stuffed his school bag under his seat and focused his gaze out the window. As the bus lurched out of the station in San Miguel and pulled beyond the city's sprawling suburban slums, he tried to imagine what his new life might look like. The photographs his mother had sent over the years and the dubbed American comedies he watched on television were his only points of reference. As he concentrated on compiling these images into a mental picture of his new home, he was almost able to forget the image of his aunt's tearful face before she turned away.

Hours later, he jolted awake. They were in Guatemala, and he and the two younger children were being ushered off the bus into another bus terminal, this one more rundown than the one in San Miguel. They waited for the bus to Mexico City to be called, and then climbed aboard for the next leg of the journey. In between naps, Daniel snacked on chips and cookies and peered groggily out the window at the blur of cacti and cities passing by. By the time they arrived in Mexico City, he had forgotten what day it was. He was separated from the two other children and put on a third bus labeled Tijuana. He waved good-bye as they trailed along behind another coyote. They were the only people he knew in this new country, although they had barely spoken during the journey. Even the five-year-old seemed to sense it was safer to stay silent.

When they arrived in Tijuana hours later, it was dark. He followed the man through a shiny station that seemed more like a shopping mall and climbed into a car driven by another stranger. The neon lights of the bars and occasional white face suggested they were getting close to their destination. They drove to a small house on the outskirts of town. There a dozen men lounged on couches and beds. Daniel was the youngest.

A week passed. The men were nice. Most were younger than thirty and on their way north to work. They cooked him the food the smugglers occasionally dropped off and took him on furtive excursions to the beach nearby. Daniel tried to enjoy the newfound freedom that allowed him to buy candy whenever he wanted with the small amount of cash his aunt had pressed into his hand. But when a new man showed up at the front door of the house and told them it was time to go, he was relieved.

It was the middle of the night. They left the house in two groups of six. The plan, Daniel soon realized, was to pass the border checkpoint in the trunk of a Honda Civic. The smuggler directed them to climb in and lay down against each other like spoons. Daniel was crammed in the middle, but the trip was short. In fifteen minutes they were over the bridge and unloading at another house, where they showered to strip themselves of each other's sweat. They were allowed only a quick nap before they were dragged from sleep and told to get back in the trunk. This time there were two more people. Daniel was again in the middle, and this time the trip was longer. The woman in the far back began to sob. There was no air in the stifling trunk, and the smell made him gag.

They climbed out into a parking garage near the Los Angeles airport. The sense of excitement and adventure that had sustained him drained away as exhaustion and fear took over. Daniel had never flown in an airplane before. The others were seated nearby, but they were told to act as if they had never met. They also were told not to talk to the stewardesses or the people sitting next to them. Daniel scooted to a middle seat, away from the window, as soon as he could. Then he clenched his fists and tried to keep from crying. He was sure the plane was going to crash. When the stewardesses came around to offer drinks and peanuts, he tried to follow instructions; he shook his head and said one of the few English words he knew, "No." They were persistent, and Daniel was thirsty, but even after four hours on the plane, he resisted the urge to ask for water, or to get up and go to the bathroom. By the time they landed at JFK airport, he was ready to give in to the tears he had kept so far at bay.

In the airport, a woman grabbed his hand. He didn't recognize her, but he followed along as she made a phone call and led him toward baggage claim, where they stood scanning the faces in the waiting area. He didn't see anyone he knew. He saw a woman running toward them with tears streaming down her face. As she clasped him in a hug, Daniel realized it was his mother—he recognized her from the photograph he had hanging in his room at home. But he felt nothing, just embarrassment for this woman he hardly knew. He didn't tell her how scared he was.

• • •

The same month in San Pablo Tacachico, a small town on the outskirts of San Salvador, another twelve-year-old was packing his bag in preparation for the journey north. Jaime Alvarenga's mother, Rosa, had called earlier in the week to say she finally had enough money to pay the coyote. It cost $5,000—money slowly accumulated over seven years of cooking and doing laundry for her neighbors, mostly male day laborers who had left their families behind, too. A few years earlier, Rosa had paid another $5,000 to bring Jaime's older brother, Alvaro.

The timing seemed good to bring Jaime to Long Island. His grandmother, who had raised him after his mother left, had died the month before. His elderly grandfather was frail, and his aunts were busy with their own children. Without his grandmother, Jaime would be left to fend for himself.

On the morning he left, Jaime hugged his grandfather good-bye and hoisted a knapsack onto his back. Jaime's aunt walked him to the bus stop. Another boy was there with his aunt waiting to go, too. Their families had arranged for them to travel together, hoping that two would get a better deal from the coyote than one, and that together they might be safer. They would cross through the Arizona desert. It was a cheaper route than through Tijuana, but also more dangerous. Jaime's aunt kissed him and turned away.

That year, in 2001, Daniel and Jaime were part of a wave of Central American children taking to the roads north. At bus stations across Central America, grandmothers and aunts who had stood in as mothers hugged them good-bye. With whispers to be good, they shepherded the children into the hands of smugglers. Rules about talking to strangers were turned on their heads. The youngest were told to stay quiet, and the older ones told to lie if border agents, military officers, or police questioned them about who they were or where they were headed. They were received at the other side as prodigal children, even though it was their families who had left them behind. Although there was no reliable gauge of tracking how many were slipping past the border, in 1997 the Immigration and Naturalization Services caught 2,375 children crossing illegally without their parents.[1] By 2002, the number nearly doubled, to 5,385, and it kept growing. By 2007, the Office of Refugee Resettlement, which took over the job of caring for unaccompanied immigrant children from the Immigration and Naturalization Service in 2003, took about 1,000 to 1,600 children into its care each month.[2] Nearly 90 percent of them were from Guatemala, Honduras, and El Salvador.

Some left on their own to escape domestic violence—nearly 70 percent of Salvadoran children reported being victims of abuse—or the crime taking over the region.[3] Most were sent for by parents who had left years earlier to look for work in the United States, some during civil wars in El Salvador and Guatemala. But many others left after, when it became clear that the peace accords and disbanding of the armies were not bringing the promised peace or prosperity.

In El Salvador, the homicide rate rose steadily upward after the war, and street killings quickly outpaced the violence of the eighties.[4] About 5,000 people were killed annually during the last years of the Salvadoran war. After the war ended, the number of people killed rose to as many as 9,000 a year.[5] The homicide rate was 114 per 100,000 people, more than in Colombia, where a civil war was still raging, and ten times the murder rate in the United States during the crack epidemic.[6] Kidnappings, armed robberies, and bus hijackings were common.[7] The criminals— gang members, drug runners, and paramilitary organizations still operating clandestinely—outnumbered the newly formed police forces, which became known for violence and corruption.[8]

Political and economic reforms did not go well, either. The competitive, open democracy the peace was supposed to bring never arrived. Instead, ARENA, the party born of a right-wing paramilitary group, stayed in power, in part by stoking fears about the gangs and rising street violence. At first, newly adopted neoliberal economic policies prescribed by Washington propelled the economy ahead of its neighbors.[9] But then the economic growth rate began to fall as inflation rose, and the per capita GDP dropped to below 1970s levels.[10] The government promoted more privatization and free trade, and in 2001 converted the Salvadoran currency to the U.S. dollar to boost the faltering economy.

Standards of living, education, and work for poor Salvadorans continued to worsen. The privatization of electricity did not improve service, although it raised costs for consumers, while the sputtering leftist movement criticized the switch to the dollar as only beneficial to the wealthy.[11] Dollarization also curbed the government's ability to control the country's rising inflation.[12] The income gap grew as wages stayed stagnant. Close to 40 percent of Salvadorans earned less than $1 a day by 2000, while the wealthiest 20 percent enjoyed 45.6 percent of the nation's income.[13]

Rural areas were deforested as farmers struggled to coax crops out of the tired land, and they soon emptied as Salvadorans flocked to the cities.[14] Some migrants tried their luck in the growing foreign-owned factories known as maquiladoras and in the service sector, sending money back to those who stayed behind in the villages.[15] But the cities couldn't accommodate all of them. Many left for the United States, gradually transforming labor into the country's most important export. More followed after Hurricane Mitch in 1998 and a major earthquake in January 2001 further decimated the country's economy.[16] By 2003, more than a million Salvadorans lived in the United States. The $2 billion they sent home each year—15 percent of the country's GDP—propped up both the Salvadoran economy and their families.[17]

The trip north was not easy, and it was expensive. Often migrants with children could only afford to pay for themselves. Once they found a job and paid their debt to the coyote for their own trip, they hoped to raise money to send for the rest of their family in stages. Many spent years sending some money home while putting aside savings to reunite their families. By 2000, thousands of Central American parents working in the United States had accumulated enough to pay for their children's trips, leading to the surge of children crossing alone. Later, stories emerged of smuggling rings that extorted money from desperate parents, sold children to adoption agencies in Guatemala, or abandoned children who couldn't keep up on the journeys across the desert.[18] But the risks of the journey had to be weighed against the option of leaving their children in countries increasingly consumed by violence and poverty. The troubles they might face in American suburbs like Hempstead appeared trivial in the face of the desperation and despair back home.

Some were granted temporary legal status by the U.S. government because of the natural disasters. Immigrants from Honduras, El Salvador, Guatemala, and Nicaragua who arrived within a certain time frame after Hurricane Mitch in 1998 were granted temporary protected status by the Clinton administration.[19] The legal status was extended for several years for Hondurans and Guatemalans. Salvadorans were allowed to apply separately for temporary legal status following the 2001 earthquake.[20] About 250,000 Salvadorans were granted temporary status, less than a fifth of the total number of Salvadorans living in the United States.[21] Temporary status allowed them to work but barred them from applying for permanent residency or a green card.[22] They would never become citizens, and to apply for the program, most had to have made the treacherous border crossing.

The trip became more dangerous during the late 1990s, just as the number of unaccompanied children trying to cross the border began to increase. Border crackdowns blocked easier paths through urban areas. Three programs launched in 1993 and 1994, Operation Hold the Line, Operation Gatekeeper, and Operation Safeguard, cut off once-popular crossings through El Paso, San Diego, and Nogales, Arizona. Under Gatekeeper, the number of border agents was doubled to 2,264 along the Tijuana route that Daniel followed. A new fence was built along forty-five miles of border near San Diego, while underground sensors turned more remote pathways into a minefield for illegal crossers.[23]

In 1996, President Clinton expanded the border crackdown begun during his first term. Passed with the enthusiastic support from the Republican Congress, Clinton's Illegal Immigration Reform and Immigration Responsibility Act increased the U.S. Border Patrol to 10,000 agents from 5,175 and gave the new troops access to equipment from other government agencies.[24] The border patrol soon took to the skies in fixed-wing aircraft and helicopters, donned night-vision equipment, and rode across the desert in off-road vehicles.[25]

To avoid the fences and agents, immigrants headed to the remote terrain of Arizona and Texas, where the fences did not reach. While dangerous paths took them through scorching desert, mountains, and the land of hostile ranchers, the numbers of immigrants crossing the border didn't decline. Between September 1999 and September 2000, there were 241 deaths along the border. During the following twelve months, as Jaime began his journey, there were 372. Most of the deaths were along Jaime's route, a stretch of border in Arizona known by the border patrol as the Tucson sector.[26]

A crossing at Sasabe, Arizona, was the new favorite route for immigrants through the sector.[27] Largely untouched by the new border initiatives, the passage led through a remote valley between the mountain ranges west of Nogales. Immigrants gathered sixty miles south of the border in squalid bunkhouses in Altar, Sonora, to buy provisions or make arrangements with coyotes if they hadn't already. Local vendors sold knit hats and gloves for the frigid desert nights.[28] Winter, when Jaime's mother arranged his trip, was one of the most difficult times to cross. It was hot during the day, and the temperatures dropped precipitously at night. Those fooled by the warm daytime temperatures into leaving coats behind were often found frozen in ditches. In later years, a community center in Altar kept track of the names of the dead by taping hundreds of paper strips to a wall.[29]

Groups like Jaime's headed north toward the farming town of Sasabe from Altar. Vans labeled "Altar-Sasabe" left frequently to carry migrants to the staging ground for the last and most difficult stretch of their journey. Their first view of the United States was of a vast yellow grassland broken only by the distant crags of the Baboquivari Mountains. The destination was the highway leading to Tucson, 70 miles away. First, they had to pass through the Buenos Aires Wildlife Refuge, 118,000 acres of desolate plains and rough mountains. Skeletal mesquite trees gave little comfort as the desert sun burned overhead. There were no houses, and few people ventured there besides the small bands of immigrants scurrying daily along the trails. Sparse patches of wetlands and a few oak-lined streams offered the only shade and water for hundreds of miles. They toted gallon jugs of water and their luggage, sometimes running, sometimes crouching in the stiff grass. After miles of walking, exhausted crossers climbed into cars and pickups that bumped along the dirt roads passing through the reserve and carried them to the expressway leading north.

The trip from El Salvador to the Arizona border crossing took Jaime a month. On the other side, an aunt was at the safe house to take him the rest of the way home, to Hempstead, Long Island, where his mother was waiting to embrace him. He was still the spindly boy she remembered, but more than a foot taller. Something else seemed changed, too. She asked him about the trip. He said he didn't want to talk about it.

Hempstead was nothing like the neighborhood where Daniel lived in San Miguel. At home, a Christmas festival each year brought neighbors—all as close as family—together in a big block party. The rest of the year children played soccer in the streets. The neighborhood was poor, but Daniel always had enough to eat and new clothes to wear to school, thanks to the money his mother wired to his aunt. The crime and violence consuming the country didn't reach into his neighborhood elementary school.

His new home in Hempstead was an old three-story brick apartment building that survived the 1941 demolition efforts to transform downtown into a series of parking lots for suburban shoppers. The building, with decorative Tudor trim, matched other buildings from Hempstead's early days, but it stood alone in the center of a strip mall parking lot. Cut off from its counterparts and surrounded on three sides by asphalt, the view from Daniel's new home was of a Home Depot, a Super Stop & Shop, and an Old Navy. The building next door was a drive-through bank, and past that was a Burger King. Older residents spent the afternoons on the building's steps, watching people come and go from the box stores and chatting in Spanish. Day laborers gathered under the trees scattered around the parking lot and waited for work in the early mornings.

Daniel's mother shared the cramped apartment with his uncle. He arrived in the spring, and his mother decided it was too late in the year to enroll him in school. Daniel holed himself up in the apartment for most of the summer, afraid to venture out into the foreign streets.

On the other side of town, in another cramped apartment, Jaime was also getting used to his new surroundings. His grandparent's house in San Pablo had overflowed with cousins who gathered for family meals on the weekends. Their games spilled into the streets in the evenings. On the days when his grandmother didn't button him into a prim school uniform, he ran wild in the nearby fields, picking mangos and diving into swimming holes in the river. The small town was struggling—there were few jobs, and most of the adults lived in America—but the money they sent back kept extreme poverty at bay. Many Salvadoran children supported by parents abroad lived relatively comfortably and had less contact with the gangs and other violence roiling the country. It was the children whose parents couldn't afford to go, or who had been abandoned, who were more apt to join gangs.

Jaime's mother also waited until the fall to send him to school. That summer she tried to re-create his life in El Salvador and bring him out of his shell. They spent several days a week at the public swimming pool. He shared a room with his older brother, who was adjusting well to his new life and walked protectively alongside Jaime every time they left the house. They came home to arrangements of fruit from the supermarket set out by his mother, but it wasn't the same as biting into a fresh mango after grabbing it from a low-hanging branch. He never talked about his trip, or his grandmother, or home. He wasn't sullen, just quiet, and he seemed to warm quickly to his mother despite the years apart. He prayed with her at night before bed, tucking her in with a kiss. She was thrilled to have him with her again, and she assumed he was happy, too.

In September 2001, Jaime and Daniel enrolled in seventh grade at Alverta Gray B. Schultz Middle School on Greenwich Street, near downtown Hempstead. On the first day of school, Daniel sat down apprehensively in the front of his assigned classroom. He was the first one there, and he wasn't sure whether to feel relief to be out of the crowds of children in the hallway or fear of what was to come once the teacher began the English as a Second Language class. Another boy walked in and sat next to him, but Daniel kept his eyes down. Class began, and the teacher introduced an icebreaker game they were to play in Spanish.

The game forced Daniel to look up from the safe beige square of his desk and turn to face the boy next to him. "*Hola. Soy Jaime,*" the boy said. Daniel said hello back. They chatted shyly in Spanish, soon discovering they were both from El Salvador. Daniel described his trip on the airplane and days at the beach in Tijuana. Jaime briefly described his journey through the desert but avoided the details. They traded stories about home and learned that each played soccer. They agreed to meet up later to play. When class ended, they stuck together as they made their way into the school's chaotic corridors. By the end of the day, they were inseparable.

The middle school had more than 1,300 students, as many as the high school down the road. Most were poor, and many struggled with academics. The state had listed Alverta B. Gray Schultz as failing for several years running.[30] Books were in short supply, and computer equipment was lacking.[31] Classrooms were crowded. The school also had a violent reputation after a series of incidents, including arson, which destroyed a classroom, and a knife assault.[32] In 2000, the year before Jaime and Daniel enrolled, the number of students who spoke limited English nearly tripled: to 20 percent from just 7 percent.[33] The number of poor students also jumped. In the 2000–2001 school year, it had been a little more than a third. When Daniel and Jaime started school, 85 percent of students qualified for the free lunch program.

The school's culture was a shock to the new arrivals. In El Salvador, school discipline was strict for those who could afford to go—which included most students with parents working in the United States. In Hempstead, schools were raucous, and fights between classes were routine. Gangs prowled the hallways, even in the middle school. High school students gathered outside the middle school at the end of the day, adding to the mayhem.

The vast majority of new students adjusted to their surroundings, however, learning to cope with the memories of the trip and to get along with new stepparents and younger, American-born siblings. School was scary, but many buckled down and attempted to learn. Jaime and Daniel tried to do the same.

On their fifth day of school, airplanes struck the World Trade Center towers in Manhattan, killing almost 3,000 people. Many were commuters, firefighters, and other first responders from Long Island. Down the street at Hempstead High School that day, students were evacuated because of a bomb threat. Other Long Island schools, fearful that more attacks were coming, sent their students home in the middle of the day.

School started up again on Wednesday, and although Daniel and Jaime had never been to Manhattan, they could feel its proximity in the somber faces of the teachers and other adults. In West Hempstead, less than a mile and a half away, one church lost more than twenty of its members in the terrorist attacks.[34] A handful of the dead were from Hempstead Village. More were finance workers who had lived in the upscale villages surrounding Hempstead. The sorrow and confusion was palpable everywhere, and the anxiety that Jaime and Daniel felt as they navigated this strange and threatening place was now reflected in the faces of the adults. There was no one to reassure them that they would be safe in their new home; instead, the fear that consumed them was amplified and echoed all around them.

CHAPTER 13

A New Threat

● ● ●

The aftermath of the attacks shook the suburban calm, cracking any remaining illusions that the island's winding cul-de-sacs and gated communities were immune from the troubles of the outside world. In New York City, the hole in the skyline became a constant reminder to city residents of their new vulnerability. For suburbanites, the nearness of the violence was just as jarring. To have terror and fear touch suburbia was "not normal," one *New York Times* reporter wrote.[1]

For some, the fear, sadness, and confusion quickly gave way to anger. They lashed out at the newcomers, who seemed to represent the shadowy threat. A *Newsday* reporter watching evacuees from Manhattan on September 11 as they disembarked from a ferry in Glen Cove recorded their reactions: some cried as they ran into the arms of loved ones; one shouted, "Bomb the Palestinians"; while another called for arrests—of whom, he wasn't clear.[2] "This way you take control of what's in this country, and then take it from there," he said. The weekend after the terrorist attacks, police stepped up efforts to thwart hate crimes. They found one man who made a bomb he planned to use "to get an Arab," and arrested a fifteen-year-old boy for calling a 7-Eleven store and threatening to blow it up because he believed the owners were "Hindu."[3]

In November, five Mara Salvatrucha members pleaded guilty for killing Eric Rivera with baseball bats a year earlier as he walked home from the Puerto Rican Day parade.[4] Police charged that Eric resisted the gang's invitations to join them. The beating was their revenge. The defense attorneys in Eric Rivera's case were insistent that their clients weren't gang members. After September 11, however, the lawyers and their clients said they were forced to reverse their pleas from not guilty to guilty. They were convinced it would be impossible to have a fair trial on Long Island—that the rising anti-immigrant sentiment would taint juries. "We could not run the risk of trying a reputed gang case in these times," one of the lawyers, Thomas Liotti, said to explain the change of course.[5]

The fear and anxiety about strangers was not limited to Long Island. Across the nation, a backlash was building.

The week before September 11, the Bush administration made it clear that one of its top priorities would be to solve the immigration problem.[6] President Vicente Fox of Mexico, a man President Bush considered a personal friend, visited the White House on September 6. He stood side by side with the president and declared forcefully that "we must, and we can, reach an agreement on migration before the end of this very year."[7] It was an unprecedented and bold move by a Mexican president, but his chances of pulling it off—if not by December 2001, then soon after—seemed plausible.[8] Mexico was the first country Bush visited during his administration, always an important signal of a president's foreign policy priorities, and Bush was clear about his intentions to create a guest worker program between the two countries that would match "willing workers" to "willing employers."[9] Bush even appeared amenable to an amnesty program for illegal immigrants—which the administration preferred to call "regularization"— although he faced an uphill battle in Congress. He said he was considering a program that would allow both new workers and immigrants living in the United States illegally to apply for temporary legal status, and later permanent status if they met certain requirements.[10]

After September 11, the plan was dropped. The Bush administration began a new campaign to seal off the country. To protect itself in the newly hostile world, the United States insulated itself from outsiders and became increasingly suspicious of foreigners already inside its borders. The rules of entry were tightened and the stakes increased for anyone perceived as a threat. The War on Terror was launched and the Uniting and Strengthening America by Providing Appropriate Tools Required to Intercept and Obstruct Terrorism Act of 2001—the USA Patriot Act—was passed. In the following months, the government detained hundreds of Middle Eastern immigrants, some of them indefinitely if they were "certified" as national security threats.[11] Wiretapping was expanded. Mandatory detention was required for all immigrants in deportation proceedings accused of crimes—even minor ones.[12]

Two years later, the Department of Homeland Security was formed. Within it, a new agency—Immigration Customs and Enforcement— replaced the embattled INS. ICE was created to focus almost exclusively on deporting illegal immigrants, especially those accused of committing crimes. Separate agencies within the department would handle the softer bureaucratic tasks of immigration, refugee, and citizenship applications, but even there the sense of siege was palpable. New requirements for FBI background checks were implemented and stretched the wait to become a citizen indefinitely for some. Often the applicants left waiting were those with Middle Eastern names, but some were from places like Canada and India. Under the Patriot Act, refugees applying for asylum were barred if they gave "material support" to groups considered terrorists by the United States, which could mean small amounts of money, clothing, or food, even if it was coerced. New regulations on remittances—meant to curb money laundering—were implemented, meaning immigrants had to show official identification when they wired money home to their relatives.[13]

The border with Mexico was another point of focus. In the minds of many Americans, the southern border was a weak link. The Bush administration, worried that terrorists would find opportunity in the expanses of Arizona desert and Texas ranchland still unmanned by the border patrol, argued for more expansive enforcement. But much of the rhetoric was symbolic: Only a handful of new agents were deployed in 2002. Thirty-three were added to the more than 9,000 agents along the 2,000-mile border with Mexico, while 15 were added to the 331 assigned to the more than 5,500-mile border with Canada.[14]

Anti-immigrant groups continued to publicize concerns that would-be terrorists would mingle among immigrants crossing the southern border, and as immigration reform stalled, legislation eventually passed allocating more than $1 billion for fences along the border with Mexico. The number of agents was again doubled, to 18,000.[15]

● ● ●

In Hempstead, police were fighting their own war against an increasingly emboldened enemy. Between 1995 and 2001, gang-related arrests tripled in Nassau County. Nassau police said the gangs were spreading and becoming more violent.[16] In September 2001, police declared MS-13 to be the largest gang in Nassau County, a notoriety that propelled them past black gangs such as the Bloods, and their rival, SWP.[17]

SWP had been less active since the RICO arrests the previous year, and as if to emphasize their new status, Mara Salvatrucha launched new attacks against its weakened rival and the black gangs. Drive-by shootings became monthly occurrences. Violent crime was still lower in the village than it had been in thirty years, but during the fall of 2001, news about the War on Terror was interspersed with updates on a spate of new gang attacks.

The first was in late August, when Mara Salvatrucha members killed a fourteen-year-old girl in a drive-by after mistaking her for a member of the Bloods.[18]

On September 8, a seventeen-year-old girl reported that she had been raped in the backyard of a house near the middle school. [19]

On September 10, a Hispanic man was killed in a drive-by in front of a bar in downtown Hempstead.[20]

On September 16, five teenagers jumped a man leaving a catering hall in Mineola, a mostly white town a few miles away from Hempstead.[21] The man died, and the five teenagers were arrested on gang assault charges.

The bloodshed continued into October. On a corner about ten blocks from the middle school, a seventeen-year-old Hempstead High School student died in a drive-by shooting on October 18.[22]

That same month, a group of men in a minivan slowed as they drove past a convenience store a few blocks from the Long Island Railroad station.[23] They fired at a group of SWP members gathered outside. No one died, but to the Hempstead police, it was the most terrifying shooting of all.

The men in the minivan weren't local. They were MS-13 members from Fairfax and Falls Church, Virginia, suburbs of Washington, DC. The group had driven up the day before the shooting. Police said it was unclear why they had come or what their connections were to Long Island. All they knew was that outsiders appeared to be feeding the Central American gang problem.

The spread of the gangs was partly explained by the rapid growth of Hispanic populations as immigrants followed jobs and family to new communities such as Long Island. A new worker in Hempstead might keep in touch with cousins or an uncle in the suburbs of DC or a town in North Carolina, and those cousins might eventually make their way north if jobs dried up in their town. The gang members—who were also plugged into the networks connecting the Central American diaspora—functioned in the same way. Young people kept in touch with each other as they moved around, either following jobs or joining their parents in new towns. The network was loose—local police still believed the gang cliques had few formal ties to groups outside of their immediate area. But there was evidence that gang members communicated with each other online. A

Salvadoran newspaper in Long Island, *La Tribuna Hispana*, published a
story about gangs at Hempstead High School in 2003 on its Web site.[24]
Within a few months, Central American gang members from across the
country and even Canada had left thousands of comments attached to the
article, many of them boasts about the prowess of their particular gang or
clique coupled with insults against commenters from rival gangs.

As the tally of gang incidents spiraled upward, the police pleaded for
more funding and officers. They said the county department was operating with a "skeletal" force and that cases were going uninvestigated.[25] But
the county was mired in a financial crisis after a decade of fiscal mismanagement by the local Republican administration, including unpaid 911
phone bills and bookkeeping that didn't track the number of employees
on the government payroll.[26] Steep salary raises for police had exacerbated
the county budget deficit. The average Nassau County officer made six
figures in 2002.[27] The police budget was cut earlier in 2001, but the top
three officers, including the commissioner, were given raises totaling
$60,000. The number of police officers had decreased by a quarter since
the 1970s, but crime had also dropped steeply.[28] Still, the county police
department said it was overwhelmed.

The new county executive, Thomas Suozzi, was not convinced. Instead
of hiring new officers, the county redeployed seventy-four of its officers
from desk jobs to street patrols and created a new crime statistics database.[29]

But around the island, fear of immigrants, and in particular immigrant
gangs, was rising.

Across the county line in Suffolk, the district attorney announced the
creation of a task force modeled on Hempstead's that would invite federal
agents to help with local gang cases.[30] The gangs were more "pervasive
and menacing" than ever before, he said. Two Suffolk-based lawmakers
took the war against gangs statewide.[31] An up-and-coming state assemblyman, Steve Levy, introduced a bill in the legislature in February 2002
to increase prison sentences for gang crimes. State Senator Michael Balboni, the coauthor of New York State's post–September 11 terrorism law,

sponsored a bill in April to make recruiting for a gang on school property a felony offense.[32]

The bill included a provision to create a statewide database. It was modeled on a similar plan in California. There, in 1997, law enforcement agencies began compiling a database on gang members that tracked everything from their friends to their tattoos. Facial recognition was added later, and police could remotely search the Cal/Gang database from crime scenes.[33] Gang experts and some law enforcement officials regularly criticized the database because police rarely expunged individuals once their names were added, and its estimates of the gang population were notoriously inaccurate.[34] Still, Balboni argued that a similar database would help New York gain control of its fledgling gang problem. He coupled his antigang proposals with promises to implement outreach programs in poor areas, although he noted it might be difficult to "cobble together" the funds.[35] In the end, Balboni's gang proposals didn't pass, but his state terrorism law was later put to use against gang members in New York City. The law defined "terrorism" as committing a crime that was intended to intimidate civilians or influence the government. In 2007, Balboni was promoted to the position of Homeland Security Chief for New York State.[36]

In the fall of 2002, in response to another Mara Salvatrucha drive-by shooting, Suozzi announced that Nassau would also launch a new antigang program, the Nassau County Taskforce Against Gangs.[37] The task force would convene a group of nonprofit leaders, ministers, corrections officers, and prosecutors, led by a Nassau County detective, to discuss gangs at a monthly meeting. They would focus on how to coordinate the various outreach programs intended to reach at-risk youth and prevent them from joining gangs. The task force would also implement "zero tolerance," which Suozzi said meant using police intelligence and statistics to "identify problem areas" and programs that could help.[38] At the same time, however, Suozzi had proposed that spring to cut $600,000 in youth programs from the county budget.[39] The county legislature restored the money, but many of the programs, including counseling and tutoring programs that reached out to immigrant teens, were already weakened after funding cuts during the previous administration.[40]

The gangs didn't go away. In Suffolk, police quietly considered disbanding a unit of gang detectives because it had done little to reduce the number of gang members.[41] In Nassau, the war between MS-13 and SWP escalated over the summer, even as the county threatened RICO prosecutions and promised "zero tolerance." The commanding officer of Nassau's gang unit, Detective Lieutenant Matthew Brady, summed up the frustrations police felt as they tried to understand what motivated the gangs' single-minded violence: "It's almost like if you're not with them, they consider you against them."[42]

CHAPTER 14

Fighting Back

● ● ●

During Jaime and Daniel's first year of school in America, as their new country went to war, drive-by shootings rendered their route to school as dangerous as the conflict-ravaged country they had left behind. Slow-moving cars were cues to duck and run, while the news flashed warnings that the terrorists could strike anywhere next.

The threats that most worried the two boys were even more immediate, however. The bigger kids leered at them in the school hallways. Their sagging pants, long belts, and colored flags communicated in a menacing language that was even more urgent for the boys to learn than English. Fights broke out in hallways, and the newest immigrants were favored targets for bullies. Jaime and Daniel dreaded leaving the safety of their ESL class for lunch and gym, when they faced the threatening looks and mocking laughter of the other students.

In the second week of school, another boy insulted Daniel during class. He couldn't understand all of the English words, but he could tell by his sneer and the grins on the faces of the other students that the boy was making fun of him. Daniel lashed out. He couldn't form a witty comeback in English, so he punched the boy in the mouth. The teacher dragged both to the principal's office, but the administrators didn't speak Spanish, and Daniel couldn't explain his side of the story to them. The boy told his version and was allowed to leave. Daniel was sent to detention. When his mother got a call from the principal, she was furious.

"Why did you come if you are just going to look for problems in school?" she asked him when he arrived home that night.

He didn't answer. He stomped to his room and slammed the door. He was struggling still to connect with his mother and the other members of his family. He missed his aunts and cousins in El Salvador, and the only person he could talk to about it was Jaime.

In class, they sat next to each other in the back of the room, where they attracted less notice, and whispered about girls, classes, and El Salvador. After school, they played soccer, and sometimes Jaime came over to Daniel's house to drink sodas afterwards.

Jaime told Daniel that his mother worked most days and was never home, so they didn't spend time there.

In fact, Rosa was a homemaker who had married a construction worker she met shortly after moving to Hempstead. She was eager to meet Jaime's friends. She bought him sneakers with her savings and cooked meals of meat and rice. Yet Jaime still seemed distant, and spent less and less time at home. When she asked him if he was enjoying his new school, he said he didn't want to go. That wasn't an option, she told him. The conversations ended there.

By the end of the year, neither Jaime nor Daniel had learned much English, although both enjoyed their class work. Jaime was the best at academics. He helped Daniel cheat on tests using the ubiquitous sign language the two absorbed by watching the gang members around them in the school hallways. Jaime would flash Daniel the answers to quizzes from across the room, smiling innocently if the teacher noticed him twisting his fingers into odd shapes. As soon as the teacher looked away, the two collapsed into fits of giggles. They absorbed other information about the gangs, too. The signals, colors, and, most importantly, the borders of the gang territories, were crucial to know if they were going to survive in their new town.

On the last day of school, they promised to call each other over the summer for pickup soccer games and trips to the public pool. But Jaime never called, and he didn't return several messages Daniel left for him. His family had moved from their apartment to a house across town, more than a twenty-minute walk away from Daniel's apartment building in the Home Depot parking lot. Jaime made new friends in his new neighborhood. Over the summer, Daniel also branched out and made new friends with boys in his building. Several went to his school. They taught him handball and English street slang.

Gradually, Daniel forgot the loneliness of the previous summer. With his new friends, he whiled away the hot afternoons smoking marijuana in the alleyway behind the building and playing handball. His new command of slang soon won him some respect from his new friends, most of them native-born Americans. He learned that they were all members of SWP, and eventually they tried to coax him into joining. They promised him protection if anyone gave him problems at school. The summer was ending, and the first day of school loomed. Daniel dreaded going back. It didn't take long for him to agree.

He learned the rules of the gang and memorized its creed. Before September, he was jumped in, solidifying his commitment to the gang.

Jaime's new house was a block from the border with Garden City on a tidy street of small Cape Cod–style homes of brick and vinyl siding. His family's was yellow. A low brick wall hemmed in the mown lawn, and two white stone lions stood sentry at the end of the front walk. Jaime's stepfather tended a garden of tomatoes and green beans that stretched up toward the living room window. The house was rented, and dingy on the inside. Like many immigrants, they shared it with other relatives and renters, but it seemed like a step up. The mall was within walking distance, and so was downtown. He stayed out more often, occasionally worrying his mother, who missed the family trips to the public pool they made the summer before. But Jaime wasn't interested. His new friends were older and tougher. Among them was Julio, who was protective, if temperamental, and who acted as something of a role model for younger boys who hung out at the pool halls downtown. Jaime had not known his father growing up, and he was about the age of Julio's own boy back in San Salvador; Julio gradually took him under his wing.

The week before he began eighth grade, Daniel heard from one of his new SWP friends that Jaime had joined a gang, too—Mara Salvatrucha.

Daniel's friends knew he was close with Jaime. They told Daniel to stop talking to him. Otherwise, both would get a beating, or worse. Daniel protested at first. He couldn't imagine seeing Jaime, whom he still considered his best friend in Hempstead, and turning away.

"That's the rule," his friends repeated, and that was that.

On the first day of school, Jaime and Daniel passed each other in the hall. They kept their heads down and lifted their eyes only briefly before looking away. They had classes together, though. In the back of one classroom, a few days after school started, Daniel confronted Jaime.

"I know you're MS, and I'm SWP, but you know I love you like a friend and a brother," Daniel said.

Jaime nodded.

"I don't do nothing to you—we're cool, so let's not do nothing stupid here. I'm going to defend you if I have to."

After that, they talked in secret. They took their old seats in the back of the classroom and passed notes. Sometimes they communicated in the gang sign language they had mastered over the summer.

By joining SWP, Daniel gained immunity from the bullies who had terrorized him the year before. The gang ruled the hallways of the school. Despite its name, most of its members were Americans of Salvadoran descent. In contrast, MS-13, the gang Julio had helped to found six years earlier, was generally made up of older members, a club of men who earned their living doing day labor or cleaning and security work; as a result, they had very little presence in the schools. Unlike SWP, most of their senior leadership had not been sent off to jail in a RICO case, and MS-13 scorned their weakened, more amateurish rivals. Mara Salvatrucha was considered more serious, although they still only dabbled with drug dealing and were known mostly for their willingness to protect their territory with violence. With MS-13, Jaime had tough defenders when he walked home from school each day, but inside the school there was no one to protect him. Daniel's friends often picked on him, ignoring Daniel's efforts to distract them. They threw wads of paper at him in the halls and splashed him with water in the bathroom. They shoved him against lockers after gym and one day stabbed him with a plastic fork in the cafeteria hard enough to draw blood. Another day in the cafeteria, one of Daniel's friends knocked Jaime's tray of food to the ground to gales of laughter.

Daniel tried not to get involved, but their friendship strained. After one attack, Daniel could tell Jaime was about to cry, but he was afraid to step in and help. Later, he whispered to Jaime that he was sorry.

"I couldn't do nothing about it—you know the rules," Daniel said.

"Yeah, I know the rules. I know it's not your fault," Jaime said before turning away.

Jaime's mother was now on a first-name basis with the principal, who seemed to call weekly to report more trouble involving Jaime. He complained every morning when she woke him up for school. He didn't want to go, but when she asked him why, he was vague.

Rosa was insistent. Jaime was thirteen, the age she had been when she became pregnant the first time. The baby was a girl who died not long after she gave birth, but then she became pregnant with Alvaro, Jaime's older brother, and then Jaime. She was forced to drop out of school and look for work in her village. Jobs were scarce though, and she eventually followed the path of other young people in the town and headed to America.

She was determined that her boys wouldn't end up like her, uneducated and scraping by. She applied for temporary protected status for herself and her sons and was waiting on the paperwork. The only way out of the poverty they lived in, she lectured Jaime, was for him to get an education—it was the reason she came here and sacrificed for years to bring him, too. Although they wouldn't get green cards if they were granted TPS, at least they would be able to go to work legally, and she hoped they could go to college. It was their best chance to make it, and she didn't want him to ruin it. Her oldest son was doing well in school, she reminded him. Why couldn't he?

He begged to be allowed to get a job instead. He could work in construction, like his stepfather—anything but school. She received a call from the school that he was skipping class. She tried to convince the school to send a bus to pick him up, to make sure he got there, but they said he didn't qualify. On some mornings she walked with him and dropped him off at the school door, but she couldn't follow him every day.

By November 2002, Jaime was going to school just once or twice a week. Sometimes he skipped for a week at a time. He moved out of his brother's room and started sleeping on the living room couch, which gave him easy access to sneak out at night. Short of strapping him into bed, Rosa had little power to keep him inside. She could tell he was depressed, but she didn't know what to do. She knew nothing about Jaime's friends. As far as she knew, none lived nearby. Downtown Hempstead and Main Street were within walking distance, but Rosa never knew where he went when he slipped out of the house at night.

One day in early November 2002, she woke up at midnight and discovered the couch empty. She checked the bedroom and the basement, but he was gone.

It was cold, but she waited on the lawn. Two hours later, Jaime pulled up in a battered green taxi.

"*Mamá*, what are you doing out here?" he asked casually as he jumped from the cab.

"Waiting for you," she said. Her voice was trembling. "You don't do this. You know that hanging out in the street at night, something could happen to you."

"Nothing will happen to me, because I always take a taxi," he said.

"What are you doing out on the street anyway?" she said.

He shrugged and said he had been hanging out with a new girlfriend. She wasn't satisfied.

"Oh, you have a girlfriend—so now you can take care of yourself?"

She tried to control the anger and tears she felt welling up. He looked down and didn't reply.

His hair was close-cropped as always, and he wore his T-shirts neatly tucked into his jeans. He didn't look like a gang member to her, but she read the newspaper and knew about the gangs proliferating around town. She had to ask.

"Do you have friends who are in the *mara*?"

"Look, *Mamí*, if I have friends who run around like that, it doesn't mean that I do," he said.

"Well, how sad for a mother to have children running in the street. You should know that we aren't like that."

"*Mamí*, I have to have friends."

He walked past her and went inside, stretching out on the couch. All Rosa could do was go to bed. The next morning, she shook him awake and sent him off to school.

A few weeks later, he disappeared again. This time, he didn't come home from school or later that night. Rosa sat up waiting, but by dawn, he still wasn't home. A second day went by, and Rosa was desperate. She called his school, but they told her he hadn't come to class and there was nothing they could do. She called the police and reported him missing to a detective. They came to the house to take a report, but they couldn't find him.

Three days passed before he came back, dirty and disheveled from sleeping in the streets.

"Jaime Alberto, what is happening to you?" she screamed as he walked in. "Do you have problems?"

"No, *Mamí*."

"So why did you leave?"

"I told you: I don't want to go to school. I already said I don't want to go back to school." He crawled onto the couch and fell asleep.

She looked for counseling at a community center and asked around about her options in family court.

A few days later, he was gone again. This time he didn't return for two weeks. Rosa got in the car and circled Hempstead, rolling slowly past groups of black and Hispanic teenagers in front of the apartment complexes across town. She stayed up each night listening for his footsteps downstairs. Eventually the sleepless nights and worry made her sick. With a high fever, she checked herself into the hospital for a few days. After she returned from the hospital, one of Jaime's aunts finally ran into him at the McDonald's downtown. She told him that Rosa was in bed, sick with worry. That afternoon he appeared in the doorway of her bedroom. She jumped to give him a long hug. After they embraced, he asked if she was okay. She shook her head—"How do you think I am?"

He said he had been working. She began her school lecture again, but he cut her off.

"I won't go," he said.

Rosa had been instructed to call the detectives when he came back, but Jaime begged her not to. He was furious when she picked up the phone anyway. The detectives arrived and questioned Jaime. He answered in monosyllables as Rosa stood by anxiously, trying to catch English words she could understand and looking worriedly at Jaime's stony face. Eventually the detectives left, and Rosa offered to make dinner. Jaime turned and replied in a low, quiet voice:

"I swear to God, I'm never setting foot in this house again."

He walked out the door. He could hear his mother sobbing, but he didn't turn back.

●　●　●

On January 18, 2003, Daniel went to the movies with his family to see *Kangaroo Jack*. The slapstick film was a welcome relief from the screaming fights he was having at home with his mother. He was getting into more trouble at school. She couldn't understand why he was messing up all that she had worked for. That night, however, they maintained a truce. Daniel even felt some peace sitting with his family in the movie theater and laughing at the jokes in English that he only partly understood. They made their way home after the movie, and Daniel went to bed early.

The next morning, one of his friends found Daniel in the hallway of his apartment building. He asked him if he had heard the news: Jaime had been stabbed. Daniel had not seen his friend at school since before the Christmas break and had been concerned. Now he felt sick.

It had been seventeen days since Jaime left his mother standing in the living room. As he promised, he didn't come back. That night, as Daniel laughed with his family at the movie, Jaime was hanging out with MS-13, his newly adopted family. They started the night near the train station, but moved on when some police detectives showed up, among them Detective Ricky Smith. They ended up at a pool hall downtown, where Jaime played a few games with the older boys.[1] At around 3 AM he ran out of money. He left the pool hall with a friend and set out into the cold.

Three men were watching as Jaime headed back toward the Long Island Railroad station. They were members of 18th Street and SWP. Police later identified them as Henry Portillo, age twenty-eight, and Elmer Romero and Darwin Reyes, both twenty-one. Henry first joined 18th Street in El Salvador, and sought the protection of SWP when he arrived in Hempstead. That night, the three started out at Illusions, a club in Uniondale. While they were in the club, someone smashed in Henry's car window.[2] They were convinced Mara Salvatrucha did it, and they went looking for revenge. The men cruised past the pool hall, a known hangout for MS members, just as Jaime and his friend were leaving.

When they saw the men eyeing them outside the hall, the two boys started walking faster. They ran when they realized the men were following them. Jaime's friend got away, but the men trailed Jaime as he headed west on Columbia Street, in the direction of his house. The men pulled out a baseball bat as they got closer. They grabbed him, holding him down as one pummeled Jaime with the bat. Another kicked at him, as the third pulled out a knife. He stabbed Jaime three times in his back and side before they fled.

Jaime was found at 3 AM collapsed on the steps of the Long Island Railroad station in a pool of blood. Someone waiting in line for a bus in the nearby depot called the police. By the time an ambulance arrived, it was too late. Jaime was unconscious and had lost too much blood. He died an hour later at Mercy Medical Center, alone in a hospital room while his mother slept fitfully across town.

Rosa didn't know until the next day. The police stood in the doorway of her living room for the third time in as many months. They looked at the photos of Jaime when he first arrived in Long Island hanging high on the living room walls. He had grown a foot since he came to New York two years earlier and had filled out from the skinny twelve-year-old in the pictures. But they could tell it was Jaime. For a moment, Rosa hoped they were going to say they had found him and braced herself to hear that he was in jail. When they told Rosa to sit down, and shooed the other children out of the room, she knew then why they had come.

Rosa didn't believe he was really dead until her eldest son returned from the morgue a few hours later. He walked toward her, his arms apart to give her a hug, and she collapsed, sobbing.

Daniel didn't know whether the gang members had learned about their secret friendship, but he knew he would have to watch his back even more closely than before. He wanted to go to the funeral, but his friends warned him, "If you go, watch what will happen to you." He watched news of the funeral on a local television station and read the newspaper to see if there were pictures of the coffin that held his friend. He thought about going to the train station to pay his respects, but he was too scared.

Henry Portillo, it turned out, had relatives from San Pablo, Jaime's hometown in El Salvador, a discovery that Rosa viewed as a cruel irony. She made a difficult decision to take his body back to El Salvador, so he could be buried beside his grandmother and his grandfather, who had died the previous year. It was almost two years to the day since Jaime had climbed onto a bus and headed north. Although Rosa wouldn't be able to tend his grave, she thought he would have liked to be home, near the river and the mango trees he had loved.

His return trip would be by plane, soaring above the desert he had snuck across in the company of strangers. Rosa had been granted temporary status, so she would be able to fly with him in her first trip home since she had left ten years before. Rosa received forms for Jaime to apply to become a permanent legal resident that December, but she never had the chance to tell him that the situation had changed, that now, if anyone asked, he didn't have to be afraid to tell them the truth about who he was and where he came from.

Julio, 2000–2005

CHAPTER 15

Jaime

● ● ●

Julio was working at a construction site a few towns away when he got the call about Jaime. He rushed to Hempstead and headed directly to the train station. Pulling his car into a parking lot, he watched from across the street as the detectives and curious onlookers milled around in the icy cold. The neon green of the Laundry Palace towers and the dots of dark blood on the concrete stood out on the gray, frost-singed street. He worried that if the police noticed him hunched in his car, they would bring him into the station for questioning, but he couldn't stay away. He was heartbroken—and furious.

Julio had had hopes for Jaime. They had become close that fall as Jaime struggled at school and with his family. Jaime looked up to Julio and confided in him. On one occasion, Julio invited Jaime over to dinner at his apartment. As his girlfriend served Jaime rice alongside her own two children, the boy suddenly begun to cry. He told Julio about the fights with his mother and about the visits by police to the house. He didn't want to go back. Julio listened sympathetically. He advised him to stand up for himself and not let his mother boss him around. And he was furious about the police. He told Jaime that the other gang members would be there for him when it got hard at home, reminding Jaime that he had rights and could stand up to the police if they harassed him.

It was one of the last times Julio saw him. Sitting in the train station parking lot, Julio considered what to do. Were the police somehow responsible for Jaime's death? He wouldn't put it past them. His experiences in El Salvador and in Los Angeles convinced him that men in government uniform were corrupt, vindictive, and never to be trusted. He was frustrated, but he was determined not to let his anger derail his plans. Julio had begun to tire of the gang violence, although he did not want to leave the gang completely—he took seriously his promise to be an MS member for life. But he spent less time with his old friends, and when he did hang out, he devoted his time to trying to persuade several of the young boys in the gang, including Jaime, to go back to school. He believed they looked up to him, and thought that he could influence them, if not to leave the gang— never an option he considered for himself or others—at least to make life better for themselves. To Julio, Jaime had been a perfect candidate for the new organization he wanted to form, Homies Unidos, Hempstead. He borrowed the name from a Los Angeles organization that was gaining attention for its work with gang youth. Julio hoped to replicate it in Long Island, and Jaime had been one of a small group he identified as salvageable. Now it was too late.

He would have to do more to save the others, and he knew what his next step would be. He had to confront the police. As Julio watched the detectives through the whirling snow flurries, conferring over the spot where Jaime crumpled to the ground with no one to help him, he vowed to honor Jaime's death.

● ● ●

Detective Ricky Smith hadn't slept. The call came in about three hours after he left this exact spot. He had been there to warn a group of MS-13 members gathered by the train station about the shooting the night before: MS-13 against SWP. SWP would be out for revenge. They were practically asking to get shot by standing around in the open. He told the kids, including Jaime, to go home, but they hadn't listened to him. Now Jaime was dead. Smith was exhausted and cold and frustrated. Another teenager killed in this stupid gang war, another set of witnesses to track down and interview, another sobbing mother to comfort. Sobbing now, but where had she been last night? Why was her child running around at three in the morning? He ran over the informants he ought to call. And he still had the other shooting to deal with from the night before. It never seemed to end, and on days like this, it felt overwhelming.

After several years living in Hempstead during the 1980s, raising his young daughter among the burnt buildings and transvestites downtown, Smith had finally moved his family out of the village, but he was still a devoted member of the Hempstead police force twenty years later. After the drug trade died down, Chief Russo had assigned Smith and his partner to examine the growing graffiti problem. The two detectives believed they were the first to acknowledge the rising gang problem in the suburbs, and now Smith was an expert. He had watched the gangs transform from three posses who defended their turf in the Hills, the Heights, and Trackside, to serious cliques with national and, in the case of MS-13, transnational reputations. Smith had sat in on the meeting when SWP had asked the police to recognize it as a social organization and had participated in the RICO case against it a couple of years later in 1999. But the violence seemed only to quiet for a year or so before Hempstead was the same as ever.

Although he didn't believe the gangs were highly organized, or tightly connected with their namesakes elsewhere in the country and the world, to Smith the spiraling gang battles were worse than anything he had seen in his two decades in Hempstead. It was moments like Jaime's death that brought this home. They all have the attitude that this is my barrio and I'm protecting my barrio, he thought; you have to shake your head at them and say, "Wake up." But the nightmare continued. To force some order on the chaos, several years earlier Smith created a system to track the problem. He tallied each arrest by gang and filed a growing number of memos on police procedure for gang-related incidents. The arrest numbers grew along with the new procedures, as the department invented new ways to deal with the problem. Neither seemed to make a dent. He had a whole drawer full of files in the gang unit's office in the old armory.

Just a month earlier, they had celebrated one success. In the federal task force's RICO case against SWP, seven of the original eleven pleaded guilty to the federal charges. One of the defendants faced as many as eighty years in jail.[1] But it was clear the guilty pleas hadn't slowed down the escalating war between the two gangs. SWP members were most likely behind Jaime's murder. MS-13 was on the rise, too. Lately, the gang acted as if it were sizing up not only its rivals but also the police. Julio in particular was one to watch. He was a perpetual thorn in Smith's side. Smith knew Julio was up to something new, and he didn't like it.

The good news was that the FBI would be helping out. They were taking over from the Drug Enforcement Administration starting that month— a positive development, since Hempstead's gangs were only minimally involved in the drug trade. From what Smith could tell, all the Central American gangs seemed to care about was violence. They had outdone themselves this time. He looked around at the blood-soaked ground and shook his head.

CHAPTER 16

The Corner

● ● ●

Julio first thought about leaving gang life behind—or at least stepping away from the violence—during a short stint in the county jail in 1998. The monotony of life in a cell gave him some time to reflect on his life. He didn't want to be gangbanging when he was an old man. Although he had sworn to stay loyal to MS-13 for life, he was almost thirty now, and it felt like time to calm down.

But calm was elusive to Julio, even after he settled down to live with his girlfriend. A petite Ecuadorian woman who already had two children, she was also the ex-wife of one of Julio's friends. From the beginning their relationship was fiery. Julio's posttraumatic stress—nightmares about bullets and explosions that woke him up in a sweat, and sudden fits of rage—did not diminish. His anger often bubbled to the surface, and when it did, she fought back. In 1997, she called the police after Julio grabbed her wallet during one of their domestic battles. Julio maintained that she took his wallet first, and that it shouldn't matter since they were a couple. But Julio was convicted of petty larceny, tampering with a witness, and disorderly conduct. They stayed together. After another fight, he was convicted of contempt and attempted assault. A month later, he was arrested when he gave a police officer a fake name during a traffic stop. He served thirty days in jail. After that, he was picked up for a fighting in Long Beach and, later, for criminal possession of a weapon. Hempstead police were getting to know him.

The convictions made it hard to find stable work. He bounced from delivering newspapers to disposing of hospital bio-waste, always moving on when he became bored or fought with his boss. In between short stints in offices or driving trucks, he ended up back on the corner waiting for day labor. There were some things he loved about the work: the camaraderie of the other men and not having a boss. If he didn't like the orders he was given, he could leave and go to the corner to wait for a better employer. He may have covered over his Wanderers tattoo, but the ethos of his first gang was still strong.

But the things he liked about day labor were often outweighed by the grueling labor and precarious pay. Employers were frequently unscrupulous, promising a certain amount and paying less, or nothing, at the end of the day. Even when they paid in full, the wages were measly, and the workdays were long. Across Long Island, the negotiated price for a day of work could be as little as $60 for as many as twelve hours, sometimes more. If he was sick or injured on the job, it was his problem. He had no health insurance, and there was no such thing as worker's compensation. If no contractors drove by his corner, or if he arrived later than the other men, he earned nothing. And always, he had to keep an eye out for the police.

Once out of jail, he went back to his daily routine. He drove out everyday to Freeport, where a new hiring site was becoming popular with workers and contractors. Because Julio was a veteran of the corner, many of the other day laborers looked up to him. He negotiated jobs for the newcomers, using his now nearly fluent English. He mediated fights over who was next in line to jump in the vans and bargained with the contractors to raise their wage offers. He enforced the rule they had settled on: never accept less than $80 a day for a job, a motivation to stick together. But by 1999, being a day laborer on Long Island was more than just a precarious way to earn a living. It was dangerous.

●　●　●

Day laborers appeared as part of the suburban scenery in many Long Island towns starting in the late eighties, as the mass exodus from the Salvadoran civil war reached its peak. Word of the island's booming construction jobs spread across the continent to villages in Honduras and El Salvador. More men joined the first trickle of refugees that had made their way east. Unemployment was only 3 percent on Long Island.[1] There was plenty of manual labor and not enough people to do it. Informal hiring sites, or "shape-up sites," appeared across the island through unspoken agreements between contractors and workers. They chose spots in Home Depot parking lots or close to train stations for the benefit of day laborers commuting from Hempstead and Roosevelt. Often, a convenience store or Dunkin' Donuts was a source of hot coffee on cold mornings. A handful of sites were located in wealthier towns, but most were in blue-collar towns, places such as Farmingville and Huntington that had once been mostly white. The contractors would swoop through, pick up a few men, and then head out to trim the hedges around the island's mini-mansions or pour concrete for new ones in the rapidly expanding resort towns and commuter villages.

One of the first towns to host a shape-up site was Glen Cove. It was a wealthy town, almost entirely white, on the northern edge of the island, and it had once hosted the estates of robber barons.[2] A century later, it was still an enclave of the wealthy. Nearby, a country club provided landscaping jobs for some of the men.[3] Workers who couldn't afford to live close by commuted from elsewhere. Some crammed into older homes near the village's downtown, while others found shelter in the woods or hedges near the train tracks. Each morning starting at dawn, they gathered at a deli downtown to wait for the daily caravan of pickups and vans. The contractors slowed, eyed the crowd of men rushing toward them, and allowed a few to squeeze in among the tools and lumber littering the truck beds.

As the number of men grew, some in the community complained. They said the men hooted at passing women and urinated in public.[4] The mayor, Donald De Riggi, heard their complaints and responded. In August 1989, he introduced an ordinance to make it illegal for more than five men to assemble at a time to seek employment.[5] Opponents of the bill who supported the day laborers, including ministers and civil liberties advocates, pointed out that the Constitution guaranteed the right to free assembly. The mayor rewrote the bill to instead ban "illegal undocumented aliens to be present in a public or private place for the purpose of soliciting or promoting employment."[6] More complaints about the bill's constitutionality prompted the mayor to rewrite the bill again several months later. This time, the mayor focused on the traffic hazards the men created by gathering in the street. The new law would make it illegal to stand on a "street or highway" and solicit work.[7]

Advocates for the workers accused the town of being motivated by racism. Proponents said race was not a factor. "They need to eat. They need to live. But we're saying they have to fit in the social pattern," a spokeswoman for the town said.[8] The advocates sued.[9] As the conflict became more heated, some day laborers, worried the town was attracting the attention of immigration agents, stayed away. But they soon returned. The immigration agents came shortly after, rounding up more than two dozen Salvadoran workers that fall, among them two who were legal residents.[10] But gradually the workers again overcame their fear of deportation, driven by desperation and lured by the continued flow of jobs. Soon they were back in full force.

Illegal immigration was the hot button issue in a contentious Glen Cove mayoral campaign in 1993. The Democratic candidate, Thomas Suozzi, did not dispute the assertion that illegal immigration was disrupting the way of life in the town. In an op-ed published in a local paper during the campaign, Suozzi wrote that "neighborhoods are being destabilized and action must be taken."[11] But a court order issued as a result of the lawsuit six years earlier meant the town could not ban the men from seeking work. The decision left only one option—build a hiring site for the workers. After Suozzi took office, the town installed a trailer near the train station with a bathroom. A sign directed contractors into an attached parking lot.[12] A worker in the trailer noted license plates of the contractors, just in case a worker was swindled out of a paycheck, or worse. The town was transformed from what advocates once called "one of the most aggressively anti-immigrant communities in Long Island" to a model of nearly peaceful coexistence.[13]

But other towns in Long Island that faced their own conflicts over day laborers were reluctant to follow Glen Cove's lead. In 1996 a fight broke out in Huntington Station between community groups struggling to move the day laborers from a busy street to a quieter park and residents who wanted them gone altogether. They shouldn't have to accommodate people who broke immigration laws, the second group argued. Long Island wasn't the only place where such a debate was taking place.

Concerns over immigration were exacerbated by stories of the ineptitude of the Immigration and Naturalization Service. In 1993, the *New York Times* published an article detailing the "porous" deportation system that allowed thousands of criminal immigrants to elude immigration agents.[14] In 1990, Congress ordered a census of the number of immigrants who committed crimes and were deported, but the agency never obtained funding for the project and never completed it.[15] The INS rarely visited city and county jails to search for immigrants who had committed deportable offenses and didn't check with parole officers about potential deportees. In state prisons, criminal aliens were often released without being deported for their crimes.

The border crackdowns of the early 1990s were soon accompanied by a broad strategy to hunt down illegal immigrants in the interior. In 1995, a series of INS raids at factories across six southern states netted more than 4,000 illegal immigrants.[16] In 1996, the INS led a high-profile raid on New York's garment industry.[17] Later that year, the Clinton administration implemented the Illegal Immigration Reform and Immigrant Responsibility Act, the broadest and toughest federal effort to curb illegal immigrants since Operation Wetback deported more than a million Mexicans in 1954.[18]

An increase in border patrol agents was just the beginning of the law's wide impact on the country's immigration system. It also limited the number of documents immigrant workers could use to verify their status, made it more difficult for refugees to apply for asylum, and cut back the public benefits available to legal immigrants. A section of the act, 287(g), allowed state and local agencies to be deputized as federal immigration agents to investigate narcotics, smuggling, and gang crimes.[19] The law took away immigrants' right to appeal deportation in federal court.[20]

In 1996, prompted by the Oklahoma City bombing, a bombing at the summer Olympics in Atlanta, and the crash of TWA flight 800 off Long Island, which was at first believed to be terrorism, the Clinton administration pushed through a set of antiterrorism measures.[21] Although Republicans in Congress resisted Clinton's attempts to expand federal wiretapping powers and a proposal to improve tracing methods for guns and explosives used in crimes, the administration was able to increase airport security measures and passed the Anti-Terrorism and Effective Death Penalty Act. The act required immigration agents to arrest and deport any immigrant convicted of a felony and serious misdemeanors. Deportation waivers for immigrants convicted of crimes who were rehabilitated and who faced separation from dependent family members were eliminated.[22]

Illegal immigrants kept coming, and Americans' anxiety about them grew. In California, Proposition 187 barred illegal immigrants from public schools and hospitals. Known as the "Save Our State" initiative, Proposition 187 passed easily in a public referendum but later faltered under judicial scrutiny. Nevertheless, the idea quickly spread to other states and cities across the country that were dealing with their own conflicts over immigration.[23] A similar state bill passed in Arizona several years later, while other local governments passed laws that banned landlords from renting to illegal immigrants. But nowhere was the conflict more heated than in Farmingville, a blue-collar town at the center of Long Island.

●　●　●

The nineties were good to Long Island. Home values rose, jobs multiplied, and unemployment was low. New businesses proliferated. Few patches of Long Island were untouched by the development spree. For contractors, real estate brokers, and wealthy homeowners, the sunny economy was especially bright.

For the residents of Farmingville, the good years seemed long past. The hamlet, once an enclave of white blue-collar residents, had changed over ten years into a hub for day laborers. By 1998, there were an estimated 1,000 day laborers among the population of 15,000. Farmingville was an obvious choice for day laborers. It was situated just off the Long Island Expressway in Suffolk County in a convenient place for the construction contractors that crisscrossed the island. Local hardware stores and Home Depots were located nearby. Much of the island was off limits to poor people. But Farmingville was made up of mostly older homes where the day laborers could afford rooms by sharing the rent. Some houses in the hamlet housed as many as thirty men. The crowded conditions meant garbage piled up, and the workers' long hours meant some houses were unkempt. Lawns sprouted weeds, and walls went unpainted. The workers' dilapidated rentals were interspersed among the neatly kept homes of working families, whose green, close-trimmed lawns were still a sign of good citizenship. To many, the new blight was untenable.

In June 1998, the Farmingville Civic Association called a meeting to discuss the workers. The meeting was packed. Those who attended estimated that four hundred residents from the little town came to complain.[24] One by one, they took the microphone to tell their stories. Some described near accidents driving down Horseblock Road as vans stopped short to pick up workers. Others reported seeing men urinating on the corners in the middle of the day. Terry Sherwood, a middle-aged housewife and mother of two, said she first noticed the men when she stopped at a local 7-Eleven. She stepped out of the car, as her twin ten-year-old sons watched from the backseat, and saw a crowd of Hispanic men nearby. They gestured at her, said things in Spanish, and laughed. She was terrified. She had never felt so unsafe in her own town. She wrote later in an op-ed in *Newsday* that she felt as if she had been violated.[25]

Sherwood joined more than a dozen others to form a new organization: Citizens for Immigration Reform. The group was led by a New York City public school teacher, Margaret Bianculli-Dyber, who said the day laborers who gathered near the corner of her house had "solicited" her daughter, expressing a growing fear around the island that the new arrivals presented a particular sexual threat to white female residents.[26] Within months, the group became known for its protests at Farmingville's shape-up site, where they used video cameras and taunts to intimidate the workers. The Suffolk County executive, Robert Gaffney, was among some officials who suggested a hiring hall like Glen Cove's would mollify the protesters.[27] The group's response was tepid. Instead, they rallied behind a new town bill that would outlaw the outdoor hiring spots outright.

The bill failed in June 1999. The Farmingville group turned its focus to opposing a separate bill introduced by a Democratic county legislator to build a hiring hall.[28] They had renamed themselves Sachem Quality of Life, the name of the school district and also a term for a Native American king. The workers were in the country illegally, and Sachem argued the government shouldn't condone illegal activity by building a hall to house them. In July, the group organized a rally of more than a hundred people across the street from the main shape-up site at the 7-Eleven.[29] The protesters waved American flags and chanted.[30]

As the conflict gained attention across the island, a nonprofit based in Hempstead, the Workplace Project, came to town to organize the workers and advocate on their behalf. The Workplace Project organizers wrote op-eds, attended community meetings, and in August held their own rally, where the workers waved signs and chanted back at the Sachems.[31]

Sachem switched tactics. They proposed a new bill to the Brookhaven town board, which encompassed Farmingville, that was reminiscent of the slum clearance efforts of the 1930s. The bill placed a limit on the number of people who could reside in rental properties and allowed building inspectors to spot-search rental properties without a warrant.[32] The Workplace Project denounced the law as racist.[33] The Sachem group pressed on. At a community meeting in October 1999, the two groups faced off. The room was again packed. The last witness was a day laborer who read slowly in Spanish from a printed script as a Workplace Project's associate director translated.[34] A woman in the back interrupted him. "Legal or illegal?" she yelled. He ignored her and kept reading. She yelled out the question again.[35]

The room erupted into chanting: Dozens of white people began reciting the Pledge of Allegiance. The worker struggled through the end of his testimony, but his last words were nearly drowned out. "How far will this situation go?" he asked before sitting down. The Farmingville residents continued chanting the pledge as they picked up their coats and filed out the door.[36]

There were four assaults in the town that fall: two sexual assaults against local women, allegedly by workers, and two against day laborers, allegedly by local townspeople.[37] Someone fired a shotgun at a house where day laborers lived.[38] The Brookhaven town board passed the housing bill in December.[39] Rental property owners were forced to register with the town, and a special fund was set up to hire new building inspectors.[40] Six homes were eventually shuttered, and a hundred men were removed from the homes.[41]

Less than a year later, two white men picked up a pair of Mexican day laborers in front of a house on Granny Road in Farmingville. The white men, Ryan Wagner, twenty, of Maspeth in Queens, and Christopher Slavin, twenty-nine, of Melville in Long Island, were tattooed with white supremacist symbols. Wagner had an anti-Semitic epithet on his neck, and Slavin was covered in swastikas and skin-head symbols, including a caricature of a Jewish man kneeling in front of a clown brandishing an ax.[42] But the workers, Israel Perez and Magdaleno Estrada Escamilla, didn't notice the tattoos. They were happy for a job.

Wagner and Slavin drove them to an abandoned building in Shirley, about twenty minutes away from Farmingville. In the basement, the white men pulled out a posthole digger and a knife. Wagner stabbed Perez repeatedly.[43] Slavin pounded Estrada with the posthole digger.[44] As Perez lay bleeding from stab wounds, Estrada, knocked down by a blow to his head, managed to pull himself up. He lunged at Slavin, who fled with Wagner close behind.[45] Estrada and Perez, bleeding and bruised, dragged themselves out of the basement, through the woods, and stumbled to the edge of the Long Island Expressway, where a driver saw them and took them to the hospital.[46]

Two years later, a group of teenagers cruising along Granny Road past the house where Estrada and Perez were picked up lobbed a bottle rocket into the window of a Mexican family's home next door. They watched the house catch fire and then drove on. The family, including a baby and a five-year-old, escaped, but the house and everything they owned was destroyed.[47] The teens were caught, and one of their lawyers claimed the firebombing was a "Fourth of July prank." Eventually, the teenagers pleaded guilty to hate crime charges.[48]

The violence was the boiling over of a conflict over the day laborers that had become more entrenched. Sachem continued its protests against the day laborers even after the building inspection law passed, but its organization fractured. Leaders with more extremist anti-immigrant views took over, and the group began attracting national attention to Farmingville. Newspaper and television reporters swooped in. One of the Sachem leaders, Ray Wysolmierski, who had called illegal immigrants "terrorists," defended the teenagers who firebombed the house, saying they were being "crucified."[49] Elsewhere around the island, politicians waded into the battle. One Suffolk County legislator proposed an English-only law for government agencies. Another went further.[50] Michael D'Andre, who represented Smithtown in the county legislature, said during a public meeting that if immigrants moved to his town, "we'll be out with baseball bats."[51] In 2002, Suffolk County launched its federal gang task force. Gaffney, the county executive who had originally supported the hiring hall, vetoed it.[52]

Gaffney, a Republican, was on his way out of office under a cloud of rumors about corruption that had also tainted his would-be Republican predecessor. Steve Levy, the Democratic assemblyman who had proposed state legislation to increase penalties against gang members, won the Suffolk executive seat easily in 2003 with the enthusiastic endorsement of the *New York Times*.[53] In his inaugural address, he promised to develop more affordable housing and foster unity, but he also promised not to "sit by idly while immigration and labor laws are being violated right before our very eyes."[54]

The anger and resentment over the day laborers was impossible to disconnect from the growing panic about Central American gangs. When leaders like Levy talked about the problems illegal immigrants brought to Long Island communities, the gang violence in places like Hempstead, Freeport, and Mineola loomed in the subtext. Many leaders also issued urgent warnings about the threat of the Central American gangs. They didn't even need to wink when they discussed the illegal immigration problem to signal that the problems were one and the same. Increasingly, they were. Some illegal immigrants, ostracized and facing a climate of escalating hostility and violence among their white neighbors, no doubt joined forces with the gangs for protection. Other workers, like Julio, had a foot in both worlds. But more and more of the gang members were born in Long Island, and many were the children of day laborers and other working-class immigrants who had brought them to what they believed was a better life. These youngsters grew up among the racial tensions that delineated the suburbs, where they heard the constant refrain that Hispanics were unwelcome criminals. When they were old enough, they were ripe for recruitment into the gangs.

CHAPTER 17

Freeport

● ● ●

As the fight in Farmingville ground on, the Workplace Project expanded its organizing efforts. In December 1999, shortly after Brookhaven passed its law allowing building inspectors to monitor rental properties, the nonprofit turned its attention to Freeport, the town where Damian Corrente had been shot a year earlier. A conflict over day laborers was brewing there, too, and they sent one of their lead organizers, Carlos Canales, to see if he could help.

Freeport had passed its own building inspection law years before, but it did little to deter the day laborers who flocked to the village that year in search of work. The shooting and the workers came at an especially bad time for Freeport. In an effort to revive the town after a rough period during the eighties and nineties, village officials were undertaking a major project to refurbish the facades of the downtown shops.[1] The cosmetic makeover had little effect on the town's reputation—a high-profile gang shooting and the day laborers crowding on the streets everyday couldn't be whitewashed by painting storefronts.

The contractors and the workers gathered in the parking lot where commuters from surrounding towns paid to park their cars before hopping the Long Island Railroad. Commuters vied for space with the day laborers rushing to the contractors' vans, and as the number of workers grew, police began fielding complaints from commuters on an hourly basis each morning.[2] Fights broke out almost daily between the two groups. The owners of the Dunkin' Donuts, which had once catered to the commuters, worried that the white-collar workers were going elsewhere for their coffee because of the crowd of men who gathered out front. Women complained about catcalls. The Dunkin' Donuts owners said the workers urinated on their property and littered.

To the chief of the police department, Michael Woodward, the day laborer problem was nothing like the crack plague of the eighties and early nineties, when calls of shots fired mustered police officers nightly in the village's worst neighborhoods. The village had calmed down, and the violence ebbed, as more Hispanics and a handful of young white professionals moved in. While Corrente's killing was a warning that new gangs had arrived in Freeport, Woodward didn't think their arrival or the day laborers heralded the village's descent back into the bad old days.

But the day laborer issue did have him flummoxed. Police officers were engaged in almost daily arguments with the workers to keep them away from the commuter parking lot. The men would move, only to come back the next day, drawn to the contractor trucks that lined up every morning. The drivers didn't ask for papers—with the economic boom they depended on this army of willing workers, illegal or not. But by hiring the men, they often faced criticism for their role in bolstering the underground construction job market that was drawing more men to Long Island. A local movement was brewing to combat illegal immigration by targeting employers, which culminated in 2006 in Suffolk County with a bill forcing all government contractors to certify that their workers were in the country legally.[3] Still, the contractors for the most part had much less to fear than their workers and mostly tried to stay out of the debate, and out of the spotlight. The police generally ignored them, anyway; it was the workers the commuters were upset about. When the day laborers and contractors appeared in a new area, the calls from angry commuters would start again, and fights would once again break out. One of his biggest worries was that a commuter car or a contractor's truck would hit one of the rushing workers. No matter what the police said to the day laborers, their desire to work was stronger.

Carlos Canales, a former FMLN rebel who had come from El Salvador and transformed his revolutionary experience into a passion for community organizing, arrived in Freeport from the campaign in Farmingville in December. He wore his hair long and dressed in plaid shirts and work pants. His skin was dark and leathery from his days out on the streets with the laborers in Farmingville, but the workers still eyed him suspiciously as he approached them. The men stood stamping their feet in the predawn cold and sipping Dunkin' Donuts coffee. One of the men stepped out of the group to confront him before Carlos could get closer, his intimidating glare reinforced by his thick arms and slicked-back hair.

"What do you want? What are you doing here?" the man demanded.

Carlos tried to keep from smiling. Here was the leader he was looking for. Julio looked him up and down slowly—not someone Carlos wanted to piss off. He began carefully, explaining that he was an organizer and that he wanted to ask them about their jobs—if they were getting paid enough and if the police were bothering them.

Julio frowned and walked away. The men turned their backs and closed ranks. Julio didn't trust this outsider, and some of the other men were scared. They knew what was happening in Farmingville. They didn't want that kind of trouble here.

Carlos came every other day for a month. He asked quiet questions of anyone who made eye contact with him. Were there any contractors they had problems with? How many police officers bothered them yesterday? Did they herd and bump you with their patrol cars? What do you think about a hiring hall?

Julio was still hostile. Carlos knew he needed his help to move forward; otherwise the workers wouldn't listen. He decided to take a break. He was needed back in Farmingville. One month later, Carlos got a phone call. It was Julio. The workers were having more trouble with the police; he had been thinking about some of Carlos's ideas. Maybe they could talk.

Carlos went to Freeport the next morning. There were four other men who were also respected among the workers, and Carlos walked them off to the side to chat. Julio led the questioning. Carlos suggested they organize a campaign for a hiring hall. It wasn't easy, but it was possible. They would have to work hard, but they had already proven they were good at that.

Julio agreed. The other men followed his lead. They held weekly meetings. The ice quickly melted between Carlos and Julio, although the two men were polar opposites. Carlos had a quiet, wry humor. He asked questions rather than telling the workers what to do. In contrast, Julio was rash and loud. He often took over the meetings and spoke over the others. Julio was eager to confront the police, but Carlos gently urged caution. The workers had to all be in agreement first.

The group of men enlisted some white residents to their cause, hoping their presence would lead the police and mayor's office to be more sympathetic. They recruited two ministers, including Bob Lepley, a former Methodist preacher who ran the island's largest social justice coalition. Lepley had left the ministry in frustration. The mainline denominations were too conservative for him. He worked as a music teacher in a public school and organized peace marches in his free time. He read in the local newspapers about the fight in Farmingville and wanted to get involved. When Carlos called, he leapt at the opportunity.

Several months passed, but Carlos worried that the group of workers had not yet solidified into a united force. There was an ingredient missing. He was mulling the problem one morning as he passed out pamphlets for an upcoming meeting. Attendance was spotty, and some of the workers never came at all. Several of the flyers fluttered to the ground unread. Then the police arrived. They ordered the men to disperse. Usually, Carlos moved out of the way along with the men. This time, he stood his ground. Like Julio, he was fed up. When they repeated the order to move, he stayed put. One of the cops bent down and picked up a pamphlet. He looked quizzically at Carlos: Soliciting for union dues? Carlos protested. Workplace Project wasn't a union. It didn't take dues. They argued. Then the officer scribbled on a pad. He handed Carlos three summonses, including one for disorderly conduct.

As Carlos grimly took the tickets, he looked back. All of the workers' eyes were on him. Julio looked furious. So did everyone else. As soon as the police left, the men surrounded Carlos. They were both angry and ecstatic. They were impressed Carlos had stood up for himself and for them. The police had treated him the same way they did the workers. As they clapped him on the back and talked excitedly, one of the workers suggested that they march down to the police precinct and demand that the harassment stop. And an apology for Carlos's tickets, Julio added. While they were at it, they would also demand a hiring hall. The next day, fifty men gathered to march. Bob Lepley came along, too, as a white face they hoped would prevent an angry reaction from the police.

Woodward saw them coming from his office window. They marched up the town hall stairs and pushed their way into the side door leading to the police department offices. The room overflowed, and some workers were forced to stand outside. They wanted to speak to Woodward in person and said that they wouldn't leave until the chief came out. Maybe something would come of this, Woodward thought. He came out and led them to the village boardroom, a cavernous hall with chandeliers and wooden pews. A Spanish-speaking detective helped translate.

Julio presented their demands: no more harassment, a hiring hall, and an apology.

The chief gave them his side: You're bothering people, you're spitting on the ground, you're whistling at women, and someone is going to get hit by a car. We have nothing to apologize for, he added.

Julio was ready to argue, but the chief hadn't finished. He refused to dismiss Carlos's tickets, but he said they could hold another meeting to talk about their options sometime soon.

The men were ecstatic. They rumbled down the stairs and erupted into the street, cheering and slapping hands. Julio stood in the center of the crowd, shouting with the rest. They did it. They made the police listen.

Carlos watched from the sidelines. He was as excited as they were. The next day, he steered them back to the drawing board. They had to gather more support and develop a clear plan to bring to the village authorities. They called the mayor's office. After several tries, the mayor agreed to see them.

Julio took charge at the meeting. He repeated the demands he made of Woodward: a hiring hall, with a bathroom, a sign, and electricity. The mayor said okay, he was happy to help. Carlos and Julio looked at each other, stunned. Just like that they had won.

Freeport averted the storm that hit Farmingville by putting the men, considered an eyesore that was ruining the efforts to beautify the town, out of sight. The only condition was that a different organization must run the hall. The Workplace Project, with its rabble-rousing, was risky. Carlos reluctantly agreed. Otherwise the men wouldn't get their hall. A year later, the workers and the city settled on a trailer in a city-owned parking lot near the Home Depot. It was off the beaten path, but the mayor promised a sign to point contractors the way.

Julio and the other men set the rules for the site. They wrote bylaws that governed how the jobs would be divvied up. Drinking, smoking, and fighting were prohibited, as was looking for work independently within a certain distance of the trailer. A part-time organizer was hired to run the place, although Carlos hoped that Julio might eventually be hired to help since the trailer wouldn't have been established without him.

But Julio had other plans. The victory with the police energized him and reminded him of the thoughts he had in jail two years earlier. The day laborers were in a difficult position, but the young gang members dying in Hempstead were worse off. If anyone needed help, they did. Near the end of 2002, he told Carlos and Bob Lepley—now a trusted friend— his plan. Julio wanted to organize gang members.

Two years earlier, in 2000, Sergio Argueta was driven by a similar passion to start his own antiviolence organization. The group, Struggling to Reunite Our New Generation, or STRONG Youth, began as a part-time operation while Sergio attended college at Columbia University. After moving to Hofstra, where tuition was cheaper, he took a job as a youth outreach worker for the Nassau County Youth Board and continued his antiviolence work. His efforts so far had consisted of leading peace marches and teaching prevention classes in the middle schools. But he hoped to develop the intervention arm of the organization to help teenagers entrenched in gangs leave the violence behind.

Julio knew of Sergio's organization but was skeptical of Sergio's ties to the government. He believed he had more pull with Hempstead's youth than the former Redondel Pride leader, since he was still an active gang member. He wanted to empower gang members to stand up for their constitutional rights and fight back against oppression. He believed being connected to the government would make that difficult. He named the organization Homies Unidos, after the Los Angeles organization. Julio was convinced he could have the same success they were having on the West Coast using the tactics he learned organizing the day laborers. He would not renounce his gang membership, however. If he left the gang, he believed his life would be threatened, but he also believed that he could do more good from his position of leadership in MS-13—which he had maintained even as he concentrated on his organizing work in Freeport.

Julio believed gang members would only listen to someone from the inside, and he also believed that violence could be extracted from the gang. It was the same thing the SWP leaders had hoped several years earlier, when they had asked for police recognition for their fledgling social group. Julio was undeterred by SWP's track record, however. Nor did he see a contradiction in his efforts to re-create a street gang as a group with positive values and peaceful intentions.

Bob and Carlos, along with the executive of a local bank in Hempstead and a professor at Hofstra University, agreed to help. Carlos was somewhat wary of the project. He knew about Julio's history with the police and worried they wouldn't look on the new group favorably. Bob was enthusiastic. He designed a curriculum for the organization and met with Julio twice a week to discuss his plans.

In the fall of 2002, as the gang war between SWP and MS-13 escalated in Hempstead, Julio was eager to begin his outreach efforts. He had identified a group of boys he believed would be open to joining, among them Jaime Alvarenga. Then Jaime was killed.

Julio was devastated but determined to continue the work. First, however, he wanted to meet the police face to face. Julio, along with Carlos and Bob, worried the Hempstead police would misconstrue Julio's organizing and think he was mobilizing gang members against them. They thought he should explain his intentions. But Julio was also angry. Just as in the meeting with Woodward in Freeport, he wanted to confront the police about a problem he saw as partly their fault.

The organizers requested a meeting with Chief Russo, and he agreed. Carlos, Bob, and two MS-13 members accompanied Julio. Chief Russo brought his gang task force detectives, including Smith. They met in the Hempstead Village public library next door to police headquarters. The chief began with a small speech and opened the floor to questions. Julio stood up and faced Russo.

If the police were trying to avoid violence, why were they the ones encouraging the rivalry between the gangs? Julio asked.

Chief Russo stared. Smith stared. Here we go, he thought.

It's convenient for you that gang members exist, Julio went on, his voice rising. He pointed his index finger at the chief. It's your business. You get money for these gangs. As long as gangs exist, you're allowed to apply for more police and for more money. If gang members don't exist, you lose business.

The police were stunned—this guy had to be kidding.

Julio wasn't finished: The gangs justify your existence—you create the violence; you create the gangs.

Soon after he sat down, the meeting ended. Carlos was really worried. Julio was a hothead, but he hadn't expected this. He had turned himself into a target. Julio was unfazed. He spoke for the other gang members and for Jaime. He saw them, and saw himself, as a victim of police abuses, and he wanted them to hear his outrage. The meeting had turned out worse than SWP's first effort to gain police sympathy. Now Julio was seen as an outright enemy of the police, not simply an unruly street tough.

He told Bob about his next mission: to call a temporary truce between the two warring gangs. Julio was determined to force the two gangs to hash out their differences and end the war. It seemed like only way to avoid another murder. He had been busy organizing in Freeport for the past two years, but he was still in close contact with MS-13 members in Hempstead. He reached out to the gang, and they agreed to meet with him. Then he reached out to SWP. They agreed, too. He didn't bother to call the police this time.

The bank executive offered a conference room on the second floor of the branch for the meeting. One evening that spring, the boys filed into the room and sat down in the bank's cushy swivel chairs, MS-13 on one side, SWP on the other. Julio stood at the head of the table. He was in his element. His voice rose with excitement as he lectured the boys about the need for them to work out this conflict among themselves. It was the only way they could throw off the yoke of police oppression, he said. After Julio's speech, the boys began to talk. They talked about the police roundups and about the violence that was spiraling out of control. Some admitted to being afraid and wanting out. They didn't agree to a truce, but afterwards Julio was excited. He was convinced he could bring them together again. This was just the beginning. Soon—he could feel it—there would be peace in Hempstead. As far as he was concerned, they didn't need the help of the police—they weren't a part of the solution, anyway; they were a part of the problem.

• • •

Detective Smith was less surprised at the outcome of the library meeting than some. But he was worried. To him, Julio seemed both crazy and dangerous. Smith checked in with his informants. They confirmed what he assumed. Julio's assurances that he had left gang violence behind were a lie, they said. Informants said he was often seen with MS-13 members and was as deeply enmeshed as ever. They still regarded him as one of their leaders, Smith was told.

Worse, Smith heard from several officers that Julio had been seen with a video camera following police officers around. He taped them as they stopped gang members, and they believed he had footage of the department's unmarked cars. Julio was using his video camera as anti-immigrant protesters had in Farmingville. The camera was a tool both to intimidate the other side and to make sure any abuses were documented. He believed that training his camera on police would help him create a record of his grievances and that it could empower the young gang members to feel confident enough to stand up for themselves. His footage would be proof of his accusations against the police.

The camera worked. The police felt threatened. The last thing the Hempstead police needed was Julio riling up gang members to turn against the police and disseminating photos of plainclothes officers. If they didn't watch him carefully, Smith thought, the police could have a dead cop on their hands.

Smith now had a lot of resources at his disposal to deal with the problem. The FBI had taken over for the DEA as the lead federal agency in the task force that winter. The INS had been disbanded in March, and now immigration agents reported to the more aggressive ICE. Several were in close contact with the task force. He decided to give one a call about Julio.

The agent had what he needed. There was an immigration warrant for Julio dated January 6, 2000. Julio's criminal record was enough to make him deportable. Smith just had to wait for an opportunity.

It came on June 8, 2003. Smith and some others responded to a distur-
bance at a Hell's Angels gathering near the motorcycle gang's headquarters
east of downtown Hempstead. Smith and a group of detectives approached in their cars and parked. Off to the side, they noticed another
man approaching. It was Julio with his video camera in hand. As Julio focused his lens on the scene, Smith marched over, pulling out his handcuffs as he walked.

On the arrest report, Smith filled out "INS 236"—the national immigration law regulating the detention of "aliens ordered removed." He also
wrote, "open container," although in the report's narrative, he kept it sim-
ple: "The defendant was arrested on a outstanding immigration warrant."

Julio was taken to the Nassau County Jail and later transferred to the
immigration detention center in Elizabeth, New Jersey, to await his deportation hearing. Meanwhile, the FBI agents on the Hempstead task
force—who shared Smith's office—began looking into his case. On July
24, Special Agent Anthony Jackson obtained a search warrant for the
apartment Julio shared with his girlfriend. In a report filed after the search,
he listed his findings: a digital camera, digital and printed photographs of
government agents, vehicles, and facilities, photographs of MS-13 gang
members, a computer, documents reflecting MS-13 gang membership,
and gang paraphernalia, specifically, a blue bandana. All, according to Jackson's report, were evidence, fruits, and instrumentalities of violations
under Title 18 of the U.S. Code, Section 1959, which covered violent
crimes in aid of racketeering—RICO. If Julio won his deportation trial,
the feds would be waiting for him.

CHAPTER 18

Iron Fist

● ● ●

Julio was terrified of going back to El Salvador. He had heard paramilitary death squads still targeted gang members. Police had been charged with extrajudicial killings.[1] Alleged acts of gang violence were regularly splashed on the covers of the tabloid newspapers in El Salvador and across the region, among them, a Honduran bus attack in which twenty-eight shoppers were killed in a spray of Mara Salvatrucha bullets. In 2004, Central American law enforcement officials estimated there were about 100,000 gang members across the region, including Mexico, with about half of those in Guatemala, El Salvador, and Honduras.[2] Murders were beginning to rise again after the post–civil war spike, from thirty-six per 100,000 in 2000 to fifty per 100,000 by 2008.[3] It was one of the highest homicide rates in the world. Riots and fires regularly broke out in the country's overcrowded prisons, where he could end up. Two prison fires in two years had killed nearly 200 gang members in Honduras. Even if he didn't commit a crime, Julio's tattoos were enough for Salvadoran police to arrest him under El Salvador's antigang law, Mano Dura, or Iron Fist.

Human rights activists and even judges protested the law, which made being a gang member illegal. Anyone with tattoos or seen associating with gang members could be arrested. Many judges believed the law was unconstitutional and often released gang members when their cases came to court. But the prisons overflowed as the police rearrested them and sent them back. In the summer of 2004, the law was scheduled to sunset, but on the presidential campaign trail that year, the ARENA candidate, Tony Saca, promised to continue the crackdown against the gangs. He was elected and promptly passed a new law, Super Mano Dura, and deployed 1,000 army soldiers to help police quell the violence.[4]

The "super" version of Mano Dura contained language that was more vague than in the previous version—it prohibited "illicit associations" instead of gangs specifically—but police still had the same latitude to arrest gang members on sight. By the end of 2004, El Salvador's prison population was 12,073, well above its capacity for 7,312 prisoners.[5] By 2007, the number would rise to more than 16,000.[6] The gangs were separated into different prisons to tamp down the violence inside. In one rural jail for youth, Tonacatepeque, children cycling through wiled away the days tattooing each other with gang signs and playing soccer. The first grade classroom was the only one that was full of students, mostly older teenagers who had never learned to read on the outside. In August, a few weeks after Super Mano Dura went into effect, a prison riot broke out in El Salvador's largest and most notorious prison, La Esperanza, The Hope, killing 31 prisoners.[7]

Elsewhere in the region, other countries were ratcheting up their response to the gangs. In the spring of 2004, Honduran Security Minister Oscar Alvarez held a press conference warning that Al Qaeda had sent an operative to attend a local gang meeting.[8] "The *maras* are no longer street gangs; now we can say that these young people are involved in terrorism," Alvarez said. The vice president of Guatemala, Eduardo Stein, and El Salvador's president of National Security, Oscar Bonilla, echoed Honduran concerns.[9] Bonilla charged that international terrorists had penetrated the gangs in order to enter the United States illegally.[10]

Their intelligence turned out to be spotty. The Honduran president later distanced himself from Alvarez's assertions because he could not confirm that his administration had any hard evidence of the terrorism links, as did the Guatemalan president.[11] In the United States, members of the FBI and other gang and national security experts, who had at first spread news of the alleged gang-terrorist ties to the press, debunked the rumors of the connections as false.[12]

In New York, as Julio awaited his deportation hearings, sixteen-year-old Olivia Mendoza and her friend were murdered within a month of each other in two wealthy Long Island towns. The murders darkened his chances to win his case. In a *New York Times* article after the arrests of the MS-13 members charged with the killings, Detective Smith, who was set to testify at Julio's hearing, and one of the FBI agents on the task force, Robert Hart, said they believed that MS-13 in particular was growing more sophisticated. Hart said:

> The cliques instead of operating independently of each other are beginning to come together. . . . The difference is by doing that, obviously you have a much tighter organization, much stronger structures and instead of having various cliques doing whatever they want, wherever they want, there is one individual who is the leader and is able to control the payment of dues, the criminal acts they engage in, and the result is very, very similar to what you would see in what we refer to as traditional organized criminal families.[13]

Smith told the *Times* that "members of the cliques from California and straight from El Salvador come to the cliques on the East Coast to organize them." It was easy to fit Julio into this description.

That year, Nassau County declared that it would pour more resources into the police department. The decision reversed the orders from two years earlier for the police to cut back its staff. The county said it would hire 150 new officers and that a third of them would be designated to investigating the gangs.[14] In Suffolk, Steve Levy also acted in the wake of the murders. He proposed deputizing the Suffolk County police as immigration agents, a step beyond the collaboration in Nassau County between police and the federal agency. The plan received heavy criticism from immigrant advocates and civil liberties groups. Levy scaled back the proposal and said instead he would push the police department to augment its information-sharing alliance with the feds.[15]

Before Julio's first deportation hearing, the Workplace Project drummed up support from community leaders, including Sergio, the LA office of Homies Unidos, and well-known Long Island ministers. Many were shocked that the police had arrested Julio on immigration charges alone and accused the police of retaliating against him because he had spoken up against them. Local police arresting immigrants solely on immigration charges was rare, even after September 11.[16] Levy's proposal to deputize Suffolk County police as immigration agents went against the preferences of most police departments, including Nassau County's, who usually sought to avoid making immigration arrests because they didn't want to alienate Hispanic residents and dissuade immigrants from reporting crimes.

The head of Hempstead's gang task force, Detective Lieutenant Joseph Wing, defended Julio's arrest in *Newsday*. He argued that it had been routine for the officers to pick him up and noted that the department knew Julio already because of his criminal record.[17] "To the best of my knowledge, there were not any discussions between federal authorities and local authorities that resulted in the warrant," Wing said. "We didn't go out and actively look for [Julio]. It was mere happenstance."[18] James Margolin, the New York FBI spokesman, added that the FBI wasn't in the business of targeting people for "exercising their constitutional right to free speech."[19]

At the trial, Julio testified that he had turned away from violence and described his efforts to expand his antiviolence organization. He admitted that he had not disavowed his gang, but said that to do so was a death sentence. His lawyers from Legal Aid argued that his affiliation with MS-13 was all the more reason for him to be given asylum. As a gang member covered in tattoos, he would certainly face imprisonment and persecution in El Salvador, they said.

The judge agreed. Although she dismissed the idea of a gang member being a persecuted class, she said Julio's political beliefs—including his affiliation with Homies Unidos and opposition to the Salvadoran government's Mano Dura policy—would put him at risk in his home country. She ruled that he should be granted asylum. The government appealed.

Later that year, Detective Smith heard that Julio's cellmate told prison authorities that Julio was threatening to kill Smith and his partner. According to Smith, the man said that Julio had arranged for MS-13 members to stalk and assassinate the two detectives. To Julio's friends, despite his hatred of police, the charge was absurd. But the alleged threat was submitted as evidence in the deportation case. The judge dismissed the allegation, however, and he won the second round. The government appealed again.

In prison, Julio stayed busy. He finished his GED. He wrote letters, including a missive to the ACLU on behalf of his fellow prisoners complaining about the conditions in the prison for women and HIV-positive inmates. He made plans for his organization. But after the government's second appeal, he began to lose hope. He had been in the detention center at Elizabeth for nearly two years. The appeal meant he was likely to be there for several more. If the government continued to appeal, the decision could go all the way up to the attorney general, Alberto Gonzales, who that year had launched a national campaign against the Central American gangs and had called for restricting the rights of immigrants convicted of crimes.[20] His lawyers, along with Bob and Carlos, tried to encourage him. But Julio couldn't take the suspense or the confinement. He wanted out. Even if he were released, the police and the FBI would be waiting for him. In the summer of 2005, Julio agreed to voluntary deportation. Within a month he was on a plane back to El Salvador.

• • •

Over the next three years, hundreds of gang members would follow in Julio's footsteps, although most went involuntarily. In February 2005, as the fears about the gangs flashed in national headlines, the Homeland Security Department launched a new initiative specifically targeting Mara Salvatrucha: Operation Community Shield.[21] The effort was part of a larger Bush administration crackdown on illegal immigration in the wake of the September 11 terrorist attacks, and it marked a sea change in how the federal government dealt with criminal aliens. No longer would the federal immigration agency be criticized for sitting idly by as immigrants convicted of crimes passed in and out of prison. Instead, ICE agents would bang on doors and arrest criminals themselves.

To do so, they were still forced to rely heavily on information and assistance from local police. Many police chiefs, including those in Long Island, were eager to help. Arresting people on immigration charges alone was frowned on, but going after gang members was another thing altogether. Within a month, ICE publicized their first bust. More than a hundred Mara Salvatrucha members were swept up in seven cities and deported.[22] Thirty were from Long Island, rounded up with the help of Nassau and Suffolk County police officers.[23]

That summer, ICE expanded its focus to other gangs, too.[24] Not all of the people caught in ICE's widening net had criminal records. Some, like Julio, had only misdemeanors, or nothing at all. Of the thousands of immigrants arrested over the next two years in gang raids, many were picked up for their illegal immigration status alone.[25]

In 2007, ICE called the Nassau and Suffolk police departments again. They had arrested more than 1,000 alleged gang members across the country over the summer, and they hoped Long Island would yield a few more. They enlisted the police from Nassau and Suffolk counties to help them plan the raids. The Hempstead police, now led by the former gang task force leader Joseph Wing, after Russo retired, also agreed to participate. The police provided lists of gang members to the federal agency. But as the raid neared, the local police agencies became nervous. The federal immigration agents had not released the final list of suspects they planned to target, preventing the Long Island police from cross-checking the names in their gang databases.[26] The ICE agents also skipped the planning meeting for the operation.[27]

The police departments went forward with the raids anyway in September. The agents consulted their list of suspects, and police escorted them from house to house. They didn't need warrants to search the homes of immigrants, as they would have if they were searching the homes of citizens. It was a right that ICE took full advantage of in its new push against the gangs. But as ICE swept through Long Island, the police became increasingly concerned. Rather than acting respectfully and responsibly, the behavior was reckless, and they feared it could stoke simmering, underlying resentments.

One of the agents wore a cowboy hat, and the agents seemed careless as they wielded their shotguns and automatic weapons. At one point during a raid, the federal agents pointed guns at Nassau County police detectives. They also barged into the homes of several U.S. citizens. At the home of one, the agents lined up children and pulled a gun on one of the residents. It was the second time ICE agents had visited the house looking for a man named Miguel.[28] The woman repeated what she had told them before—that she was a citizen and that she didn't know who Miguel was.[29] They moved on. Another citizen who was arrested and taken into custody had to be driven home later.

Among the immigrants arrested were fathers of young families.[30] Most of the immigrants brought in held down at least one job, and some worked as many as three.[31] Several men were such fixtures in their communities that their employers hired lawyers at their own expense to represent them in immigration court.[32] Only 6 of the nearly 100 people ICE was looking for were actually found.[33] But 186 people were arrested anyway.[34] Fewer than a third had committed crimes that were deportable offenses. But all faced deportation. In Nassau County, only 3 of the dozens arrested were gang members. In Suffolk, it was 15. A few were released while they fought their cases, but many disappeared for months into the immigration detention system.[35]

On the last scheduled day of the week-long raid, Nassau County backed out of the final operation. The decision to break with the raids came the same day the Hempstead police officer found a hangman's noose in the department's locker room. [36] Wing had recently promoted a black officer to assistant chief of the department, and the noose was apparently hung in response as a Jim Crow–era racial threat.[37] A month later, a pair of nooses was found hanging in a Hempstead sanitation garage.[38]

Later, the police said they ended their support because they were stunned at the recklessness of the raids. They said they had been particularly worried when ICE agents told them their next armed raid would be on a Hempstead bar after dark.[39] The police believed the plan was a recipe for a shooting, and wanted no part in it. ICE was forced to cancel the raid, since they did not have the jurisdiction to go in alone.

The following week, Nassau police and Tom Suozzi took the unusual step of publicly denouncing the federal agency.[40] Nassau had enthusiastically invited the feds two years earlier to join its gang task force, while Hempstead Village had been calling for cooperation with federal agencies and working with immigration agents for nearly a decade. But the feds had gone too far.

At a press conference, the Nassau County police commissioner, Lawrence Mulvey, expressed concern about the department's efforts to build rapport with the Hispanic community. Nassau County officials said they were "misled" and called for Homeland Security investigation into the alleged misconduct by the federal agents during the raids.[41] They threatened never to cooperate with ICE again. Even in Suffolk County, where police applauded the raids, a detective who helped the immigration agents said he had some regrets. The agents had deported a gang member before the detective could bring a criminal case against him. The criminal justice and immigration systems were working against each other, he told the *New York Times*.[42]

But his point rang true at a deeper level as well. The immigration agents left a trail of fear and mistrust extending beyond the homes they visited. The local police were now associated with immigration enforcement. The raids also split up stable, two-parent families. Fathers were deported, and mothers had to cope with the separation from their husbands. They were left alone to raise their children in poorer, more isolated households. The raids, intended to alleviate the Long Island's gang problem, created the perfect conditions for the gangs to spread.

Jessica, 2003–2007

CHAPTER 19

Quinciñera

＊　＊　＊

The dress was pink and frilly. Jessica climbed in and attached a crystal tiara to her head. Jessica's cornrows had been unraveled and her hair combed straight. One of her friends offered lipstick. Jessica grimaced and smeared it on. The photographer snapped pictures, and her mother, Ana, beamed proudly. To humor them, Jessica twirled the satin skirt. It billowed out around her ankles, a little too long without the clear high-heeled shoes she had picked out. Her favorite uncle, the only one among her mother's brothers who had stayed clear of the gangs and had always treated her nicely growing up, would slip them on her feet later at the party. It was a ritual ushering her into adulthood that was supposed to be carried out by her father, but she hadn't seen him in more than a decade. Her uncle was the closest thing to a father she had. She glanced in the mirror. The dress, which fit her torso closely before ballooning out, emphasized the thin waist she usually hid under a baggy T-shirt and jeans. She smiled tentatively as the camera flashed.

It was July 2003, a month after her fifteenth birthday, and Ana was throwing her a party—her *quinciñera*. She had offered to buy Jessica a car instead when she turned sixteen, but Jessica said no. She didn't want to wait a year, and she wasn't certain her mother would follow through. She wanted the party—and the dress.

They went together to pick it out. It was the only girls' outing with her mom she could remember. Jessica knew what she was looking for as they rifled through the racks of prom dresses in the strip mall gown shop. It had to be pink. Something a princess or a ballerina might wear. She had imagined this dress since she was little—silly, she realized, but she wanted this almost as much as she wanted the boys in the gang to accept her as one of them, maybe more. Jessica couldn't wait to see all of her SWP friends dressed up. Fifteen of them would be her "court" for the evening. They would escort her and join her in the waltz she had been practicing to perform in front of everyone. One of her homeboys, dressed up in a white suit, would be her dancing partner. The other girls would wear purple and waltz around her with partners from the gang.

Her family had rented a hall downtown, and there would be plates of food and cases of beer—even champagne. The cake was the best part though. Little dolls dressed to match Jessica and her friends paraded down the three tiers of icing on a miniature staircase.

After she posed for more photos, she wiped off some of the mascara and went to show off to her brother. She was almost a grownup, and he couldn't boss her around anymore, she said as she strutted into his room in her dress. He laughed and shook his head. She may be turning fifteen, but as far as he was concerned, she was still a little girl. Jessica stalked out in a pout.

She refused to let anything ruin her party. She had escaped a juvenile detention home to make sure she didn't miss it. She was in the group home only two days before she walked out the front door and made a run for it. She knew the police probably wouldn't bother looking for her, and Ana didn't seem to care that she was on the run. The party was just as important to her mother. It was their one chance to act like a normal family. Jessica climbed into the car with her family, and the pink satin puffed up around her. She felt as if she were in a fairy tale.

Dozens of people filed into the hall, which had once been an old Polish clubhouse. The building was a remnant of the days when white ethnics ruled the town, but now it was dedicated to events like *quinciñeras* and baby baptisms for Hempstead's Hispanic community. The room was filled with balloons and seemed magnificent to Jessica. Noticeably absent were several of her uncles and her aunt, Angela. She was forced to invite them because they were relatives, but Jessica didn't expect them to come. They were hard-core Mara Salvatrucha members, and this was an SWP party. They knew to stay away. The party started, and Jessica twirled around the dance floor to pulsing reggaeton and tinny bachata music, pausing only to sneak drinks from the buffet. She couldn't remember a time when she felt so happy.

The meal was served, and her brother stood to give a toast. The room filled with the sound of clinking glasses. Everyone fell silent. But he had only uttered a few words before he his speech was interrupted by the sound of shouting outside. He put down the glass. It sounded like a fight, and a few men jumped up from the tables to go see. Mara Salvatrucha had arrived.

They surrounded the entranceway to the hall. Women screamed as more men ran outside. Jessica tried to make her way through the crowd, but she was tipsy and the heels slowed her down. By the time she made it to the door, the MS-13 members were gone, and one of Jessica's uncles was bleeding. One of the crashers had stabbed him with a garden fork. The party was over. People pushed to get out of the hall through the swirl of balloons. The cake sat uneaten. Jessica climbed into a car with her friends, not caring that she was crushing the pretty pink dress. They sped to her house.

Inside, she let the dress fall to the floor and pulled on baggy jeans and a T-shirt. She was furious. She knew one of her family members told the

MS-13 about her party, and they had ruined her perfect night. She wanted revenge. There was an MS-13 party that night down the road. She ran back out to the car, and they headed there.

Armed with a baseball bat, she followed the boys into the house. The party had been going on for a while, and people were drunk. They were easy targets. Her friends attacked the partygoers, and Jessica took her anger out on the windows and electronics. Then they fled, laughing, back into the night. Jessica felt a little better. They jumped into the car and drove until they reached the shore in Long Beach. Out on the sand, they sat in a circle and passed around joints until the sun came up.

* * *

Jessica had given up on schoolwork by the time she turned fifteen. She was hopelessly behind in her classes and nearly illiterate. She missed most of the beginning of her first year at Hempstead High School, but she didn't care. She had other accomplishments she was more focused on. In the gang, she had learned how to be successful. Her willingness to be cruel and her fierce loyalty won her the praise and respect of the leaders.

On an afternoon not long before her fifteenth birthday party, she arrived late to the gang's weekly meeting in Bradley Park. The girls were sitting on the playground equipment looking sullen. They pointed to the gathering of boys on the other side of the park. No girls allowed, they explained, but Jessica ignored them. She marched across the park's brittle, unkempt grass.

This was their usual hangout, rain or shine. The park was surrounded by a chain-link fence and, beyond that, blocks of cookie-cutter homes that had deteriorated into drab ghosts of their former selves. If any of the residents had come out onto their lawns, they would have seen a formation of boys kneeling in a circle. They looked druidic with their hands raised above their heads, their fingers twisted into cryptic symbols, chanting quietly in unison. But people in that neighborhood stayed indoors.

Jessica shored up her confidence and knelt next to one of the older boys. After they finished chanting the Spanish prayer in unison, Jessica asked the leader, "How come the females are not over here?"

"We'll let you stay here, but them, no."

She was elated.

They went forward with the business of the meeting: a discussion of how to punish an enemy gang member who had attacked one of their own. When they finished, the leader turned to Jessica and announced to the rest of the group that she would from now on have "control of the females." Jessica tried to keep from smiling too widely and revealing her excitement.

As president of the girls' clique she wasn't expected to be democratic. There was no voting in the gang; she could order them around as she wished. She ruled tyrannically. She had the power to issue "violations," which meant an infraction against gang policy that required a beating as punishment. The gang's rules were followed rigidly, and she could add more to the list of regulations when she pleased. She loved the strictness—she implemented a regime almost as tough as the group home rules. No snitching, no showing up late, no skipping meetings. She thrived on the strict rules in the gang; they were the opposite of her chaotic home life, where her mother barely paid attention when she arrived home after midnight. When one of the girls broke a rule, Jessica ordered her to be beaten for several seconds by the other members. If two girls had a dispute—a frequent occurrence since they often vied over the boys—she ordered them to resolve it by fighting each other for fifteen seconds. To inspire them to fight harder, Jessica decreed that whoever lost the fight then had to endure another fifteen-second beating by the whole group of seven girls.

Jessica skipped school nearly every day that winter. She got a job, at the gang's encouragement, to help pay dues. They made her a fake ID so employers would think she was old enough. Her first job was at the McDonald's downtown, but she didn't like the work. She preferred selling marijuana. Her cousins provided a steady stream of pot from home, so she focused on expanding her clients. She supplemented her small income with shoplifting. Her favorite target was JC Penney; she resold clothes on the street or at thrift stores. She always tithed a percentage of her various entrepreneurial ventures to the gang.

Most of the money was saved to buy guns. The bestowing of a gun was an important moment in the gang, although a girl was almost never given a gun unless her boyfriend shot someone and she needed to hide the evidence. Jessica was different. When she became leader of the girls, the gang entrusted her with a small 9-mm. pistol. She had been waiting for this. She took the gun home and stuffed it carefully under her mattress. Feeling the lump under her at night filled her with a sense of pride and also made her feel safer.

But there were some days she came crashing down. On several gray winter afternoons when everyone else in the family was off at work, Jessica sat on her bed, pulled the gun from under her mattress, and lifted it to her temple. Seconds ticked by as she held it there, the cold little circle denting her skin, and wondered if her family would care that she was gone. Later, she wondered what stopped her from pulling the trigger.

With the gang, she never let on that she was scared or sad. The leaders decided to give her a new role. They wanted her to make friends with a Bloods affiliate in Freeport known as Thugged Out Posse, which had access to guns. She already knew a few of the members. Once the other gang trusted her, SWP hoped to use her as a source to buy weapons.

She had learned from the boys in SWP how to break car windows and extract the radio for sale. She showed off to her new friends. The boys in TOP were impressed and soon she was spending as much time with them as with SWP. They spent the days smoking pot and searching for targets. Walking around with TOP one day in Freeport, Jessica noticed a car idling in front of a bodega. She bragged to them that once she had stolen a car on her own—a 1997 Honda Civic. It had been in good condition. She found it in a gas station, radio blaring and owner gone. She hopped in and headed to a chop shop to sell it. She didn't tell them that the men in the garage had only offered her $50. She tried to bargain with them for $100, but they laughed at her. They knew she was desperate and refused to budge. She took the $50.

She told TOP her plan as they approached the bodega. She would climb into the driver's side while one of the group blocked the door of the bodega so the owner couldn't get out. Once the others were safely in the car, they would let go of the door, make a run for it, and jump in. The plan went off perfectly.

They headed out of town in the car, laughing and passing around a joint. They pulled over once they were several towns away and looked in the trunk to see if they could find any valuables. They found a shotgun. They spent the next day joyriding around Long Island. Later, they got a phone call about a party back in Freeport. Jessica wasn't so sure. In Freeport, police might know about the stolen car. She resisted their pleas to turn the car around, but then gave in. She didn't want to seem scared. Flashing lights appeared behind them almost as soon as they crossed the Freeport border. She hit the gas pedal, but in her panic she turned into a parking lot with no exit. The police blocked their way out. They quickly concocted a story. Within minutes, they were handcuffed and headed toward the Freeport police station.

At the station, she told the detectives that the car belonged to her grandmother. Her friends told the cops the same thing: She told us it was her grandmother's; we didn't know it was stolen. Same thing with the gun—they played innocent. After a few hours in the Freeport police station, Jessica was sent to the Westbury Juvenile Detention Center, her first time in jail.

Long Island had only one detention center for juveniles in Nassau County. Suffolk County was also supposed to send its underage inmates there, but had occasionally been caught illegally keeping children in the adult jail.[1] The conditions in the Westbury juvenile jail weren't much better than an adult facility. In the early nineties, a scandal erupted when a teacher at the juvenile center had an affair with one of the young prisoners.[2] In 2000, the center failed a state inspection for the third year running because of fire code violations, soiled mattresses, and a dirty kitchen.[3] The same year, a *Newsday* reporter, Lauren Terrazzano, catalogued a list of more problems, including abusive and under-trained staff.[4] For three years, the center, which housed both boys and girls, had ignored requirements that it update its staff training, waiting until one of the employees was caught roughing up a teenager. The center struggled to fill its staff to capacity, and a quarter of its employees had been arrested in the past for offenses including assault and larceny. In one incident, an inmate was locked up overnight without access to a bathroom. In another, a girl was left locked in a closet while the only employee with a key ran an errand to the bank. Employees allowed inmates, often members of rival gangs, to fight uninterrupted.

In 2002, guards at the center were charged and later pleaded guilty to extorting $20,000 from the parents of an inmate for protecting their child from beatings and harassment. They also admitted to selling alcohol and marijuana to the teenage inmates.[5] Five years later, investigators found that the center was still understaffed, that a dining room ceiling was near collapse, and that the building was rife with fire hazards.[6]

Jessica didn't stay long. She was fourteen, and it was her first offense. After two weeks, she was released on probation and told not to mess up again.

When she arrived back home, the fights with her mother became more vicious and often ended with Ana kicking Jessica out of the house. Sometimes Jessica stayed with Nadia, an older woman with three children who often hosted parties for SWP. The parties were wild, despite the fact that her youngest child was less than a year old. On nights when she didn't go to Nadia's, Jessica curled up under a tree in the park. She skipped showering and went for days in the same clothes.

Her brother was also fighting with her mother. After one brutal fight, Ana took him to court and filed a petition designating her son as a "person in need of supervision," or PINS. Although a PINS designation was different from being identified as a juvenile delinquent—which required committing a crime—the two groups were housed together in group homes and often considered interchangeable. Everyone knew the PINS kids usually ended up becoming juvenile delinquents eventually.

Soon after, a social worker came to the house to check on the case. She didn't speak Spanish, so she brought along a friend, Sergio Argueta, to help her communicate with Ana. He had been appointed Nassau County's first gang specialist and was working to transform STRONG, his nonprofit organization, into a full-time operation. Sergio's job description didn't include house visits with social workers, but he agreed to accompany them sometimes because it allowed him to meet young people he might be able to recruit for his antiviolence programs. From what the social worker told him, it sounded like he might find some candidates in Jessica's family.

Jessica's brother was livid at the intrusion. He yelled and cursed at his mother, the social worker, and Sergio. Why didn't they deal with his sister? She was worse than he was, he argued. Jessica's mother conceded his point. It was nine in the morning, and Jessica, a freshman in high school, had just arrived home two hours earlier. The social worker and Sergio exchanged glances. They asked to meet her.

Jessica's mother disappeared into a bedroom. Jessica did not want to be woken up. The screaming went on for several minutes. Finally, a tiny girl stalked out into the living room. She was in the rumpled clothes she had been wearing the night before, and her mascara was smeared. She started cursing as soon as she saw Sergio and the social worker.

"What the fuck do you want? Why don't you people leave me the fuck alone!" she said by way of introduction.

They couldn't get a word in as she continued her tirade. Her mother yelled back. Jessica stormed out.

Sergio was stunned. He had seen some kids in bad situations, but that little girl was a mess. He would leave this case to the social worker.

Ana was fed up with Jessica. One morning, she dragged her to the car and drove her to the family court building in East Garden City, a crumbling structure built in 1960 a few blocks down from the Garden City mall. Fifty years later, the building was bursting at the seams and had numerous fire violations, much like the Westbury juvenile detention center on the other side of the Nassau County golf course. Jessica met a lawyer seconds before they went in and stood mutely as the adults talked over her head in legalistic terms she couldn't understand. Her mother nodded at the judge as he read aloud documents that described Jessica's drinking and drug habits, her short criminal record, and her alleged gang ties. She thought her mother looked kind of smug. The judge looked at her with calm, knowing eyes.

Jessica's rage boiled over. She started shouting at the judge. She screamed that he didn't know who she was and added that he could go to hell. With that, the court hearing was over. She would be going to a group home for an extended stay. The adults said they hoped more time in detention would be beneficial and that Jessica could get the help she obviously needed.

The days in detention were monotonous, except when she made them interesting by fighting with the other inmates, a dozen other girls about as angry and disturbed as she was. The doors weren't locked at the home—it was a nonsecure facility—so sometimes the inmates escaped. They melted away into Hempstead's suburban streets, not to be seen again until police caught them committing another crime. During her first stay, Jessica didn't try to escape. The home was located in the middle of MS-13 territory. She was safer inside.

She had her own room, furnished with a bed, a hard mattress, and no door. Each day, the inmates woke up at 6 AM and descended downstairs to eat breakfast. They had class, taught by a teacher provided by the nonprofit that ran the home. Jessica got into as much trouble there as she had in the public schools. In the afternoons, the young inmates marched around the backyard for exercise. For variety, one of the staff members taught them capoeira moves, the Brazilian fighting-dance, but Jessica was banned from the lessons after she used some of the moves in a fight against another girl. Another staff member sat them down occasionally to read from a book about drug addiction that described the tragic fates of teenagers who didn't just say no. Jessica held on to the book, but she shut out the social workers, only paying attention to them when they reminded her of court dates or passed along phone messages from home. Jessica's mother came to visit once.

When Jessica returned home, life there was just as tumultuous as it had been before she left, and only a few weeks passed before she was caught drinking at a party and shipped back to a group home. This time she escaped so she wouldn't miss her *quinciñera*. A few days after the party, police came looking for Jessica to question her about the fight.

Ana was happy to give her up to the detectives, but Jessica was out again that night. Instead, Ana gave them a photograph from the wall. That evening, when Jessica arrived in Bradley Park, her friends told her that a police patrol was cruising through town with her picture in hand. She turned around and headed to Nadia's house, across the park. Police had just been there, Nadia said. Jessica headed home. As soon as she walked through the door, her mother picked up the phone to call the police. Jessica glared at her and turned to go outside. They were waiting for her down the block. When she began her fourth stint in detention after the party, she decided to stay. She was too angry with her mother to go back home and worried she would just be kicked out again anyway. At least in the home she had a bed.

◆ ◆ ◆

One of the group homes where Jessica spent time was in an old Victorian house near downtown. It had been founded in the mid-1970s as the country deinstitutionalized its juvenile jails and mental hospitals. Neighbors on the block, including a funeral home and Catholic church across the street, fought against the opening of the home viciously. They didn't want the blight in their neighborhood. But the home—run by an organization founded by a veteran civil rights activist—won. It stayed as the neigh-borhood turned over from white to black and Hispanic. A second group home for girls was opened nearby a few years later.

By the time Jessica was sent there, the original brown siding was re-placed with sterile white vinyl. Thick bulletproof glass had been installed in the windows, and a four-story-tall tree that had shaded the front yard had been chopped down, but the daily itinerary and programs offered to the youth had stayed the same for thirty years. The stories of the children were similar, too. All came to the home deeply troubled, mostly from fam-ilies torn by domestic abuse, alcoholism, drugs, or all three. When they walked in the door, the children were told that there would be no fighting, no drugs, and no talk of gangs. They were forbidden from even mention-ing the word. The rule curbed the fighting and also—in the minds of the administrators—turned their time there into a break from the stress out-side. Usually the children, who ranged in age from ten to seventeen, seemed thankful for the time-out. Others, like Jessica, kept their guard up.

Most only stayed for ten days at a time, but the beds stayed full. For many children, such group homes were their first encounter with the ju-venile justice system and usually not their last. Across the nation, the num-ber of juvenile delinquency cases jumped by 42 percent during the nineties.[7] By 2000, there were more children in jail than ever before, and nearly 60 percent of minors who came into contact with the juvenile jus-tice system were arrested at least once more before turning eighteen.[8] New York was especially active in jailing children. The state had more than 4,000 children in detention in 2003. Only Texas, California, and Florida had more underage inmates, but New York was one of only three states, in-cluding Connecticut and North Carolina, where childhood in the eyes of the courts ended at sixteen, not eighteen.[9] Jessica's brother might have laughed at the idea of Jessica acting grown up, but by the time she cele-brated *quinciñera*, the state considered her childhood almost over.

CHAPTER 20

American Mano Dura

* * *

The rise in the number of youth in jail came in response to a wave of fear about youth crime during the 1980s and 90s. Paradoxically, juvenile arrests dropped dramatically during the nineties—by 18 percent between 1994 and 2003.[1] But the reality that youth crime was decreasing didn't diminish broad concern that juvenile delinquents were running wild in the nation's streets.

Concern about youth crime was nothing new. In 1838, Abraham Lincoln warned on the campaign trail that violent lawlessness was the "No. 1 domestic problem."[2] The first juvenile court was later established in 1899. Its mission was relatively soft, however. It was designed as a surrogate parent for wayward children, particularly second-generation immigrants living in homes where poverty, violence, alcoholism, and other problems increased the risk that they would become violent themselves. Judges and other officials in the system believed they could turn children who dabbled in crime—assumed to be more vulnerable and malleable than their adult counterparts—into productive members of society.

In 1929, one of the first prevention programs, the Police Athletic League, was formed in New York City in response to fears that "trouble-making" young immigrants in the city's poor enclaves would fuel an adult crime epidemic once they grew up.[3] The country began keeping track of crime officially only in the 1930s, however, and didn't have comprehensive national statistics until 1958. In 1961, shortly after the newly available numbers showed what seemed like a shocking proportion of crime committed by youth, Congress passed the Juvenile Delinquency and Youth Offenses Control Act, which allowed for experiments in new methods of preventing delinquency. In 1967, the Katzenbach report on crime was released. President Johnson commissioned the report following the contentious 1964 presidential campaign, when Barry Goldwater put him on the defensive about his crime policies.[4]

It was a huge undertaking. Besides laying the groundwork for RICO, the report was the first comprehensive study of crime undertaken by the federal government, and it warned that crime—juvenile crime in particular—was worsening. Surveys at the time found that Americans were deeply preoccupied with juvenile delinquency. One 1963 Gallup poll found that Americans complained about juvenile delinquency almost as much as local real estate taxes, their top source of anxiety.[5] The majority of Americans felt that crime was getting worse in their neighborhoods. Almost none believed that it was improving.[6]

The nineteen commissioners spent two years churning out more than three hundred pages filled with analysis of the problem and two hundred recommendations. The commission acknowledged the perennial nature of American fear of crime and noted that it wasn't only related to fear of injury or death, "but, at bottom, a fear of strangers." It also suggested that sometimes those fears were unwarranted.[7] When it came to street gangs in particular, the commission found that the problem was not so bad as Americans generally perceived it. Although gangs were "commonly blamed for much of the street crime that presently alarms the Nation," gang violence was "less frequent, less violent, and less uncontrolled than is generally believed."[8] In a major two-year study of gangs, researchers found that only 17 percent of gang offenses were violent and that half of those were against rival gang members.[9]

In keeping with Johnson's Great Society liberalism, the report was progressive in its analysis and solutions. It was released at the height of the civil rights movement, and the commissioners proposed that ending segregation and inequality in the schools should be the focus of efforts to curb crime. "Money for schools is money against crime," they said.[10] The commission applauded efforts by nonprofits to reach out to "gang boys," but "with little more permanent to offer than bus trips and ball games, they have rarely managed to convert boys from total gang involvement."[11] The commissioners suggested that youth be recruited as community organizers and involved in political activities "to give him a reason to care about what happens to his world—a stake in a healthy society."[12]

The commission also criticized the juvenile justice system. The number of juveniles referred to court was growing faster than the youth population itself, and recidivism was worsening.[13] The commission blamed a lack of resources and other obvious flaws: At the time, many juvenile judges had not even graduated from college. It also found that a quarter of the 400,000 children detained for nonviolent crimes had been jailed with adults—a surefire way to shape them into hard-core criminals.[14]

The commission suggested that the juvenile justice system turn back to original efforts to rehabilitate children.[15] Detention in low-security residential centers and other such shelters was recommended only in cases in which the parents seemed incapable of supervising the child. It suggested that troubled kids—the ones who seemed most in danger of committing delinquent acts—should be engaged in intensive programs to prevent them from getting in trouble again. Above all, they should not be "labeled for life."[16]

The report's suggestions for more emphasis on alternative treatment culminated in the 1974 Juvenile Justice and Delinquency Prevention Act.[17] The law extended a series of previous federal youth crime laws and set into motion a plan to partially deinstitutionalize the juvenile system.[18] Like the efforts going on at the time to move people with mental illness out of asylums, the plan was to move youth out of prisons—especially those charged with crimes that only applied to children, like truancy—into softer programs where they would receive the "gentle and friendly" care envisioned by the Johnson commission. States were given block grants as encouragement to create new alternative programs and group homes.[19]

But the commission's good intentions met with a harder reality in the world of American politics. Youth crime was skyrocketing. Juveniles arrested for violent crimes tripled in the early 1970s.[20] In 1974, sociologist Robert Martinson published a major study arguing that rehabilitation programs didn't work.[21] Other researchers later proved him wrong, but at the time his findings were widely publicized and embraced.

It was the era of the Saturday Night Special, when the nation's streets seemed awash with cheap handguns. Even the suburbs were affected. There, the rise in the crime rate was outpacing that of cities.[22] James Q. Wilson, the conservative criminologist who invented the Broken Windows crime theory, predicted that a new "critical mass" of young people would send crime soaring even higher in the next decade.[23] In a special address to Congress in 1975, President Gerald Ford proclaimed the billions spent on law enforcement efforts over the previous decade a waste. "For too long, law has centered its attention more on the rights of the criminal defendant than on the victim of crime. It is time for law to concern itself more with the rights of the people it exists to protect," he said.[24] He recommended tougher sentencing for convicted criminals, including children, and mandatory incarceration for a wider array of crimes and for repeat offenders.

"There should be no doubt in the minds of those who commit violent crimes—especially crimes involving harm to others—that they will be sent to prison," he said.

New York, where the city was tumbling into a financial crisis, became the symbol of the crime wave gnawing at distant corners of the nation and a leader in the new movement to fight it. A 1976 New York law extended sentencing for juveniles who committed certain felonies beyond the former limit of eighteen months and shifted the mission of juvenile courts to public safety, away from the previous focus on the welfare of minors.[25] Two years later, the case of Willie Bosket, a fifteen-year-old boy who fatally shot two men in a subway, fueled more angst and worry. In response, New York passed even harsher juvenile laws. Since 1922, children sixteen and up in New York had been considered adults.[26] After the Bosket murders, the state passed a law making it possible to charge children as young as thirteen as adults if they committed murder.[27]

In the 1980s, the panic over a perceived youth crime epidemic spread. Child murderers and rapists seemed to be everywhere. In California, officials announced that Hispanic gangs were on the rise and competing for space with black gangs. The state responded with one of the most expansive efforts yet to fight youth crime and gangs—which were by then closely linked in the minds of the American public. The Street Terrorism Enforcement and Prevention Act passed in California in 1988. Gang crime was defined as offenses committed by individuals who had to "actively participate in any criminal street gang" and was differentiated from other criminal acts.[28] Other states clamored to copy the legislation, and soon gang crimes were defined in criminal codes across the country.

In New York in 1989, a group of teenage boys were accused of assaulting a white female jogger in Central Park. The incident fueled the sense of urgency for new laws to crack down on young criminals and gangs. In the aftermath, the press and politicians beat the drums about young savages rampaging across the city and country. The term "wilding" gained currency to describe the latest worrisome trend among youth.[29] It was a "kill-or-be-killed world," one *New York Times* reporter wrote in 1993 in describing the year's "countless murders."[30] In the story, the reporter quoted a man in Little Rock who "talked wistfully of times when people could leave their doors unlocked and children could play outside." "I never used to worry about gangs or violence," he was quoted as saying. "Now I'm aware of it all the time."[31]

FBI statistics repeated in newspapers and on campaign trails were dramatic: Between 1965 and 1990, the number of children arrested for murder jumped by 332 percent.[32] Crack cocaine was partly to blame, but so was the spread of guns, poverty, urban blight, and so many other factors that devising a coherent prevention and intervention strategy seemed both daunting and naïve. Politicians across the country had a simpler answer: Put them in jail.

State after state passed laws that strengthened punishments for young people who committed murder, but also for those who committed property crimes like robbery and burglary. One preferred strategy was to automatically push youth charged with the most egregious offenses out of the juvenile court system altogether—where mandatory limits on sentencing were often in place—and into adult criminal courts. In the first half of the nineties, forty states expanded the circumstances under which juveniles could be sent to adult court.[33] The number of children sent to adult jails jumped by nearly 5,000 cases nationwide between 1988 and 1992.[34]

But the homicides in 1993 weren't "countless." In fact, the count, tallied by the FBI each year, showed that murders fell significantly between 1991 and 1992.[35] Youth crime hit a plateau in 1994, and then went into a precipitous decline for the next decade.[36] Later, it turned out that the five teenagers who were charged in the attack on the jogger were innocent. Like "wilding," the youth crime epidemic was also largely fictitious. Among youth, arrests were going down as a percentage of all serious crimes by 1994.[37] And while there had been a slight uptick in the percentage of youth arrested for violent crime in the preceding decade, it was minimal, rising to 0.5 percent of all juveniles, from 0.3 percent.[38]

But some of the harshest new laws against youthful offenders were still on the horizon. In 1994, crime was the top issue for voters in the November election, even though murder rates had been worse in 1931 and 1979.[39] In February that year, James Frier, the deputy assistant director in the FBI's criminal investigative division, testified in Congress that youth crime was increasing. Frier told a Senate subcommittee on juvenile justice that the "alarming" rise in youth crime could be attributed to one problem: street gangs.[40] And not just any street gangs. "These gangs have become national in scope in terms of membership, organizational structure, objectives and criminal activity," he testified. Frier characterized the gangs as brutal and mafia-like and reported that they were spreading out of the inner cities into areas never thought of before as gang centers, including Kansas City; Smyrna, Georgia; and the suburbs around Washington, DC. In 1992, the FBI had implemented the "Safe Streets" initiative focused almost exclusively on gang crime, but there was more to be done, Frier said.[41]

A few months later, Congress passed the $30 billion Violent Crime Control and Law Enforcement Act.[42] The focus of the law was prisons. Nearly $9 billion was authorized to build new prisons and $2 billion for boot camps, an alternative to incarceration later proven to be largely ineffective.[43] The law also expanded the application of the death penalty, instituted a three-strikes rule at the federal level, lowered the age of juveniles eligible for adult treatment in federal courts to thirteen, increased the penalties for gang members, and created new gang-related offenses.[44] It funneled more than $3 billion toward dealing with criminal aliens, including money for a criminal alien tracking center and for reimbursing states that imprisoned illegal immigrants convicted of crimes.[45] It also created the COPS program, which provided money for 100,000 police officers to be split up among cities and towns across the country.[46]

Crime prevention provisions included in the law, ranging from domestic violence programs to rehabilitation for drug offenders, were allocated $7 billion. Ten percent of that—or about 2 percent of the total amount—was designated to help various school and community programs working with at-risk youth.[47] Still, many scoffed at the prevention programs as pork and criticized the law as incoherent and not tough enough. James Q. Wilson told the *Times* the bill was a "Christmas tree designed by Salvador Dali." The *Times* reporter suggested the bill was a "flimsy bauble to dangle before voters."[48]

In New York that fall, crime was also a main issue for voters in the heated gubernatorial campaign.[49] The sitting governor, Democrat Mario Cuomo, called for doubling the sentences of young people accused of crimes, fingerprinting juveniles who committed serious offenses, and allowing more people access to juvenile records.[50] His plan also called for preventative measures, including a proposal to keep some schools open later at night, but on the campaign trail Cuomo frequently boasted of the number of jail cells built in New York during his tenure.[51] George Pataki, Cuomo's Republican challenger, campaigned with an even tougher crime plan and won the election.[52]

Three years later, the U.S. prison population was exploding, and crime was plummeting, but the hysteria didn't taper off.[53] In 1997, President Clinton declared a "war on gangs." Violent crimes rates among young people had been falling sharply for four consecutive years, but in his 1997 State of the Union address, Clinton said it was time for "a full-scale assault on juvenile crime."[54] Soon after, the administration introduced the Anti-Gang and Youth Violence Act of 1997, sponsored in the House by Representative Charles Schumer of New York. Promoting the bill in Congress in February, Attorney General Janet Reno acknowledged that juvenile crime was dropping, but predicted it would worsen as the youth population grew.[55] She applauded new efforts to turn RICO against gangs but said there were still "serious and violent juveniles on the street right now."[56]

Clinton's plan included $200 million for states to prosecute juvenile crime and create gang task forces.[57] It also eased the process of funneling juveniles into the adult criminal system and called for tighter gun rules and new prevention measures.[58] Clinton hoped to replicate an antigang program receiving rave reviews in Boston that had combined intensive policing with prevention efforts.[59] Congress rejected the plan. The law was too soft compared to harsher penalties for juvenile crime supported by the Republican majority.[60] The country needed to treat thirteen- and fourteen-year-old criminals as the "predators they seem to be," one Republican congressman said. In the House, an alternative bill passed that would have required juveniles who committed violent crimes to be tried as adults.[61]

Neither bill was signed into law, but one of the goals professed by both sides was met. The number of states with laws allowing judges to send youth to adult courts grew to forty-six.[62] During the nineties, the number of children sent to adult jails rose by 300 percent.[63] In 1999, a third of young people in the adult system and four in ten youth inmates in juvenile jails were charged with nonviolent crimes.[64]

The swell of young inmates had the century-old juvenile justice system on the verge of collapse. Between 1985 and 2000, the number of juveniles incarcerated in juvenile detention centers rose by more than a third.[65] The number of juveniles in detention was more than 100,000 on any given day in 2000, compared to less than 80,000 in 1991, the year when youth crime spiked.[66] Between 1997 and 2001, the number of youth held for more than six months on nonviolent offenses grew by 15 percent to more than 17,000.[67] More than a third of juvenile detention centers reported being overcrowded.[68] Some criminal justice experts cautioned that it wouldn't be long until the juvenile courts and jails were completely dismantled and dissolved into the adult criminal court system.

Minority youth bore the brunt of the crackdown. Studies showed that African American and Hispanic teenagers were arrested at higher rates, given harsher sentences, and kept in jail longer than whites.[69] One study found that parole officials and others in the court system regularly described minority youth in their case files and in presentations to judges more harshly than they did white youth accused of the same crimes.[70] Between 1997 and 2003, the number of Hispanic youth placed in detention centers for nonviolent offenses such as property crime, drugs, or parole violations grew, while the number of white and black youth sent to detention centers for such nonviolent crimes fell.[71]

By 2002, murders committed by young people had plummeted 65 percent since 1994.[72] Arrests of minors for other crimes had fallen at twice the rate of decline for adults.[73] The number of youth in gangs had dropped by nearly 100,000 nationwide after a spike in the 1990s.[74]

The economist Steven Levitt argued in a 2004 article that the increased incarceration rate was the primary reason for the crime decline, an argument that became a chapter in the book he wrote with Stephen Dubner, *Freakonomics*.[75] More criminals in prison meant fewer on the streets, and there were more people in prison than ever. In the article, he wrote that the ebb of crack, the legalization of abortion, and the rise in the number of police had contributed but were not the primary explanations behind the decline. "The one factor that dominates all others in terms of predicted impact on crime . . . is the growth in the prison population," he wrote. It was a neat solution, but it was also a short-term one.

One study in Florida—among the most aggressive states when it came to cracking down on youth crime—found that putting children in prisons, especially adult prisons, raised the recidivism rate.[76] The longer they were in detention, the more likely it was that they would go back to crime after their release, the study found. Another study compared juvenile recidivism in New York, with its tougher laws, to New Jersey, where juveniles were largely kept out of the adult criminal court system.[77] It found that the New Jersey youth were less likely to be arrested again after their release. New York's system, in contrast, was a revolving door. A Centers for Disease Control report also recommended against sending juveniles to adult jails, finding that it "generally resulted in increased arrest for subsequent crimes, including violent crime."[78] But by the time the report was published, hundreds of thousands of young people had already passed through adult jails.

Some experts worried the hodgepodge of gang laws enacted in the eighties and nineties also increased the potential that crime would again grow. Thousands of young African American and Hispanic teenagers were listed in gang databases—suspects before they had even committed a crime.[79] Gang experts noted that the efforts of law enforcement officials to label the gang members complemented the work of the gangs by fostering cohesion and further alienating the members from mainstream society.[80] At the same time, the definitions of gang membership varied widely across states and jurisdictions and highlighted the difficulty social scientists, police, and policymakers encountered when it came to defining what exactly a gang was.

During the nineties, nearly every state enshrined in law its own set of characteristics that defined a gang, a gang member, and a gang crime. Nearly every definition was different. In Illinois, a gang was a "combination, confederation, alliance, network, conspiracy, understanding, or other similar conjoining" of three or more persons, "with an established hierarchy that, through its membership or through the agency of any member engages in a course or pattern of criminal activity." In Indiana, it had to be five members, and the group had to require as a condition of membership the commission of a felony or the "offense of battery." In Arizona, the gang only had to have one member, and its member, or members, had to "individually or collectively" attempt to commit felonies. Besides the wide variances in state law, local law enforcement agencies often had a lot of discretion in deciding what counted as a gang-related crime.[81] The most reliable data to measure crime across the states was by using gang homicides—although more than two-thirds of places that reported gang problems never reported any gang murders. Most other cities reported three or fewer gang-related murders a year. The confusion about what constituted gang membership had done little to stop the widespread panic about its growth, however.

In 2004, a group of Long Island police chiefs, among them Chief Russo of Hempstead and Chief Woodward of Freeport, released a joint report with a youth advocacy organization, Fight Crime: Invest in Kids. The report warned that gang homicides were increasing, gangs in Long Island were growing, and the members were getting younger and younger.[82] Quoting Chief Russo, the report called gangs "domestic terrorists," who "intimidate entire neighborhoods and entire communities."

But throwing more of them in jail would backfire, the Long Island police argued. They pointed to a decade of cracking down against juveniles

to prove their point. "Locking up youths in juvenile facilities may only increase the likelihood that they will continue a life of crime," the report
said.[83]

In Long Island in particular, the influx of young inmates had strained
the already embattled juvenile justice system. In 1999, 1,000 children were
held in Nassau and Suffolk annually, about a quarter of the state juvenile inmate population and more than during the crime wave in the seventies—
even though crime among youth dropped 20 percent in Suffolk County
and 29 percent in Nassau County over three years.[84] The swell of new
cases meant children waited longer in the island's dilapidated detention
center for their cases to wind through court and became more likely to act
out again when they left.[85]

The police report was critical of the Pataki administration's introduction of a new antigang initiative that year, Operation IMPACT. The program pumped more than $7 million into new gang task forces around the
state, promoted information sharing, and trained law enforcement and
educators in how to identify gang members.[86] More law enforcement was
"only a partial solution," the report said.[87] Identifying gang members was
only half of the battle.

Their recommendations weren't innovative. They echoed the fifty-year-
old Johnson crime commission report, dusting off proposals to enhance
intervention, address poverty, and improve public schools that had been
discarded in the anti-rehabilitation movement of the 1970s. The report
was novel only in that it was written by a group of police officers begging
to expand the response to gangs beyond more funding for their departments. "Law enforcement cannot solve the juvenile crime problem themselves," the report concluded. "We can deal over and over with disasters,
repeatedly repairing the expanding leak, or we can find the money to fix
the hole in the roof."

CHAPTER 21

Second Chance

● ● ●

After her fourth release from detention, Jessica immediately went back to fighting with her mother and cutting school in Bradley Park. She occasionally visited the TOP members in Freeport, too, but her relationship with the Bloods gang soured after she clashed with one of the girl members. To Jessica, it wasn't worth it to make peace—she had her own gang, anyway. But it would not be easy to cut off ties with TOP, despite the fact that she was not an official member. She set up a meeting with them to tell them she was thinking about calming down. She knew she might face a beating, the ritualistic "blood out" that would free her from the gang, but she wasn't afraid of a fight.

TOP agreed to the meeting, but they were not pleased. They had trusted her, and now she knew too many of their secrets. They were not going to let her off with just a beating. At school on the day Jessica was set to meet them, someone whispered the rumor to Jessica. TOP would beat her up, and then they would stab her.

Jessica was tough, but she knew the threat was real. They wanted to kill her. As she wandered from class to class, she thought about what to do. She couldn't escape—if she left school grounds, they might be waiting for her. Besides, she had no money. She had rarely left Hempstead on her own. SWP probably wouldn't step in to defend her—she doubted they would want to risk their affiliation with the larger gang just to protect her. They would probably be angry with her for cutting off the flow of weapons to their gang. She certainly couldn't call home. At the end of her last class, she waited behind. She would have to trust her teacher—there was no one else to help.

The teacher brought her to the security guards, who called a police detective. The detective arrived and told Jessica he would make a few calls. He left her in the classroom to wait. Soon, the shuffling of hundreds of feet in the hall outside was replaced with the eerie quiet of an empty school building. Then the door opened. It was Sergio. He cocked his head at her and forced a smile. Oh no, he thought.

She stared back and laughed nervously. She remembered when he had barged into her house with the social worker. She hated this guy. Not long after his appearance at her house, she had been forced to attend one of his gang presentations at school. She led SWP in a walkout.

Sergio sat down with the detective. She was surprised he stayed—she expected him to laugh and turn around. But he looked at her with an intent gaze. They didn't have many options, he said. He had done research for the Nassau County Youth Board on what to do with gang youth who wanted out and found that there was no official mechanism for dealing with children already involved in gangs. Instead, there were prevention programs, like G.R.E.A.T., or detention. There was a state shelter program for homeless runaways, but technically she was neither. And even if he could pull strings, they could only keep her for three days before she would have to come back to Hempstead or be placed in another group home.

The biggest hurdle, however, would be Jessica herself. If Sergio was going to help her, she must promise him that she really wanted to change.

She stared down at her feet. If she were somehow lucky and they didn't stab her, inevitably she would end up back in trouble or in jail again. No one had ever offered her a way out. She would have to grab her chance now. She nodded. Yes, she wanted out. She said she would do whatever was necessary.

Sergio got to work. There was no formal process for dealing with a teenager like Jessica, but she couldn't wait. He would have to bend the rules.

After dozens of phone calls, he found a home that would take her temporarily in Wantagh, a mostly white, middle-class town near the entrance of Jones Beach. She could stay for a few days while Sergio looked for other options. The home wasn't used to kids like Jessica. She had promised to behave, but she chafed at the rules and didn't like the other kids or the staff. Sergio got a call within a week. Jessica had thrown a flowerpot at someone. She scared the counselors. They couldn't keep her.

Sergio called a group home in Albany. The goal of the home was to help teenagers become self-sufficient, and the facilities were state-of-the-art. He asked if they might take Jessica, even though she was young and she wasn't local. They agreed.

He drove her up to Albany, four hours away, and dropped her off. Jessica was impressed. The home was new and clean. The staff was energetic. For the first time in years, Jessica started going to school regularly. But she was far behind in her classes and quickly got frustrated. She could still barely read. At first she was lonely, but she soon made new friends. They were outcasts and troublemakers like her. They smoked, sold marijuana, and drank. The staff at the home caught her sneaking out after curfew. They told her if she did it again, she would be kicked out.

One of her new friends had a shoplifting habit, something Jessica was an expert in. Only a couple of months after she arrived, the two were caught in the mall as her friend stashed clothing into her bag. She was going back to Hempstead. A court hearing in the Garden City family court was scheduled for the next week.

Sergio drove the four hours back up to Albany to pick her up. He was angry. Jessica was his first and probably his last chance to prove that an entrenched gang member wasn't necessarily a lost cause and that intervention could work. In the short time she was gone, Sergio had been working to expand his contacts. He had an idea for a yearlong "university," in which gang members trying to get out could study for their GED, do group therapy, and give antiviolence presentations in school as a part of their own rehabilitation. He had also been giving more presentations, holding peace marches, and giving interviews to the local newspapers to get the word out.

But if Jessica failed, he could lose his chance to convince the county and state authorities to consider a new approach for dealing with gang members. He knew it took patience, but he was losing his. Maybe this case was hopeless. They loaded her few bags into the minivan, and as they drove away, he started to vent his frustration. She interrupted.

"You need to stop wasting your time with me. I'm not worth it—you've already done so much," she said. She was staring out the window. Even with her baggy pants, tattoos, and cornrows, she looked vulnerable. At her age, Sergio had been going to Kmart to buy a gun to avenge his friend's murder—trying to prove to the world that he was grown up and didn't care about anything, especially himself. He took a breath.

"Listen, we're not going to stop trying. We're not going to give up, no matter what you do," he said.

She kept staring out the window, but she looked relieved. He asked her what went wrong in Albany. Jessica talked the whole way back, unburdening the story of her childhood and her family to Sergio and talking about what she should do next.

In Hempstead, Sergio went to the court hearing with her. The judge would probably order her back to jail or, if she was lucky, another group home. But Sergio had one last idea.

Several months earlier, a man had come to visit him in the offices of the Youth Board. The man belonged to an Anabaptist sect, the Bruderhof, a group related to the Amish. They preached peace and shared resources communally, but unlike the Amish, they also participated in outside political causes. They had read about Sergio's efforts and wanted to invite him to a conference on forgiveness. To entice him, they had baked him a batch of cookies.

After the man left, Sergio turned to his boss and shook his head.

"You're out of your mind—I'm not going there. And I'm not eating those cookies," he said.

But the Bruderhof were persistent. They attended one of Sergio's presentations and a talk he gave at Hofstra University. Eventually, Sergio gave in. He drove up to the conference. It was held in a rustic building in the rural oasis the Bruderhof had constructed on hundreds of acres of farmland upstate. Sergio was impressed that they would want to invite in the troubles of the outside world to disturb their tranquility. After the trip to pick up Jessica in Albany, he picked up the phone. If the Bruderhof really wanted to help his cause, they could take her in.

The Bruderhof agreed, and, to Sergio's amazement, so did the judge when he made the proposal in court. But this was her second last chance; there wouldn't be a third. Sergio explained the conditions to Jessica: no television, no music, no going out, no drinking, and no smoking. She would be living with a new family, and the rules would be strict. She would have a job and go to school. She could only make phone calls to a short list of approved people. And she would have to stay for a year.

To Jessica, the alternatives seemed worse. She agreed. Sergio packed her bags back into his minivan, and they headed north.

The commune was near the Catskills, in the middle of the woods. The Bruderhof put Jessica to work doing laundry, canning vegetables, and learning to read as soon as she arrived. For a while, she was subdued as she absorbed the vastly different new world. They assigned her two tutors, and she spent hours studying. She also went to classes in the community high school, although she sat in the back of the room and rarely raised her hand. Gradually, she caught up.

She spent most of her time with the women on the farm, but for the first time, she lived in a family with a father. He was strict, and she sometimes bristled at the rules. But for the most part she followed them. Still, she was ambivalent about her new home. The woods were beautiful, and the women were nice to her, but the culture was alien, and she often felt uncomfortable. She felt like even more of an outsider than she had in Long Island. After six months, she decided she wanted to go home. She called Sergio and told him she was ready. He was astonished. She had lasted five and half months longer than he predicted she would.

She couldn't bear the thought of going back to her mother's house. She got a job at a Friendly's diner to pay for her own apartment. She didn't go out much, fearful that TOP might find her. SWP was also angry at her sudden disappearance. They had made threats to her mother and brother while she was gone. When they realized she was back, they began threatening her, too. She told Sergio she was too scared to stay in Hempstead. Sergio put her up in a room in his mother's house in Uniondale and enrolled her in the newly open STRONG University. She gave presentations in schools, where she told other kids her story: the cold nights in the park when her mother kicked her out, the time she held a friend in her arms after he was shot, desperately trying to staunch the blood with her hands. She also told them about the times she considered suicide. She explained how helpless and out of control she had felt. Girls sometimes came up to her after her speeches to tell her their own stories. The helplessness transformed into purpose. She studied for her GED and was hired as a counselor at a summer camp. She was a natural with small children. The camp hired her to work throughout the year in an after-school program. By the time she turned eighteen, her life had been transformed.

The thought of prison hadn't scared her straight before, but it did now. Jessica was slowly picking up the pieces of her life. She was able to tamp down her anger when it welled up. She met new friends in STRONG with pasts as brittle and bruised as her own and began to feel less lonely. She formed a fragile but workable truce with her mother. She was no longer a child. She had grown up.

After graduating from the STRONG program, she moved back in with her mother, who had broken her ties with her brothers and MS-13 with the help of a charismatic evangelical church. Ana now lived in North Amityville, a black suburb a few exits down the highway from Hempstead. Ana hoped the move would keep her twin boys from joining Hempstead's gangs, although North Amityville was also becoming known for its crime.[1] Jessica didn't want to stay long. She was thinking about her future and saving money. Her dream was to get out of Long Island, and the suburbs, as soon as possible.

CHAPTER 22

The Gathering Storm

●　　●　　●

In 2005, a New York State government commission held a series of hearings on the status of the state's gang problem. Sergio told officials how young gang members sought respect and discipline that was missing elsewhere in their lives. They heard the testimony of Pamela Corrente, who had joined forces with Sergio and transformed from an anti-immigrant activist to an immigrant advocate in the years since her son Damian's murder. Just as she had flipped her frustration at the police into a partnership with Chief Woodward, her natural optimism—the same optimism that had led her to write a letter to the editor defending her town from allegations that it was plagued with crime—eventually transformed her grief into sympathy. She was still passionate about solving the gang problem, but she now saw the problem similarly to Sergio. "Youth gang members are made, not born," she was quoted as saying in one *Daily News* article at the time. "It's just common sense to invest in them now."[1]

The following year, the commission published its findings, which suggested the reports that the gangs were organized on a national scale were exaggerated: "The adoption of a well-known gang name does not necessarily connote ties to a nationwide hierarchy."[2] In particular, they wrote, Mara Salvatrucha's reputation for being highly organized and especially brutal was overblown.[3] The gang did not "appear to be as organized as, for example, traditional Italian organized crime."[4]

The report also criticized the state's prisons, the majority of which lacked "adequate substance abuse treatment, mental health services, educational opportunities, and job training."[5] It noted that gangs ran rampant in the state's juvenile detention facilities, which had implemented gang intervention and prevention programs only the year before.[6] Alternatives like group homes were often counterproductive, the commission wrote, because they exposed children to their more violent and deviant peers.[7] Even the No Child Left Behind Act was problematic because it made it easier to isolate problem students.[8] The more isolated children were from their well-behaved, better-performing peers, the more likely they were to get worse, they concluded.

Despite its skepticism of prisons and punishment, seven of the eight recommendations by the commission involved strengthening laws against gangs and increasing punishments. The report proposed enhancing penalties for gang crimes, criminalizing gang recruitment, authorizing roving wiretaps against gang members, and removing legal obstacles for prosecuting gang members. The report also revived calls for the formation of a statewide gang database.

Sergio was disappointed. In his testimony, he had tried to convince them that the focus on incarceration was the problem, not the solution. But the chairman of the Commission of Investigation, Alfred D. Lerner, a Pataki appointee and former Queens assemblyman, defended the report. "Before you can really get into the enhancement of the social programs, you have to first restore a civil society," he said.[9] Sergio's hopes for an official mechanism to help teenagers like Jessica were dashed.

In October that year, a group of police chiefs from across the country published another report that predicted that the years of declining crime rates were over. A 2 percent increase in crime nationwide foretold "a gathering storm," the report said.[10] Although crime decreased in the Mara Salvatrucha stronghold of Prince George County, the report blamed the spread of MS-13 in particular, "with its vicious reputation," as a major reason for crime increases.[11] The country was at "the front end of a tipping point of violent crime," poised to fall into the chaos of the late 1980s and early 1990s if something wasn't done.[12] *The Miami Herald*, *New York Sun*, and *Minneapolis Star Tribune* ran stories warning of a coming crime wave among youth.[13]

The police chiefs' recommendations departed from the crackdown measures suggested in the New York State report, however, instead echoing those of the Long Island police chiefs published two years earlier. They warned that the increases in incarceration rates in the nineties were coming back to haunt them as convicts were released after decade-long sentences in prisons with few rehabilitation programs.[14] The report called for more community policing—a "holistic" approach that had been experimented with in some jurisdictions like Boston in the 1990s. One of the police chiefs pointed out that the rate of high school dropouts and the rate of homicide in a jurisdiction were closely linked. The police report suggested that schools should become a focus to stem youth crime and that social services should be beefed up instead of cut back. Early intervention and education was the answer, the police chiefs said, not prison.

The next year, national lawmakers listened. Congress passed the Second Chance Act in 2007 to replace resources for prevention and prisoner reentry programs that had been siphoned away during the 1990s. The law—signed by President Bush and praised by lawmakers from both parties—authorized annual spending of up to $360 million on prevention and rehab programs.[15] It wasn't much, proponents admitted, but it was something. That year, several states also revisited laws requiring juveniles to be tried as adults. Connecticut reversed its law that automatically sent sixteen- and seventeen-year-olds to criminal court.[16] New York was among a handful of other states that considered doing the same.[17]

Later that year, Congress whittled the appropriation for the Second Chance Act down to $45 million in the House. In the Senate, it was cut down to $20 million.[18] New York decided to keep its requirements that sixteen-year-olds be tried as adults. Education and prevention would have to wait for another year.

Daniel, 2004–2008

CHAPTER 23

Adam

* * *

The scorching August day warmed the liter of Grey Goose vodka that sloshed inside Daniel's backpack. He wiped sweat from his forehead and walked up to the edge of the foamy gray water. He let it touch his toes before he retreated toward the drier edge of the beach in search of a place to nestle the bottle in the sand. The others—his girlfriend, her friend, and Adam—laid out blankets nearby. Daniel poured cups of the vodka surreptitiously and passed them around. The girls giggled as they took nervous sips. Older girls strutted past in bikinis, and white families spread out in the shade of umbrellas. Daniel eyed the crowds, but he didn't see anyone he recognized—no MS-13 members. His gun was tucked under the extra clothes in his backpack just in case.

He had called in sick to his job bussing tables at a catering hall in Queens to join Lara, his girlfriend, on the outing to Long Beach. He liked her friends, and it was one of his first days off all summer. It felt good to dig his toes in the sand and forget the worries at home. Adam kept them entertained. He was a class clown whose antics often made teachers chuckle even as they shushed him in class. He was Hispanic, but he wasn't in SWP or MS-13, and the two gangs mostly left him alone. Adam wasn't interested, and his jokes acted as a shield. Daniel liked spending time with him, away from the seriousness of the gang.

It was 2007, and Daniel was due to begin twelfth grade in the fall. He had failed eleventh grade once, but he was on track to graduate—if he decided to go. His mother had recently moved from Hempstead into a new house in Uniondale. She didn't realize that the new neighborhood was MS territory. Daniel wasn't going to tell her. After years of scraping pennies, the family had finally saved enough to bring all of their children from El Salvador and to buy their own house. During his free hours that summer, Daniel helped his uncle, a manager at a construction company, renovate the little Cape Cod on a tree-lined street. They added new siding and a new roof and planted colorful cabbages in the front garden. A chandelier twinkled from inside, framed by a bay window hung with lace curtains. Nearby was a soccer field where Daniel's younger siblings could play. It was a vast improvement over their cramped apartment building in the Home Depot parking lot. Daniel didn't want to ruin it for them.

Daniel's baby cheeks, once smooth and plump, were now flecked with scars from the fights that had won him a respected position in Salvadorans With Pride. He now knew better than to think Uniondale was really an escape from Hempstead. The only difference was that Uniondale High School was ruled by MS-13. There was no way he would survive there.

After a few hours of splashing in the waves, the group, tanned, damp, and tipsy, climbed back on the bus to head home. On the way, Lara complained that she was hungry. They headed to one of their favorite haunts, Taco Bell. The fast food restaurant sat along a dilapidated strip a block from Hempstead High School. It was in SWP territory, although Mara Salvatrucha often lurked around the auto body shops across the street. They lingered over the tacos and talked loudly, trying to hold onto the day as the sun slipped from the sky. But soon it was time to go home. They trailed slowly out of the restaurant and beyond the safe neon glow of the purple-and-red sign. Daniel walked ahead with his arm draped across Lara's shoulders. Adam lingered behind and chatted up Lara's friend.

A movement across the street caught Daniel's eye. He looked back to see a mass of people crossing toward them. He squinted as the low hanging sun stung his eyes and tried to make out their faces. It was Mara Salvatrucha. It looked as if there were at least a dozen of them.

He yelled at Adam to run and took off, dragging Lara beside him and trying to urge her ahead. He scrambled to pull the zipper of his backpack as he ran and tried not to stumble as he sprinted across the parking lots of the auto-body shops. He wrenched open the bag and reached in. The sand stuck to his hand as he felt under his towel and soggy bathing suit for the gun. Finally he felt the cold metal in his hand and pulled it out. He turned around.

He saw the bottle sailing through the air before it hit Adam, who had only just turned to see the men hurtling toward him. It was a Snapple juice bottle, and it nailed Adam in the eye. Seconds later he crumpled to the ground as the men swarmed over him.

Daniel turned and sprinted in the opposite direction, toward Adam. He was shouting, still yelling at Adam, even though it was too late. The vodka and tacos sloshed in his stomach and brought on a wave of nausea. The men peeled away from Adam's body and left him slumped on the ground. They were gone by the time Daniel reached him. The gun hung lamely in his hand. Blood pumped out of a puncture wound in Adam's neck and seeped into the cracks in the sidewalk from another wound in his back. Adam's eye was mashed into pulp.

This is what Jaime must have looked like in the seconds before he died. For a second, Daniel felt paralyzed. He had never lost the sense of guilt that he felt about Jaime's death. If Adam died, he would be at fault again. The Mara Salvatrucha members weren't after Adam—they didn't even know him. They were chasing Daniel. He ran out into the street, looking for help. He was determined not to let another friend die.

● ● ●

After Jaime's death, the fear that had gripped Daniel during his first months navigating Hempstead transformed into something else. He was called into the principal's office for questioning on his first day back at school after the murder. Before he went in, he hid his gang belt in a friend's locker. The detectives made him take off his shirt in search of any revealing tattoos and peppered him with questions about the murder. He told them he had no idea who killed his friend. Still eyeing him suspiciously, they let him go. He couldn't believe his teachers and the police regarded him as a possible suspect. He would never tell them anything about the gang or his grief.

He was reluctant to reveal too much about his feelings to his gang. Jaime and Daniel weren't supposed to be friends in the first place. As the year went on, he embraced the gang life that before he only dabbled in with lunchroom fights and locker room brawls. He spent more time on the handball court, smoking pot and skipping class. When he felt sad, he lashed out. By the end of eighth grade, he had become one of the bullies he once feared.

When he started ninth grade at Hempstead High School the following fall, he felt invincible. The onset of puberty granted him a low tenor and helped to banish the scared, skinny boy who had once been afraid to step outside of his mother's apartment into Hempstead's foreign streets. On his first day of school, he masked the nervousness with a slow swagger. His low-hanging jeans swished as he walked, and his gang belt slapped against his leg. A white SWP bandana wrapped around his forehead felt like protective armor against the chaos ahead. As he approached the school's blue doors, he searched for his friends among the hundreds of students swarming through the metal detectors and past the bored stares of the security guards. They were unmistakable in their black and white. The school didn't have uniforms, so it was difficult to control the myriad of clothing colors—blue, black, white, gold, and red—that the gang members used to identify themselves, while gang belts and bandanas were often strapped on once the kids entered the building.

He followed behind them as they were swept along through the crowd of sticky, hot teenagers churning through the halls. They emerged into a large, open central hall. Students slammed metal doors in a maze of lockers in the center. Three stories of classrooms circled the space and opened onto walkways suspended above, in an arrangement reminiscent of a prison cell block. Most classroom windows were shaded in weak attempts to keep the outside turmoil at bay. The architecture of the cavernous room magnified the shouting, as girls hugged each other in delight and boys wrestled in mock fights on the main floor and along the walkways. A few administrators marched through the crowds. They yelled in vain over the roar for everyone to get to class. Some kids hurried along, but most looked impassively at the strained faces of the assistant principals and continued their raucous reunion. Daniel was thankful for the protection of his friends. Otherwise he would have felt lost.

The frenzied energy on the first day was joyful, but the school had one of the worst reputations on Long Island. Teachers and administrators met the first day of the school with hope that this year would be better, but held their breath for the inevitable moment when the chaos would erupt into violence.

CHAPTER 24

Golden Years

● ● ●

Hempstead High School had once been the pride of Long Island. It was the oldest school in Nassau County, and its original incarnation was a two-story, wood-frame building built in the mid-1800s on an acre of ground downtown. On April 5, 1919, the building burned to the ground.[1] The town built a new, sturdier brick building at the same location.[2] It was three stories high and soon bursting with offspring of the new suburbanites. The school thrived along with the town in the postwar boom. In 1958, Hempstead High was the subject of a cover story in *Life* magazine. Half a dozen seniors from the school posed on the front cover, their white faces captured in the middle of a hearty laugh for an article headlined "Golden Years at Hempstead High."[3]

A decade later, the golden years were over. Hempstead was fading as its white middle-class residents moved on and black newcomers from the city took their place. By the time the school integration fights of the 1970s were in full swing across the country, Hempstead High School was 70 percent black.[4] The drastic shift did not sit well with the whites who were still hanging on, and racial tensions in Hempstead switched to full-blown confrontation in March 1970.

The first incident broke out in a downtown pizzeria. The owner called police to help him eject six black Hempstead High School students who were eating lunch.[5] The owner said the girls were being disruptive and rude. The girls told police they had just been laughing loudly. After that, the tension that had been building in the town for years exploded. The conflict was focused in the school. White students from Hempstead beat up a black girl downtown. Back at the school, the sophomore class government became split along racial lines when black students suggested donating class funds to the Black Panthers. In the Hempstead High School cafeteria, a fight between a white girl and a black girl ended with the black girl attacking the teacher who tried to break up the fight. In the final incident, someone set fire to the curtains in the school's auditorium as a group of black students held a meeting. The fire was put out, but school was cancelled for two days while the school administration tried to figure out how to quash the unrest.[6] Nine students—eight black, one white—were suspended, and parents were brought in to monitor safety in the halls.[7]

The uneasy peace didn't last long. That summer, someone lit the school on fire again, minutes after summer school students were dismissed from the building.[8] The fire raged through the building, collapsing the roof and reducing classrooms to rubble. The school was destroyed again, nearly fifty years after the first building burned down. That fall, students were scattered among schools in neighboring districts until a new building could be built.[9]

The school reopened a year later in the center of a grassy valley near the highway and the hospital. The grounds, on the border of Garden City, were rimmed with woods. It could have been the campus of a private school. No doubt the school district hoped the peaceful surroundings would help the school mimic a private school's performance and tame the conflict raging inside.

But by the eighties, downtown Hempstead had deteriorated, and most of the white residents were gone. Hempstead's black residents were left behind to make do in isolation. As the income gap widened between Hempstead and its neighbors, the village saw the tax base it needed to fund its schools shrink. Throughout the decade, village voters routinely rejected the school budget as too expensive.[10] Library books and extracurricular activities were the first things to be cut.

In 1989, the town's black population was being supplemented by the new wave of Hispanics, who sparked more racial tension. As in the previous conflicts between whites and blacks, the troubles centered on the school. Fights broke out regularly. That year, the state issued a report on the strain between the blacks and Hispanics inside Hempstead High School. The report highlighted the school's other difficulties, too.[11] A quarter of Hempstead's students lived in poverty.[12] Almost all were now either black or Hispanic.[13] The school buildings around the village, including elementary schools and the high school, were contaminated with asbestos and falling apart.[14] The state forced the school district to submit to "austerity" measures because it hadn't been able to pass a budget for two years, meaning programs like arts, sports, after-school activities, and other "extras" were now cut by state mandate.[15] The same year, the school's principal for the past three decades, Charles Mills, who was also its first black principal, resigned.[16]

In 1991, Hempstead took last place on Long Island in student achievement in almost all subjects, leading *Newsday* to publish a damning, magazine-length article detailing daily life at the high school.[17] Students interviewed for the article called the school "a waste of time." Many veteran teachers said they felt the same way. More than a third of students were absent or late to school every day. Teachers often didn't bother to come, either. Three different principals and four different district superintendents cycled through in a single year.[18] For several months, high school students were moved into the middle school as asbestos was removed from their building. Drugs were reportedly sold in the hallways, and fights among students were routine occurrences throughout the school day. Students who had graduated, or dropped out, gathered in the parking lot with the dozens of students who skipped class each period. Students in one Advanced Placement class were barred from taking the test because school administrators assumed they would fail anyway. The year before, administrators were accused of telling poorly performing students to stay home on testing day so they wouldn't bring down the school's scores.[19]

The state education department put the school on a list of the state's worst schools and demanded that it turn its performance around fast, or else. Hope came in 1994, when a new principal, Ronald Ross, was installed.[20] For a while, it appeared Ross had whipped the school into shape. He pushed down the dropout rate, from a staggering 12 percent in 1994 compared to 4.1 percent statewide, to 1.1 percent in two years. Ross left, and other principals came and went. The progress didn't last.

By the time Daniel started there in 2003, the school had cycled back to the Wild West days of the previous decade. But a new principal took over that year: Reginald Stroughn. It was his first principal job, but he was tough and determined. He knew many of the students from his years as an assistant principal at Alverta B. Gray Schultz Middle School. The odds were against him. There were thirteen white students in the entire school, and the percentage of students signed up for free lunch had soared to 74 percent of the student population, compared to 26 percent in 1999.[21] His experience with the Hispanic students, who made up a third of the student population, was limited. He didn't speak Spanish, and neither did most of his staff.

In contrast, next door in Garden City that year, there were only 2 students who were poor. A total of 20 black and Hispanic students was enrolled, out of a student population of more than 1,000. There, the four-year graduation rate was more than 95 percent in 2003. In Hempstead, the dropout rate was about to reach 18 percent—transforming the embarrassing 12 percent dropout rate from the early 1990s into a worthwhile goal.[22]

To add to the chaos, the four gangs that divided up the school hallways, the Bloods, the Crips, SWP, and MS-13, were in a struggle to assert their dominance over the campus. Around town, Mara Salvatrucha was more feared and involved in more serious crimes. But at the high school, SWP had the upper hand, since most of its members were younger. The two black gangs, the Crips and the Bloods, concentrated mostly on each other, so the two gang wars occurred side-by-side. The result was mayhem.

● ● ●

Daniel enrolled in a mix of regular and ESL classes, since his English was still halting after three years in Long Island. He liked most of his classes and passed his assignments with ease. Several of his teachers were friendly and enthusiastic, although others shared the same bored expressions of many of their students. It was the minutes between each class when he got into trouble. The tone sounded, and students erupted into the hall. Immediately, the gangs began shouting and signaling to each other across the high school's large central chamber. They fought in the bathrooms and other nooks that went unpatrolled by administrators and security guards. The fights broke out every other day, and often Daniel was involved. Soon, he was spending as much time in the suspension hall as in class. The school's assistant principal, Henry Williams, quickly learned Daniel's name, and his mother received regular calls about his problems at school.

Each call left his mother devastated. She screamed and cried for Daniel to leave the gangs behind and focus on his schoolwork. Daniel would yell back that he did all his homework and was even passing his classes. She threatened to send him to boot camp or back to El Salvador, which made Daniel even angrier. He didn't want to go back there anymore. Hempstead was his home now. Usually, the arguments ended the same way. Daniel's mother had known Jaime from the afternoons he came home after soccer games in middle school and had watched the news when he was found dead outside of the train station. When the arguments reached their climax, she screamed that Daniel was going to end up dead like Jaime. At that, Daniel stormed out of the room.

During one fight that erupted outside of school grounds, Daniel was arrested. He went for only a short stint to the Nassau County juvenile jail, but the experience was scary. This was nothing like the detention room at school where he spent many of his days. He wanted to go home. But as soon as he was released, he found it was worth it. His friends greeted him like a hero.

"You're almost an OG," they told him: an original gangster. He only had to do one more thing to secure his place in the upper rungs of the gang: shoot someone.

The night after his release, one of the SWP members gave him a .22-caliber pistol, and they piled in a car. They circled slowly through the town and looked for a target. The boys around him laughed and heckled him. He was the center of attention, and if he did this, he would secure their permanent respect. Not long ago, he had been the one cowering as he walked along these streets. Now he was the one to be feared. They passed a group of shadowy figures on Franklin Street, Mara Salvatrucha territory. He held up the gun, steadied it, and fired.

The car screeched away. He turned quickly to try and catch a glimpse of his victim. He thought he saw him: a man holding his shoulder as the rest scattered. He only nicked his target, but it didn't matter. He was in now. He had respect. No one could dispute his love of the gang or his loyalty.

As the year went on, the fighting between the two Central American gangs in Hempstead kept up its fierce pace, but inside the school, SWP was winning. The handful of Mara Salvatrucha kids at the high school might be able to call on older, tougher guys to defend them outside of the school walls, but during the day they were on their own. SWP ruled the central hall and dominated the handball court down the hill from the school. When his first year in high school ended, Daniel and his friends declared the high school their territory.

The summer was a blur of days filled with handball, fast food, and occasional fights along the borders of the gangs' territories. The gang now let Daniel sit in on meetings, and he watched the older kids—among them Jessica, who had taken over leadership of the girls—with awe. The following September, they filed into the school cocky and determined to protect their claim. Daniel was excited to be back.

The fighting continued, although the number of students affiliated with Mara Salvatrucha had dwindled further. Among those who remained was one of Daniel's old soccer buddies from seventh grade, Olman Herrera. Olman had arrived from El Salvador a couple of years earlier than Daniel, but he had trouble picking up English and didn't mind hanging out with the newcomers.[23] Skinny and fast, he played striker on the middle-school soccer team with Daniel and Jaime during their first year in Long Island.[24] He was mild-mannered and affable back then, but by tenth grade, Olman, linked to Mara Salvatrucha, and Daniel, a member of SWP, regarded each other as bitter enemies.

For Daniel, it wasn't hard to turn against his old friend. Olman joined JROTC and bragged often about his membership in the military prep organization.[25] More annoying was Olman's flaunting of his affiliation with MS-13. He wore his light blue bandana hanging out of his pocket and starting shoving matches in the bathrooms. Daniel questioned whether his boasting was a sign that he was really just a wannabe.

Daniel heard rumors that Olman was having trouble at home and that he slept on the streets some nights or stayed at friends' houses.[26] Some days, he came in reeking of alcohol and sipped cheap vodka out of soda bottles in the bathroom. On these occasions, Daniel felt sorry for him, but if he didn't calm down, SWP would have to take action.

On November 16, 2004, Olman came to school wearing a light blue sweater.[27] He didn't go to classes that day but just hung around in the school hallways.[28] It was too much for his rivals to bear. As classes changed for sixth period, Daniel and his friends confronted Olman and a few of his fellow MS wannabes in the central hall. They didn't wait to take the fight into a bathroom. In seconds, the two groups were mashed together in a jumble of fists. The Mara Salvatrucha members were outnumbered, but soon security guards were dismantling the scrum of bodies. Mr. Williams was running toward them, too. They were in big trouble. The adults herded the grumbling, sweaty boys into the in-school suspension hall. But not Olman. He knew he was faster than any of the lumbering guards, so he took off running. They didn't bother to follow. Neither did his friends. Moments later, he was past the parking lot and home free.

But he was also alone. He didn't see the red car cruising up behind him until it was too late. A group of boys jumped out of the car and surrounded him. One pulled out a knife and stabbed him twice in the chest. Olman stumbled out of their grasp and tried to get away. The boys climbed back in the car and drove off. Olman fell a few feet from where they attacked him, steps from the school grounds.

Inside the in-school suspension room, the boys were winding down from the fight. They laughed with the guards, who chastened them for picking a fight with Olman and his friends when they were so badly outnumbered. They should know better, the guards ribbed them. Take it outside next time. Then, one of the guards' walky-talkies squawked. He walked out of the room. When he returned, the good-natured expression on his face from moments earlier was wiped away.

"Who knows Olman Herrera?" the guard asked. The room was silent.

"He just got killed."

As the news spread, the silence in the suspension room soon fell across the school.[29] Teachers couldn't understand it. Olman was always so polite. He skipped classes, but when he came, he was well behaved, even sweet. He had brought one of his teachers flowers once.[30] Earlier in the month, his parents called police when Olman drove away in their Chevrolet Suburban after a family fight.[31] Mr. Stroughn had met with his father to discuss his behavior problems and the stolen car. But no one had suspected he was a gang member. They believed Olman was attacked because he refused to join one of the gangs.[32] Olman's flaunting of his real or imagined affiliation with MS that so irritated Daniel was invisible to adults. His disciplinary problems had not raised a red flag, partly because the school administrators had little information about how the gangs operated. The police had long been frustrated with the school for denying the problem instead of dealing with it, and when Olman died, they were mystified.

Only two months earlier, the bodies of the Mara Salvatrucha victims, sixteen-year-old Olivia Mendoza and a man, both whom the gang believed to be police informants, had been discovered in the wealthy, white enclaves of Bethpage and Old Westbury. Their deaths, along with that of seventeen-year-old Brenda Paz in Fairfax County in 2003, had fueled fear that the gang violence was reaching beyond the borders of suburban slums such as Hempstead. Chief Russo wrote a letter to the *New York Times* calling for a new way of thinking in the wake of the murders.[33] "My police department is working vigorously to arrest Olman Herrera's assailant. But the police cannot solve the gang problem alone," he wrote. Rather than more police, he reiterated the recommendations of the Fight Crime: Invest In Kids report released that October, including intensive family therapy programs for troubled kids.

"Long Island gang violence is increasing. Before we panic, let's prevent kids from joining gangs in the first place," he concluded in his letter.

In response to the murders, the county executive, Thomas Suozzi, created a new post: a gang czar.[34] A Nassau County deputy police inspector, Robert Turk, whose experience included commanding the mounted police unit that provided crowd control at rock concerts, would get the job.[35] It had been two years since the county gang task force known as TAG was created and began holding monthly meetings to discuss the gang problem. A press release described the czar's duties as reaching out to community groups like the Nassau County Youth Board and HEVN, a gang prevention group run by a local Baptist minister, which were already involved in TAG. Turk would coordinate the group's coordinating activities.[36] Turk would also administer the funds already budgeted for the police department's prevention efforts and act as a point person for the law enforcement efforts to fight the gangs.[37]

"We must use every resource at our disposal to deter and prevent kids from joining gangs while keeping parents and teachers informed about signs of gang activity in our neighborhoods," Suozzi said.[38]

In a scathing editorial a few days later, the *New York Times* labeled the appointment as empty spin. "In the case of Inspector Turk, the word 'czar' vastly overstates his power. The 50 or so officers who deal with gangs in the Nassau Police Department do so only part time, and the inspector's role is to put a public face on an effort that has been disjointed, underfinanced and little-coordinated," the editorial said.[39] The paper praised the $500,000 in antigang funding the county had announced it was allocating earlier that year, but suggested that a better solution than a new bureaucratic position would be more money for social services.

A year later, the police union also mocked the gang czar, saying the lack of any police officers working under him full-time on gang issues made the position pointless.[40] The police commissioner, James Lawrence, defended Turk's efforts, even though the number of gang-related homicides, and homicides in general, had ticked upward in the tenth months of his tenure as czar. Turk responded that the police department was working on deploying more officers, including three supervisors and twelve detectives who would be investigating gang activity as a part of a special unit. Later, however, the gang czar position was quietly dissolved.

As the county scrambled to respond to Olman's death, Hempstead High School was dealing with its own problems. The school administrators scurried to bring in counselors and borrow security guards from other schools. The murder was off campus, but Hempstead was in the cross hairs of the state education department anyway. The department was getting ready for a visit in December.[41]

Five months later, in April 2005, the state issued another report that detailed a long list of problems at the school.[42] Less than half of the kids at Hempstead graduated on time. Of those who did graduate, only a handful earned the Regents diplomas viewed as adequate by most colleges. The school was not providing basic instruction. ESL teachers were isolated from the rest of the school and planned their classes without regard to the rest of the curriculum. The school's open campus policy meant students came and went as they pleased. Showing up late wasn't punished. The state officials said they found evidence of gangs. More asbestos, left over from the shoddy cleanup a decade earlier, was discovered.[43] The school was placed back on austerity, ordered to buy more textbooks, and told to reorganize its staff.[44]

A few months later, in the fall of 2005, a state audit by the comptroller's office found even more problems.[45] The school board was in shambles as members wrestled for power. One meeting had erupted into violence.[46] The audit found that the district made $5.1 million worth of questionable purchases with school money, among them $2.3 million paid to house students in portable trailers after the board neglected to repair buildings.[47] More than a million was spent in noncompetitively bid contracts. The district also spent hundreds of thousands on employee benefits for workers who quit or were fired and on undocumented meals for administrators. New computers were bought for $27,000 but then went missing. The audit also noted that the superintendent, Nathaniel Clay, who was suspended the year before and then reinstated, earned more than $74,000 during his suspension.

The Hempstead school district was named in another comptroller audit published the following May. The audit investigated schools suspected of covering up their violent incident records.[48] In the audit, Hempstead—where a student had been killed across the street—was not cited for lying about the amount of violence inside its walls, as other schools had been, but only for its bad records. Administrators at the high school did not record as many as 250 violent incidents—among them criminal harassment, thefts, and bomb threats—that occurred in 2005.

On top of everything, the school was labeled as failing under the Bush administration's No Child Left Behind law.[49]

CHAPTER 25

No Child Left Behind

No Child Left Behind was an ambitious expansion of the federal government's involvement in the states' administration of public education four decades after it had stepped in to overturn legal segregation in the South. The law was based on the conviction that the public education system could, and must, close the achievement gap between the races that persisted a half century after the *Brown v. Board of Education* Supreme Court decision. It was the fruit of George W. Bush's 2000 campaign for president, when he repeated his goal to end the achievement gap several times a day on the campaign trail. "This nation of ours must challenge what I like to call the soft bigotry of low expectations. Every child can learn," he said.[1] The law borrowed from the Texas school system's tough accountability requirements for schools that were based on standardized tests. It was premised on the belief that schools could help poor and minority children overcome the disadvantages they faced in relation to their white, wealthy peers by holding their feet to the fire.

After some haggling over how much money to add to the federal education budget, the law passed in Congress in 2001 with broad bipartisan support and set a deadline of 2014 for the nation's racial achievement gap to be erased. The line about ending the "soft bigotry of low expectations" became a favorite mantra among a new set of reformist city school superintendents trying to meet the new standards, among them the commissioner of schools in New York City, Joel Klein.

A year earlier than required by the new law, New York reported its test scores by race for the first time in its history.[2] The statistics showed a gap of thirty-four points between Hispanic and white students on fourth grade tests across the state. Between blacks and whites, the gap was thirty-nine points. In affluent districts, the racial gaps were much smaller between the races, but in a few wealthy suburban towns the gaps were also stark.

Nationally, the gaps were also striking. In 2004, the difference in scores between black and white seventeen-year-olds was twenty-nine points on national reading tests, better than the fifty-point gap in 1980, but unchanged since 1990.[3] Between white and Hispanic high school students, the gap was widening. In 1984, there was a twenty-seven-point difference between white and Hispanic reading scores, a difference that had gradually narrowed during the eighties but then widened again in 2004 to twenty-nine.

Lifting minority, particularly Hispanic, student achievement was not only a moral imperative but an economic necessity. The percentage of limited English speakers, the majority of them Spanish-speaking, had doubled between 1979 and 2005. By 2050, Hispanic children would outnumber white children in the United States.[4] They were the fastest growing group of students nationwide. This was good news for a country in desperate need of a young workforce to provide for retiring baby boomers. The white population was aging, but Hispanics had provided a new generation to take on the burden of caring for them.

But many Hispanics were abandoning school. The number of Hispanic youth who didn't finish high school rose to more than half a million in

2000, from 347,000 a decade earlier.[5] About a third of those never attended or only briefly attended American schools. Hispanics who were born in the United States fared better. For them, the dropout rate decreased slightly during the nineties, but they still dropped out at nearly twice the rate of white students.[6]

The decline in the graduation rate and widening achievement gap occurred during a decade when Hispanic students were increasingly confined to segregated schools.[7] The number of schools with a minority student population of more than 90 percent doubled in the nineties, and these schools educated 29 percent of Hispanic students in 2005, up from 25 percent in 1993.[8] A third of all Hispanic students were immigrants, a group that was even more severely segregated. By the time No Child Left Behind was passed, 90 percent of the new immigrants in New York were clustered in segregated schools where less than 5 percent of the student body was white.

At the same time, research showed that English language learners did significantly better when they were placed in integrated schools alongside white middle- and upper-class students.[9] Educating the white, wealthier students and English language learners together wiped out eight percentage points from the gap that usually existed when the two groups were educated separately. The researchers theorized that the schools and teachers in mostly white schools were simply better.

But the findings were supported by three decades of research showing that integrated schools also led to better academic performance for blacks and other minorities.[10] A 1966 study commissioned by the federal government known as the Coleman report found that the racial and socioeconomic backgrounds of classmates had more bearing on the academic performance of a student than teacher quality, school spending, and curriculum.[11] Specifically, the report showed that poor black and Hispanic students who were exposed to wealthier students did much better in school than when they were isolated with poor, minority peers. The argument was supported by subsequent research showing that especially if black students were placed in integrated schools with good facilities, teachers, curriculum, and extensive teacher training, the improvement in achievement was very significant.[12] Taking into account the long-term outcomes for black students who attended desegregated schools—better jobs, higher incomes—especially reinforced arguments in favor of integration.[13]

Mixed results from other research, however, left the nation unconvinced that integration could affect the achievement gap between whites and minorities.[14] Part of the problem, some pro-integration researchers argued, was the methods of the other studies: studies that found limited effects of integration were either limited in scope or focused only on short-term outcomes.[15] The other problem was that many desegregation efforts were often ineffective in bringing about meaningful change because of resistance inside the school districts and academic tracks that separated the races within schools. The pattern was similar to the prison rehabilitation efforts that barely got off the ground in the 1970s before they were abandoned: It wasn't that integration failed, but that it was barely tried, as the black historian John Hope Franklin put it.[16] No studies found that white students were ever adversely affected, but since the effects on minority students in integrated schools hadn't been proved uniformly positive—and white parents, along with some black parents, often protested busing, the main strategy for implementing desegregation programs—the goal of integrating the nation's public schools was gradually swept under the rug.[17]

No Child Left Behind injected the federal government back into the fray over racial inequality in the schools. Under the law, schools and districts would be held accountable for the difference in achievement between races and ethnic groups, and even the test scores of special education students and immigrant children still learning English. Schools who couldn't continue to elevate the test scores of all of their students would be labeled "failing" and then closely monitored. If they didn't improve, they would eventually be closed down. Besides threatening closure of schools that didn't measure up, the law also hoped to spur improvements using school choice, a concept backed by a powerful education movement sweeping the country. Its proponents, who cheered the spread of charter schools and private school vouchers, argued that competition between schools would prompt struggling institutions to work harder and improve. Flexibility would allow them to hire and fire teachers more readily and experiment with different education models. Accordingly, under the law, students in schools listed as failing had the option of leaving and going to other schools in their districts. It was a market-based concept that assumed the combined threat of closure and hemorrhaging of students would push bad schools to perform better.

The news that Hempstead made the No Child Left Behind failing list—a relative rarity in the suburbs—was no surprise to the residents of Hempstead or its neighbors. But it was unclear how the new light shining on Hempstead's failures and the set of federally mandated consequences would make a difference. Beyond the threats, the law provided schools with few tools to help them accomplish the mission of erasing the achievement gap. Federal funding was increased for poor schools under NCLB, but education experts argued it was not enough to bring most struggling schools up to par with their wealthy, suburban counterparts.[18] And for Hempstead students, the school choice provision of the law was meaningless: There were no other high schools in Hempstead for the students to go to.

The solution seemed within arm's reach. Hempstead was surrounded by white districts with high incomes and high test scores, many, like Garden City, which were less than a five-minute drive away. The law included a provision allowing for other, better-performing districts to accept students, but the administration and Congress did not make it mandatory that successful districts accept children from struggling ones.[19] No transportation was provided, and it was unlikely most students and parents knew about the obscure provision in the federal law, which had received little publicity—even within larger districts, only a tiny fraction of students eligible to transfer out of their schools ever did so.

Without a federal mandate or a set of incentives, school choice across district lines was a remote option. In Long Island, the public schools were largely untouched by national efforts to integrate the education system following the *Brown v. Board of Education* decision. The fledgling suburban schools had been brand new back then, but fifty years later, minority students in places like Hempstead faced disadvantages more severe than soft bigotry—the Long Island schools were among the most segregated and unequal in the nation.

Local government in Long Island developed in the independent and exclusive spirit of the suburban creed, with each locality striving to have as little to do with their neighbors as possible. It was a pattern repeated around the country. In places like Minneapolis, St. Louis, and Washington, DC, suburban and urban schools had become starkly segregated, and when the older suburbs became racially isolated and fell into disrepair, their fate followed that of the inner city. The trend was facilitated by a 1974 Supreme Court decision that struck down efforts to desegregate the Detroit schools by combining the largely minority city district with several largely white suburban districts. In the *Milliken v. Bradley* decision, the majority of the justices argued that the separation of the races between the city and suburbs in the Northeast wasn't de jure segregation like in the South. The suburban school district lines had not been drawn to create racial segregation, at least overtly, and therefore the districts shouldn't have to accept the black students from the city that the white suburban residents had left behind.

The outcome on students was predictable. In Long Island, despite their proximity and the sharing of some countywide services like the police department, the suburban villages and townships managed to keep their distance in most other matters, including schools. Rich districts—in Long Island almost exclusively white—lavished money on their students, who did well on tests, went to college, and generally excelled. Poor districts scrimped on resources like books, security, computers, and staff salaries and were continually roiled by corruption scandals. Their students did terribly on tests, and half as many went to college as in the rich areas across the district lines.

There were few attempts to disrupt this pattern until 2001, when the state education department tried to save the Roosevelt school district. When it came to poorly performing schools in Long Island, Roosevelt was at the bottom of the pile. The tiny unincorporated hamlet was one of the few places in Long Island where aspiring middle-class black suburbanites were able to obtain mortgages and join the suburban housing boom at the turn of the century. Soon after they moved in, their white neighbors departed. In 1960, the black population in Roosevelt was 20 percent, but by the 1980s white flight had transformed it into a nearly all-black community supplemented by a growing Hispanic population.[20]

In 2000, the school district was more than 99 percent students of color.[21] The district's students were half as wealthy as the state average compared to other nearby Long Island districts, where families earned twice and three times the incomes of the state average.[22] Fourteen percent of its students lived in poverty.[23] Home values were low, and there were few businesses to tax to pay for school expenses, so the school district had the smallest property tax base in the county.[24] As a result, for years the district spent thousands of dollars less per student than neighboring districts.[25] When Jonathan Kozol, the education writer, visited the district in 2002, he found an elementary school where students had been barred from half of the building after it was condemned and high school students taking mandatory sewing lessons.[26] An elementary school principal there told him his school was "the worst place you could ever put a child."

Roosevelt had been on and off the state's failing school for a decade.[27] While it was heavily in debt thanks to mismanagement by the school board and school administrators, voters regularly voted down the school budget—always a signal of major dysfunction. By 2001, the year before Kozol's visit, the situation in Roosevelt was so bad that the state education commissioner, Richard Mills, proposed dismantling the tiny district entirely and sending its 2,000 students elsewhere.[28] A pair of university education experts suggested merging Roosevelt with the nearby Bellmore-Merrick district.[29]

The surrounding districts didn't want Roosevelt's students.[30] Bellmore-Merrick's students were more than 160 percent wealthier than the state average, and the school district spent as much as $2,000 more a year on each of its students than Roosevelt.[31] It was also 93 percent white.[32]

In a letter to the editor published in *Newsday*, a resident of North Bellmore, Ron Geelan, called the proposal "an unfair burden."

"Asking the residents of only a few neighboring communities to provide a default solution is not equitable. The state needs to realize that you cannot address the problems facing one community by busing the children to another," he wrote.[33]

More angry letters poured in.

The superintendent of the Bellmore-Merrick school district, Thomas Caramore, wrote to *Newsday*. "Bellmore-Merrick had no part in the origination of Roosevelt's problems," he wrote, arguing that siblings would be split up and children would have to spend too much time on buses instead of participating in extracurricular activities—although Roosevelt's austerity budget over the past decade had ensured there were few such activities, anyway.[34]

Another North Bellmore resident wrote that the proposal's supporters "seem more interested in making a case for integration than they do helping the troubled Roosevelt."[35] The writer, Keith Grubman, wrote that "busing is inherently wrong because it's premised on the patronizing belief that blacks are inherently inferior."

A Bellmore woman wrote, "It seems they believe that integrating a failing school with a successful one will somehow be better for both—that racial desegregation is the solution to Roosevelt's woes. It seems to me that this would only add to the problems."[36]

A telephone campaign was organized among Bellmore-Merrick residents to dissuade state legislators from voting for the merger.[37] The idea died. The state education department apparently preferred to deal with the problem itself than mediate a heated busing conflict.

Instead, in an unprecedented move, the state took control of the district in 2002.[38] Following the takeover, some things improved, such as attendance.[39] But for the most part, the Roosevelt district continued to wallow in debt and pathetic student performance.[40]

No Child Left Behind offered little relief. In passing the law, Congress and the Bush administration weren't inclined to disrupt the rapid resegregation of the nation's schools. The schools could stay separate; the goal was to try to make them equal.[41] Across the country, only a fraction of the students eligible to transfer out of their failing schools under No Child Left Behind actually did so.[42] Many students in larger inner-city districts were left with a series of bad choices when their schools were labeled failing. Students in small suburban and rural towns were left with none.[43]

Although Roosevelt continued to struggle under the state's care, the state education department turned its gaze to Hempstead following Olman's murder.[44] Hempstead was also failing, and the federal government demanded improvement. But the state education department decided against taking over the district. Instead, the department would keep a close eye as Hempstead tried to repair itself.

In 2005, the challenges included a student population with family incomes that were 60 percent of the state average. More than a quarter of students lived below the federal poverty level, a fifth were still learning English, less than two-thirds went on to college, and only 40 percent had graduated in 2003. The school was more than 99 percent students of color.[45]

To begin, Principal Stroughn focused on the fighting among the gangs and began funneling gang members and other students with poor attendance records and violent histories into night school. With his assistant principals, he formed smaller "learning communities" that acted as mini-schools within the school and brought on the Institute for Student Achievement, a nonprofit service organization, to help. The organization came into badly performing schools like Hempstead High to set up small learning communities, another education movement that had become popular nationwide among reformists trying to bridge the racial achievement gap. The goal was to mimic the atmosphere of private schools and richer suburban schools. The institute's first project had been the Roosevelt school district during the early years of the district's long struggle to get off the state's failing schools list.[46]

Under the new program, fewer students were assigned per teacher, magnet concentrations were added, and preparation for college was emphasized. Stroughn tallied which seniors were missing the Regents courses they needed to graduate with the state diploma and followed up with them and their parents. In 2005, the school was almost half Hispanic, but there was still only a handful of teachers who spoke Spanish and no administrators who did. So the school hired more bilingual and Spanish-speaking staff, and Stroughn visited Central America on a weeklong trip to learn more about his students' home countries.

In 2006, outside help arrived for Hempstead in the form of a lawsuit filed on behalf of New York City school children. The Campaign for Fiscal Equity had sued New York State thirteen years earlier to force it to overhaul the state's education aid formula for school districts, which critics described alternately as Byzantine, backward, and racist. CFE lawyers based the suit on the state constitution's guarantee of a sound basic education for every child. It was a standard that was clearly lacking in New York City's schools, where the graduation rate had been below 50 percent for years, and the lawyers demanded more state money be sent to supplement the city's local tax revenue so it could improve its offerings to meet the minimum constitutional guarantee for its students.

Despite its name, the lawsuit demanded adequacy, not equity. Its supporters seemed to realize that asking to bring the city's schools up to the funding levels of its wealthier suburban districts was too much to ask. All they asked for was the basics. Other so-called adequacy lawsuits were also being filed elsewhere around the country as hopes for the more radical solution of racial integration waned.[47] The demands were relatively humble, but the lawsuits still faced significant obstacles. In New York, Governor Pataki and a group of Republican senators, mostly from wealthy Long Island districts, fought the lawsuit tooth and nail.[48]

For years, the appeals churned through state courts. State judges ruled repeatedly in CFE's favor, and the governor responded with appeals. The Republican state senators and other leaders from wealthy suburbs fed fears of a "Robin Hood" outcome that would end with the poor children grabbing most of the state funding from their rich neighbors, many of which received significant help from the state to supplement their education budgets.[49] A "Robin Hood" effort in the early 1980s by Governor Mario Cuomo had sputtered and died in the face of the same criticism.[50] Cuomo made the mistake of proposing a redistribution of money between wealthy schools and poor schools. After protests in the capitol, the idea was dropped.[51]

As a result, the supporters of the city's lawsuit tread carefully when they talked about where the money would come from. They asked for more money, not redistribution of wealth. As the lawsuit chugged along, groups representing poor suburban districts like Roosevelt and Hempstead eagerly hitched their cause to the city suit. They hoped that a win would mean more money for their districts, too.[52] The American Civil Liberties Union filed a federal suit in 1998 on behalf of Hempstead and several of its neighbors that mirrored the city's claim.[53] In their suit, the suburban districts said they needed the funding for hiring more licensed teachers, remedial classes for struggling students, and more rigorous courses so that high-performing students would have a chance to earn honors diplomas.[54] The ACLU was careful not to suggest that the money should be sucked away from wealthier districts to pay for the expense.

The Republicans battled on. The Campaign for Fiscal Equity took the lawsuit to the state's highest court and won, but the money wasn't allocated in the state budget until Governor Pataki left office. In 2007, a new governor, Eliot Spitzer, inserted the extra state aid for schools in his budget. Every district in the state was allocated a 3 percent increase, no matter how wealthy or poor they were, and the poor were given extra on top of that.

For Hempstead, the budget added 9.5 percent more in state education funding than the previous year, nearly double what all of Long Island as a whole was receiving. It seemed like a banner year was ahead. That fall, administrators planned the first Homecoming Dance in more than a decade to reward students for the reduction in violence. That summer, the state department of education announced that Hempstead's graduation rate was 64 percent in 2007, up from 51 percent in 2005 and higher than the state average of 55 percent. More students were on track to graduate with Regents diplomas, and the number of Advanced Placement classes was nine, up from two at the beginning of the decade.[55] The high school had been removed from the list of failing schools under No Child Left Behind. Mr. Stroughn appeared to have beaten the odds.

There was still work to do: The overall graduation rate masked the fact that only 53 percent of the school's Hispanics graduated. Seven percent of students dropped out, lower than the 18 percent of the 1990s, but the same percentage as in 2005. And the school had a long way to go to close the achievement gap with its next-door neighbors. In Garden City, the dropout rate was zero percent. There, 99 percent of students had graduated in four years by 2007, and nearly 90 percent of those planned to go to a four-year college. Of the graduates in Hempstead, a third planned to go to college, a quarter were going to community college, 7 percent had jobs, and a quarter didn't have any plans at all.

In January, Michael Alguera was stabbed on the handball court. The school tumbled back into crisis. Mr. Stroughn struggled to explain how it could have happened. "We've never had a problem with Hispanic gangs here," he told reporters.[56] It was unclear if he believed the statement, or if he had been instructed by the school board to follow the line they had towed for years in denying the gang problem. Admitting to violence inside school walls was a difficult choice for a school principal: The state kept a list of "persistently dangerous schools" that was announced publicly each year, and to be placed on it risked the schools' reputation and even viability. Such schools had faced closure in nearby New York City. Later it came out that he had begged that year for more security guards but was rebuffed by the district, which said it didn't have enough money.[57] Another student was stabbed at night school in March. The student survived, but Clay, the district superintendent, announced his retirement the same week.[58]

In April, the School Administrators Association of New York State officially named Stroughn principal of the year for his accomplishments in bringing the school under control. But Stroughn was distracted. He worried that all he had worked for was going up in flames in the wake of Michael's death. He faulted himself for a dip in the four-year graduation rate that August, which dropped to 58 percent from its record high the year before.[59] Security and gangs once again overshadowed academics. Instead of spending the semester tracking down students who hadn't finished their Regents requirements, he fielded phone calls from worried parents and tried to restore calm. That summer, he was offered a job in his old district in Freeport. Other districts also called. Stroughn decided to stay. Next year, he believed, would be different. He would not leave these students behind.

Meanwhile, the police were stumped as they tried to solve Michael's murder. His death came near the day of the tenth anniversary of the village's federal gang task force. The village police department added fourteen new officers to its force in response to the murder and assigned them to patrol the troublesome Heights neighborhood, where MS-13 was based.[60] But the police made little headway, and months dragged by as they tried to turn up clues.

Sergio organized a peace demonstration. Oscar and Clementina Alguera marched with him through the streets of Hempstead with a newly painted cardboard gravestone bearing their youngest son's name. They begged for peace and for answers.[61]

A few days after the murder, *Newsday* ran an editorial about the "other Nassau County" that Michael's death highlighted.[62] The island might be one of the wealthiest places in the United States, the nation's "safest suburb," the article said, but his death was a reminder that all was not well under the surface. It was "sad but not shocking." The editorial board then urged Hempstead's villagers to do something about it. They should "speak loudly, in one true voice, to a county that prefers not to listen."

CHAPTER 26

Garden City

● ● ●

At Roosevelt Fields, the mall in Garden City, the shooting and its rever-
berations in Hempstead seemed far away, not just a two-mile meander
along tree-lined suburban streets. A month after the stabbing, middle-aged
Long Island ladies toted Nordstrom's and Bloomingdale's bags, and teenage
girls flitted in and out of Claire's Boutique. The gray winter had dissolved
into a torrential spring rain, but in the mall the yellow track lighting banished the gloominess. Trails of umbrella drippings winding behind the
shoppers were the only evidence that it was an ugly day outside.

Daniel draped himself across one of the mall's leather chairs. His
scarred face and baggy clothes drew an occasional glance, but he ignored
the stares. He came here often, mostly just to wander aimlessly and absorb
the manufactured peace. He rarely bought anything except at Christmas,
when he splurged on presents for his mother and his girlfriend. It was
one of the only places in Garden City he visited often, although even here,
he sensed he was an outsider. The racks of clothing and shelves of new
shoes and perfume were beyond his means. He could only look. Still, to

Daniel, the mall was an oasis where the grit and despair of Hempstead didn't penetrate.

Other temporary refugees from Hempstead occasionally passed by, but the hatred between rival gang members relaxed here. The mall, brightly lit and immaculate, magically diluted the anger and fear Daniel felt when he was on Hempstead's streets. Lately, the Garden City mall was the only place he felt safe.

Daniel had been on his way to work in January when he got the call about Michael. He wore a balaclava to cover his face, a disguise he adopted after several Mara Salvatrucha members chased him on his way to the bus in Uniondale. He hunched down into his coat and flipped open his phone. It was one of his friends from SWP. Mikey had been killed at Hempstead High, on the handball court. SWP knew MS-13 was behind the murder, and they were planning revenge.

Daniel kept walking and pressed the phone harder against his ear. Mikey had loved handball almost as much as Daniel. He had been a sweet kid, not as tough as Daniel, but Mikey was hard to beat on the court. Daniel couldn't understand who would want to hurt him. SWP thought they knew who did it. They were going to wait outside of the man's house and attack him when he came home.

Daniel pictured the MS-13 members who stabbed Adam. They had been waiting and watching, too. He glanced behind him. They thought the guy who did it might live in Uniondale, Daniel's town. His friend finished talking, and Daniel told him he would call him later.

After Olman's death three years earlier, Daniel was left to cope with the second murder of one of his classmates in as many years. The murderers were members of his own gang, SWP, so Daniel was supposed to act as if he didn't care about the death. As the year went on, he spent more time with the gang, skipped classes, and eventually failed eleventh grade. But sometimes he dreamed about moving away.

When Adam was stabbed, Daniel became even more conflicted about gang life. That evening in August, as his friend lay near the Taco Bell with the blood pooling under his head, Daniel flagged down a taxi. He pulled Adam into the cab, and they drove to Mercy Hospital with Daniel cradling his friend's head. He refused to leave him alone in the emergency room. Jaime had died alone; Daniel wouldn't leave Adam. Even after Adam's mother arrived, frantic and sobbing, Daniel offered to stay. She glared at his tattoos. He lied and told her he wasn't a gang member. She still looked at him suspiciously, but she didn't force him to leave. He was cool-headed and tried to be helpful and comforting. He had been through this before.

In the morning, doctors told them Adam would make it. The knife came close to arteries in Adam's neck, but it missed. Adam made a full recovery. After several weeks in the hospital, he was released and started school at Hempstead only a few days late. Daniel's relief that Adam had survived was mixed with guilt. The murder would have been on his head if Adam had died. Daniel didn't go back to school. He only had two classes left to fulfill his graduation requirements, but instead he dropped out. His girlfriend, Lara, had become pregnant. Her father was furious when he found out, and Daniel was forbidden from seeing her for several days.

After the initial shock, Daniel realized he was excited about the baby. He was determined to step up and take responsibility. Daniel eventually convinced her family to let Lara move in with him in Uniondale, while he worked and saved money to support them.

He used the excuse of the pregnancy to tell his friends in SWP that he was leaving the gang and calming down. They were sympathetic. Having a baby was an allowable excuse for getting out. Daniel increased his hours at his catering hall job and now only passed by his old haunts on his way to and from work. His girlfriend moved into the crowded house, and they prepared for the baby, a boy.

But the gang still called often. And now Mikey was dead. They wanted revenge, and they wanted his help.

Daniel sat in the mall and thought. He loved the gang. They were his family and his defenders in the hostile world of Hempstead, but he didn't want his baby to turn out like him, working twelve-hour days and scurrying home at night in fear. He wouldn't stop talking to the gang. He didn't think they would allow that. Instead, he would just avoid them and work harder to save money so that someday he could escape with his family to somewhere safe.

EPILOGUE

Barack Obama was elected the first black president of the United States on November 4, 2008, a victory that swept away the "last racial barrier in American politics," the *New York Times* reported. Less than a week later, another murder roiled the Long Island suburbs. This time, however, it was a gang of seven white youths on the hunt for "a Mexican" who stabbed a Hispanic man to death.

Marcelo Lucero was walking to a movie in Patchogue, a village in the center of Suffolk County. He had lived in the town of mostly Italian and Irish families for about sixteen years after immigrating to the United States legally from Ecuador. The town's Hispanic population was growing, but his friends said that Lucero, thirty-seven, was afraid of harassment by whites and rarely went out at night.[1] A few miles away in Farmingville, two Hispanic men were almost beaten to death by white supremacists, and a Hispanic family had been firebombed.

Just before midnight, the group of white teenagers stopped Lucero and a friend as they neared their destination. The other man ran for help as the teenagers punched and kicked Lucero. One stabbed him in the chest as he tried to fight back. They left him to die in a parking lot.[2]

The boys were students at Patchogue-Medford High School, where 80 percent of the 3,000 students were white. There had been other incidents reported before Lucero's murder. Some students at the high school said groups of area boys attacked local Hispanics for sport.[3] Before coming across Lucero, the group of seven attacked two other men, calling them "beaners." They shot one in a drive-by with a BB gun. The other they punched before he was able to get away.[4] A prosecutor compared them to a lynch mob.[5] Lucero's brother, Joselo, blamed Steve Levy, the Suffolk County executive known for his battle to rid Long Island of illegal immigrants. Levy brought about Lucero's death, Joselo said, because he "planted the seeds of hate indirectly by making people hate Hispanics."[6]

One of Lucero's attackers, sixteen-year-old Christopher Overton, was defended by attorney Anthony LaPinta, who had defended Mara Salvatrucha members against federal racketeering charges. Overton had previously been involved in a burglary in which the owner of the house was shot in front of his three-year-old son and left to die in his backyard. At first the district attorney, Thomas Spota—who had led the gang crackdown in Suffolk—charged the stabber, Jeffrey Conroy, with manslaughter as a hate crime, not the more serious charge of murder. He later upgraded the charge to second-degree murder after protests by Lucero's family and the Ecuadorean government.[7]

A few months after Lucero's death, Suffolk police began investigations into past attacks against Hispanics in the area by the same group of boys. Although law enforcement officials never referred to the white teenagers as a gang, despite the patterned nature of the group's violence and their apparent focus on defending white suburban turf from outsiders, they said they believed the violence had involved many others in a "yearlong rampage" against Hispanics.[8] The attacks were not isolated incidents—hate crimes against Hispanics had increased by 40 percent nationwide in five years.[9]

Gang violence continued to be cast as a problem of racial minorities, a problem that, in the case of Hispanics, authorities still believed could be uprooted with deportations. In October 2008, ICE conducted its largest sweep ever. The agency arrested 1,700 immigrants across the country who were alleged to have affiliations with Hispanic gangs.[10] ICE officials said the operation removed the "worst of the worst off the streets" and made neighborhoods "immeasurably safer." The deportees would join Julio back in El Salvador, where jobs were limited and the economic crisis that hit the United States in the fall of 2008 was hitting even harder.

• • •

Six months earlier, in April 2008, Daniel's baby had been born. The same month, both Jessica and Julio also had babies. The three were happy to become parents, but they each worried about the world where their children would grow up.

Julio spent his days puttering around San Salvador in an old pickup truck he had bought with the remnants of his day laborer earnings from Long Island. The investment was worth it because he feared riding the bus, where he was more likely to run into 18th Street members who controlled the routes that ran through downtown. He also worried that on public transportation he would be easily spotted by police, who could arrest him on sight if they caught a glimpse of one of his tattoos. He lived in his mother's house and earned $10 a week working as a lifeguard. On weekdays he supplemented his income by selling sandwiches out of a blue cart he rolled down the mountainside and set up outside office buildings at lunchtime.

After work Julio sometimes picked up his son from school in his pickup. He was trying to make up lost time. The two had become close. Julio was especially proud that his boy seemed destined for college, not the streets. It was unclear what opportunities would be available to him once he graduated, however, and going to school cost money, something Julio had very little of. The daughter who was born in April 2008 he saw less often. He couldn't afford a home for his small family, and the girl lived with her mother in a neighborhood claimed by 18th Street. Although he didn't want his children to join MS-13, Julio had never cut ties with his gang. His neighborhood lay next to one of San Salvador's MS-13 strongholds.

Convinced they would retaliate and maybe kill him, he refused to turn his back on the gang, even for his children.

Jessica learned she was pregnant around the time Daniel's girlfriend, Lara, did. Her baby, a boy, was heavy and healthy with a shock of thick dark hair and wide brown eyes. Like Daniel and Julio, she was hopeful about what he could become some day, if she could just find a way out of Long Island. Her boyfriend, a former member of SWP, worked full-time to support them, but like Daniel, the couple couldn't afford a place of their own. They lived in her mother's house with several other boarders her mother kept on to help pay the bills. Jessica worked part-time and saved her money. They had picked out a city in Ohio where they thought the schools would be better and the opportunities wider for their little boy. But they were often forced to raid their savings to pay rent to Jessica's mother or to fill the car with gas. At the rate they were going, it seemed that they would be trapped in the Long Island suburbs forever, surrounded by the nation's wealthiest neighborhoods but denied access to their glittering promise.

Obama's election left many racial barriers in American society intact, but his presidency held out possibilities for the three babies born that year. On the campaign trail Obama promised he would reform the immigration system, which at the end of George W. Bush's term was increasingly focused on tracking down and deporting illegal immigrants and blockading the border. His successor vowed to continue shoring up border defenses, but he also criticized the ICE raids as ineffective and harmful. He proposed "bringing people in from out of the shadows"—promising a chance at legalization for illegal immigrants in return for a fee and English lessons. He said he would work with Mexico on economic development.

His resolve would be tested by the economic crisis that hit just before Election Day and pushed immigration lower on the list of priorities. A Democratic majority in Congress improved the chances for a new immigration bill to pass, but rising unemployment rates made it politically risky for legislators to support legalizing illegal immigrants or to set up work exchange programs. Hundreds of thousands of Americans were losing their jobs. Finding a way to bring illegal immigrants out of the shadows seemed to be something that would have to wait, as Wall Street banks and the American housing market collapsed. The economic crisis seemed to release some of the pressure: The number of illegal immigrants decreased by an estimated half million in 2008. But the problem of illegal immigration and the street gangs it helped feed had not really gone away.

The nearly 350,000 deportees sent home in fiscal year 2008—most from Mexico or Central America and a third of whom had been convicted of crimes—arrived in countries embroiled in the most devastating economic crisis in several decades. Worse, an escalating drug war between rival cartels and the Mexican government sent violence and crime soaring upwards. In Mexico, the border region descended into anarchy when President Felipe Calderón launched an assault on the cartels and they fought back. Numbers released the same year showed that the main source of the drugs fueling the violence, Colombia, was churning out more cocaine in 2007 than in 2000, despite $6 billion from the United States poured into eradication efforts there.[11] The murder rate in El Salvador, a stop on the drug road north, grew by 25 percent between 2004 and 2007 according to the State Department. Yet the United States was repeating its strategy of the 1990s: depositing hordes of immigrants, many of them with criminal records, into a cauldron of violence and despair.

The hardened criminals either headed back north or were drawn into the gangs and cartels that had threatened the region's stability for decades. The dearth of economic activity and legitimate job options would likely lead some deportees with previously clean or minor records to join the underground economy, further ballooning the ranks of the criminal armies. The rest would either struggle to survive in their countries or take the chance of crossing into America, where jobs might be scarce, but at least it was safer. They would likely face the same dilemma many of their parents had confronted: whether to leave their children behind or to bring them along the dangerous and expensive journey north.

In May 2008, Matthew Quirk suggested in the *Atlantic* that the United States could better solve the Central American gang problem by keeping the gang members in American prisons instead of deporting them, since Salvadoran police estimated that 90 percent returned north anyway.[12] American prisons were better funded and equipped to keep dangerous criminals off the streets than overcrowded Central American facilities, he argued, noting that wannabes were more likely to find rehabilitation and intervention programs here. But in the United States, there was little guarantee or evidence that gang members who passed through the prison system would go on to live productive lives after they were released.

The American prison population had nearly tripled following the wider implementation of three-strikes rules and sentencing enhancements during the 1990s, when the Violent Crime Act of 1994 and new state laws added to the list of gang-related crimes and increased penalties for other offenses. By 2008, one in a hundred Americans was in jail or prison, more than three times the rate in Central America.[13] For black men the number was one in nine, and for Hispanic men it was about one in thirty. American prisons tended to do a miserable job of rehabilitating them. Among state parolees, 42 percent were re-incarcerated before the end of their parole, compared to 41 percent who finished successfully, while the recidivism rate in the United States was around 68 percent. The overwhelming majority of those released from American jails and prisons would be back behind bars in three years.[14] Chances were slim that federal policy would change dramatically under President Obama: Vice President Biden had authored the 1994 crime bill, a policy accomplishment he touted during the campaign. In October 2008, a few days before it approved a $700 billion bailout to banks on Wall Street, Congress shelved a few million dollars in funding for the newly passed Second Chance Act, which would have funded programs that help the country's more than 2.3 million inmates readjust to life on the outside when they were released.[15]

The bailout was deemed necessary to prevent a complete meltdown of the economy; rehabilitation money was noncrucial. But on the state and local level, voters and policymakers were beginning to see cutting prison budgets and investing in rehabilitation and gang intervention as economic good sense. They were questioning the wisdom of imposing increasingly harsh sentences and building ever more costly prisons that didn't seem to work as cures for crime. Imprisoning more people may have helped lower the crime rate in the 1990s, but 95 percent of inmates would eventually be released back into a society where jobs were increasingly scarce, even for people without a criminal record.[16] Every year states spent more than $49 billion of taxpayer money on prisons, a number the Pew Research Center estimated would grow by $25 billion in 2011.[17]

The states with the largest prison populations, and the most public dollars spent on housing prisoners, led the reform attempts. On November 4, 2008, in California, a proposition to emphasize drug treatment over imprisonment for offenders was defeated, but so was a proposition to enhance gang crime penalties and charge fourteen-year-old gang members as adults. In Texas, courts increasingly used alternatives to prison and gradually cut down its prison population, which was the largest in the nation. The number of Texas inmates shrank by more than 300 in 2007.[18] New York State, which had led the way in charging minors as young as thirteen as adults in the 1970s, was in the midst of overhauling its juvenile justice system. More than 80 percent of youth were rearrested after their release, and while the state's juvenile offender population was down to 2,000 from 4,000, many were incarcerated for committing misdemeanors. The state scaled back this ineffective system by closing six juvenile jail facilities—many were more than half empty—and focused on community-based alternatives to deal with delinquent youth.[19]

The tentative steps toward reforming the country's immigration and criminal justice systems would not erase the draw of the gangs for many Hispanic teenagers in Long Island, however. In *Gangs of New York,* his history of nineteenth-century gangs, Herbert Asbury observed that a young person joined a gang "because of a yearning for fame and glory which he was unable to satisfy except by acquiring a reputation as a tough

guy and a hard mug."[20] The observation applied a century later to the Long
Island suburbs, where slums were growing amid prosperity, producing
new street gangs among the isolated and desperate second-generation immigrant populations, just as they had the isolated Five Points tenements
Asbury described.

   In the deeply segregated American suburbs, where escape routes were
largely blocked and fear permeated the lives of many young people, the
gangs would continue to find a ripe crop of recruits even if the immigration system was overhauled and rehabilitation programs were well-
funded. The teenagers in Hempstead heard the stories about how
Hispanics were hated and attacked just down the road. Just over the fences,
they could see the all-white schools where success was a given, not a miracle. Just down the block, the gangs beckoned as a way of fighting back,
promising them the possibility of becoming someone who inspired respect. And as Detective Smith had observed, it was in the dysfunctional
Hempstead schools where the gangs had the most hours in the day to find
new members.

   Some education experts said that reforming a school system where
poor minority children chronically underperformed had to take a back
seat to more fundamental problems. Housing segregation and poverty
would have to be resolved first, they argued, so that at-risk children could
access good schools and find more support at home. Other education experts argued vehemently that the schools were the place to start. They
called for better teachers to be brought in, for bad teachers to be fired, and
for stricter standards. By this argument, holding minority children to
higher, more rigorous expectations would implant in them the pride and
respect some found in gangs instead of school. Many in this school of
thought saw charter schools or the small learning communities tried by
schools like Hempstead High School—models that were supposed to
allow high-poverty schools to replicate successful white, suburban
schools—as the key to success. The schools would remain separate, but
by refiguring their administrations, replacing the teachers, and adding

more bells and whistles with funding from adequacy lawsuits, they could perhaps be made equal.

A handful of education scholars held on to an old idea that had largely fallen out of fashion: desegregation. To erase the stark inequities between minorities and whites that persisted despite the promises of *Brown v. Board of Education*, they called for large-scale, long-term desegregation. In the few places where it had been tried, it seemed to work. The racial achievement gap decreased, more minority children graduated, and even white students tended to benefit compared to their white peers in isolated school districts. This group suggested that renewing the efforts to desegregate schools could bring benefits beyond the academic. Mixing children from diverse backgrounds was becoming crucial as the United States entered the era when whites would be a minority, particularly in places like Long Island, where the new demographic changes were provoking ethnic warfare.

By 2008, the nation's schools were becoming as segregated as they had been in 1968. The Northeast had long hosted the most segregated school districts after the South was forced to end de jure segregation in the 1970s. But the South was resegregating at a fast pace as its court-ordered desegregation programs were phased out.[21] It was also the newest hotbed for the Central American gangs. The states where Hispanic students were the most segregated from their white peers—including California, New York, New Jersey, Maryland, and Florida—also happened to have the worst Central American gang problems.[22]

A Supreme Court decision in 2007 had made school desegregation efforts more difficult by ruling that school districts in Louisville, Kentucky, and Seattle could not assign students to schools based explicitly on their race. The two cities had maintained the programs voluntarily to reduce black-white segregation, and in 2005 Kentucky and Washington ranked among the top five states with the smallest achievement gaps between blacks and whites in the nation. The ruling meant school districts nationwide had to abandon their desegregation plans.[23] In the wake of the decision, some districts adopted alternative methods to disrupt de facto segregation. They began assigning students based on their socioeconomic background and neighborhood, hoping that income and geography would also act as a proxy for race. Assigning students based on their language ability was another option that some education researchers believed was constitutionally sound.[24] New immigrant students could be spread throughout a district, where they would learn the language faster, be exposed to better schools and new peers, and learn to navigate their new country without the help of gangs. Their white peers would be exposed to the newcomers, too, ideally decreasing the levels of hostility that had led to the murder of Lucero.

Yet for many school districts that were small and racially homogenous, including those in Long Island, such options were out of reach. In Hempstead, there was only one high school and one middle school. The only way to integrate by race and income was to cross school district lines. Despite the obstacles, there were proposals for facilitating desegregation plans even in places as balkanized as Long Island. Financial incentives could entice suburban schools to take in struggling students from inner-city and poor suburban schools. School districts that agreed to accept the students could gain exemption from No Child Left Behind accountability standards and the grim threat of being labeled "failing" as their new students adjusted. To induce white students to enter school districts like Hempstead, they proposed a connected program to establish quality magnet schools in the struggling districts. As a new Congress prepared to take up the reauthorization of No Child Left Behind in the winter of 2009, there was hope that some of these options might be implemented at the federal level.

But Obama had never talked much about segregation in schools, in part, no doubt, because of the studied efforts to downplay race during the campaign and to maintain his image as a "postracial" candidate. Instead, he promoted an agenda that revolved around early childhood education (a focus that thrilled educators across the board), charter schools, improving the quality of tests required by No Child Left Behind, and improving teaching quality. But bridging the divides in American society and reducing the racial achievement gap, as Obama had promised he would try to do, would be a difficult task in a moment when schools and neighborhoods were returning to the stark segregation of the 1960s. Obama might have been perceived as postracial, but America was not. The spread of the Central American gangs, the rise of anti-immigrant activism in places like Farmingville, the increase in hate crimes against Hispanics, the growth in the minority prison population, and the racial achievement gap in schools were interrelated issues connected to the larger problem of racial inequality and distrust that the nation had battled for generations.

The problem had been cast as an inner-city problem, or a border problem, but increasingly gang conflicts and fights over immigration in places like Long Island made it clear that America's troubles with race were becoming firmly rooted in the suburbs. And in the suburbs it would be more difficult to implement change. The suburbs had been built on the assumption that neighbors, and their problems, were contained behind privacy fences and could be ignored. The sentiment extended to the family next door, the inner-city residents across the county line, and the countries south of the border. Persuading the white community to recognize that the problems of the newcomers were their own would be a struggle. But even in Long Island that November there was hope that a turning point had been reached.

Immediately after Marcelo Lucero's murder, the Suffolk County executive, Steve Levy, suggested the hate crime was just a "one-day story."[25] He angrily dismissed suggestions by journalists and immigrant advocates that his campaign against illegal immigrants had fueled tensions between whites and Hispanics. A few days after the murder, he retracted his statements, admitting he was wrong. It was a rare acknowledgement by a man who had made his career in part by demonizing illegal immigration. The murder was "a reminder of how far we as a society still have to go," he said in his apology, although his suggestions for reform were limited. He promised to create a Hispanic liaison to the Suffolk County police, called on schools to consider holding anti-hate trainings, and asked local preachers to talk about tolerance from the pulpit.[26]

Asbury observed that the gang member was "primarily a product of his environment; poverty and disorganization of home and community brought him into being," but he said it was "political corruption and all its attendant evils [that] fostered his growth."[27] In the 1800s, politicians kept gang members on their payrolls to help them get elected. In the 1990s and first decade of the twenty-first century, politicians used gang members in more subtle ways—as a crime issue that could scare up votes or as evidence they could be tough on crime when they announced a crackdown. Official bluster had fed the gangs for years. Exaggerated warnings about their ruthlessness and power inflated their reputations with each press conference. Money poured into police departments and prisons with little result; gangs persisted. The real problems in American society that fostered the growth of the gangs—and led to the deaths of Michael Alguera, Jaime Alvarenga, and also Marcelo Lucero, killed by white youth brought up in the same toxically segregated environment as Central American gang members—could not be summed up in a sound bite or solved with harsher punishments. Reversing decades of failed criminal justice, immigration, and education policies was a beginning. Levy had taken a small step forward, and it would be up to people like him, and Obama and Biden, to push for deeper changes that could mend the divides in America stoking the spread of violence and hatred.

ACKNOWLEDGMENTS

This book would not have been possible without the cooperation of Julio, Jessica, and Daniel, who welcomed me into their lives and were incredibly gracious with their time. George Yudice and Daniel Flores y Ascencio were there from the beginning to point the way. Judith Matloff and Mary D'Ambrosio were inspiring role models and tough editors in the early stages of this project. Thank you also to the many people in Hempstead, El Salvador, and Los Angeles who agreed to sit down with me and share their stories, with special thanks to the Algueras, Rosa Alvarenga, and Pamela Corrente.

I'm very thankful for the wisdom and enthusiasm of my editor, Ruth Baldwin, and my agent, Kathy Anderson, who believed in this book from the start. I'm also grateful for the hard work of Michelle Welsh-Horst, Claudia Dizenzo, Beth Wright, and others at Nation Books and Perseus Books Group. Thank you to the diligent and resourceful Marissa Colon-Margolies for going above and beyond in her role as a researcher. I'm thankful for the guidance and support of my first writing mentors: my parents, David and Diana Garland. My husband, Matthew Sweeney, was my editor and cheerleader; I couldn't have written the book without him.

NOTES

NOTES TO CHAPTER 1

1. Zachary R. Dowdy, "Ex-Gang Member Forges New Role from His Past," *Newsday*, October 22, 2003.

NOTES TO CHAPTER 2

1. U.S. Department of Homeland Security, "Remarks by Homeland Security Secretary Michael Chertoff to the Heyman Fellows at Yale University on 'Confronting the Threats to Our Homeland,'" Yale University, New Haven, April 7, 2008, http://www.dhs.gov/xnews/speeches/sp_1208280290851.shtm.

2. "Guatemalan Gangs Threaten to Keep Up Killings Unless Left Alone," *Deutsche Presse-Agentur*, January 28, 2004.

3. Sergio De Leon, "Gunmen Kill 28 on Honduran Bus, Escalating War Against Government," *Associated Press*, December 24, 2004.

4. Monica Guzman, "Federal SWAT Team Kills 2 Men in Anti-gang Initiative, 4 Others Nabbed in Joint Raid by FBI and HPD," *Houston Chronicle*, November 5, 2005.

5. "Smugglers Planning to Kill U.S. Border Agents, Federal Memo Warns," *Associated Press*, January 10, 2006.

6. William Kleinknecht, "Newark School Board to Fight Survivors Lawsuit," *Star-Ledger (Newark)*, August 27, 2008.

7. Federal Bureau of Investigation, "The MS-13 Threat: A National Assessment," January 14, 2008, http://www.fbi.gov/.

8. Matthew Quirk, "By Deporting Record Numbers of Latino Criminals, the U.S. May Make Its Gang Problem Worse," *Atlantic*, May 2008.

9. Federal Bureau of Investigation, "How We're Ganging Up on MS-13, and What You Can Do to Help," July 13, 2005, http://www.fbi.gov/.

10. Traci Carl, "U.S., Central American Law Enforcement Unites Against Gangs, U.S. Worry Gangs Will Aid Al-Qaida," *Associated Press*, February 18, 2005.

11. Matt Woolsey, "America's Richest Counties," *Forbes*, January 1, 2008.

12. Federal Bureau of Investigation, "Uniform Crime Reports," 2001, 2003, 2004, 2005, 2006, 2007, http://www.fbi.gov/ucr/ucr.htm.

13. Jerry Markon and Maria Glod, "Giving Up a New Life for a Gang Death," *Washington Post*, August 10, 2003; Jamie Stockwell, "In MS-13, a Culture of Brutality and Begging; Gang's Women Panhandle, Men Plot in Motels, Testimony Shows," *Washington Post,* May 2, 2005.

14. Dan Rather, "The Fight Against MS-13," *60 Minutes*, December 4, 2005.

15. Jerry Markon and Jamie Stockwell, "Two MS-13 Members Convicted in Killing, Two Others Acquitted in Informant's Slaying," *Washington Post*, May 18, 2005; Jerry Markon, "Protecting a Witness Who Doesn't Want Protection," *Washington Post*, June 12, 2005.

16. Markon and Stockwell, "Two MS-13 Members Convicted."

17. Ibid.

18. Ibid.

19. Jamie Stockwell and Jerry Markon, "Gang Member Says He Saw Va. Slaying, Defendant Denies Killing Witness," *Washington Post*, May 5, 2005.

20. Ibid.

21. Matthew Barakat, "Prosecutors Make Case for Death Against Convicted Gang Members," *Associated Press*, May 23, 2005.

22. Andrew Romano, "The Most Dangerous Gang in America," *Newsweek*, March 28, 2005.

23. Lisa Ling, "World's Most Dangerous Gang: Emails from the Ground in El Salvador," *National Geographic Explorer*, August 25–28, 2005, http://ngccommunity .nationalgeographic.com/ngcblogs/explorer/2006/01/worlds-most-dangerous -gang.html#more.

24. Ibid.

25. Michelle Malkin, "A Mockery of Homeland Security," *Kansas City Star*, September 2, 2005.

26. Chris Echegaray, "Middle Tennessee Gang Leaders Plead Guilty," *Tennessean*, July 29, 2008; Paul Elias, "Triple Murder Turns Focus on S.F. Sanctuary Policy," *Associated Press*, July 24, 2008.

27. Michelle O'Donnell, "Mineola: One of Two Murder Victims Identified," *New York Times*, September 23, 2004.

28. Kieren Crowley, "Gang Vengeance, L.I. Girl Is Slain After Wanting Out," *New York Post*, September 23, 2004.

29. Shelly Feuer Domash, "Leaders from Afar Bolstering a Gang," *New York Times*, November 7, 2004.

30. Carrie Melago, "Stunned Over Slayings: Bodies Turn Up in Two Tranquil Communities," *New York Daily News*, September 26, 2004.

31. Matthew Barakat, "Kilgore Visits Murder Site to Tout Anti-gang Initiatives," *Associated Press*, August 19, 2005.

32. Ibid.

33. Markon and Stockwell, "Two MS-13 Members Convicted."

34. Jamie Stockwell, "Convicted Gang Members Urged to Help Teens: In Sentencing, Judge Reiterates Jury's Hope of Keeping Youths from MS-13," *Washington Post*, September 10, 2005.

35. Federal Bureau of Investigation, July 13, 2005.

36. U.S. Immigration and Customs Enforcement, "Operation Community Shield: Targeting Violent Transnational Street Gangs," http://www.ice.gov/pi/investigations/comshield.

37. United States Department of Justice, "About the National Gang Targeting, Enforcement, & Coordination Center (Gang TECC)," http://www.usdoj.gov/criminal/gangtecc.

38. National Drug Intelligence Center, *Attorney General's Report to Congress on the Growth of Violent Street Gangs in Suburban Areas*, United States Department of Justice, April 2008, http://www.usdoj.gov/ndic/pubs27/27612/dept.htm.

39. Judith Greene and Kevin Pranis, *Gang Wars: The Failure of Enforcement Tactics and the Need for Effective Public Safety Strategies*, Justice Policy Institute, July 2007, p. 69, http://www.justicepolicy.org/content-hmID=1811&smID=1581&ssmID=22.htm.

40. National Drug Intelligence Center, *Attorney General's Report*.

41. Ibid.

42. Tom Jackman, "Youth Activists Decry Anti-gang Fund Cuts: White House Proposals Slice into Programs That Win War Against Gangs," *Washington Post*, June 4, 2004, p. B4.

43. Bureau of Justice Assistance, "Gang Resistance Education and Training (G.R.E.A.T.) Program," http://www.ojp.usdoj.gov/BJA/grant/great.html; Finn-Aage Esbensen, "How Great Is G.R.E.A.T.? Results from a Longitudinal Quasi-Experimental Design," *Criminology and Public Policy* 1, no. 1 (November 2001): pp. 87–118; David B. Muhlhausen and Erica Little, *Gang Crime: Effective Constitutional Policies to Stop Violent Gangs*, Heritage Foundation, June 6, 2007; State of New York Commission of Investigation, *Combating Gang Activity in New York: Suppression, Intervention, Prevention*, May 2006, p. 38.

44. United States Department of Justice, "Prepared Remarks of Attorney General Alberto Gonzales," Fraternal Order of Police, New Orleans, August 1, 2005, http://www.usdoj.gov/archive/ag/speeches/2005/080105agfraternalorder.htm.

45. Donna Lyons, *Crime Falls, but Not Everywhere*, National Conference of State Legislatures, June 2008, based on FBI Uniform Crime Reports.

46. Ibid.

47. Greene and Pranis, *Gang Wars.*

48. Cheryl L. Maxson, G. David Curry, and James C. Howell, "Youth Gang Homicides in the United States in the 1990s," in *Responding to Gangs: Evaluation and Research*, edited by Winifred L. Reed and Scott H. Decker (Washington, DC: U.S. Department of Justice, Office of Justice Programs, National Institute of Justice, 2002).

49. Ibid.

50. Ibid.

51. Jodi Lane and James W. Meeker, "Fear of Gang Crime: A Look at Three Theoretical Models," *Law and Society Review* 37, no. 2 (June 2003): p. 426.

52. Ibid., pp. 427, 432.

53. Ibid., p. 431.

54. Ibid., p. 429.

55. Jeffrey S. Passel and D'Vera Cohn, *U.S. Population Projections: 2005–2008*, Pew Research Center, February 11, 2008.

56. Roberto Suro and Audrey Singer, *Latino Growth in Metropolitan America: Changing Patterns, New Locations*, Center on Urban and Metropolitan Policy and the Pew Hispanic Center, July 2002, p. 1.

57. Passel and D'Vera Cohn, *U.S. Population.*

58. Suro and Singer, *Latino Growth*, p. 1.

59. Ibid., p. 7.

60. Ibid.

61. Julia Preston, "Immigrants Becoming U.S. Citizens at High Rate," *New York Times*, March 29, 2007.

62. U.S. Census Bureau, *The Changing Shape of the Nation's Income Distribution: 1957–1998*, June 2000; John Cavanagh and Chuck Collins, "The Rich and the Rest of Us," *Nation*, June 30, 2008.

63. Lyons, *Crime Falls.*

64. Sarah Hammond, *Gang Busters*, National Conference of State Legislatures, June 2008.

65. Ibid.

NOTES TO CHAPTER 3

1. Ebenezer Howard, *Garden Cities of To-morrow* (London, 1902); Jane Jacobs, *The Life and Death of Great Cities* (Random House: New York, 1961).

2. Jacobs, *Life and Death.*

3. Chauncy Harris, "Suburbs," *American Journal of Sociology* 49, no. 1 (July 1943): p. 1.

4. Ibid., pp. 2, 10.

5. Hempstead Village, *Hempstead 1941: A Report of the Village Government of Hempstead for the Year 1941*, edited by Philip Sparacino, p. 30.

6. Ibid.

7. Ibid.

8. *Hempstead 1941*; William Karlin, "New York Slum Clearance and the Law," *Political Science Quarterly* 52, no. 2 (July 1937): p. 241.

9. *Hempstead 1941*.

10. Ibid.

11. Ibid.

12. Rosalind Tough and Gordon MacDonald, "The New York Metropolitan Region: Social Forces and the Flight to Suburbia," *Land Economics* 37, no. 4 (November 1961): pp. 327, 331; U.S. Department of Housing and Urban Development, "HUD Historical Background," http://www.hud.gov/; Kenneth Jackson, *Crabgrass Frontier* (Oxford: Oxford University Press, 1985).

13. Robert A. Caro, *The Power Broker: Robert Moses and the Fall of New York* (New York: Random House, 1974); Jackson, *Crabgrass Frontier*, pp. 222–230.

14. Tough and MacDonald, "New York," p. 328.

15. John T. McQuiston, "A&S in Hempstead Closing After 40 Years," *New York Times*, June 10, 1992.

16. Tough and MacDonald, "New York," p. 333.

17. See Jackson, *Crabgrass Frontier*, pp. 274–276; Tough and MacDonald, "New York."

18. Tough and MacDonald, "New York," p. 336.

19. Jackson, *Crabgrass Frontier*, pp. 234–243.

20. Ibid., pp. 81–86.

21. Ibid., p. 81.

22. Jackson, *Crabgrass Frontier*.

23. Bruce Lambert, "At 50, Levittown Contends with Its Legacy of Bias," *New York Times*, December 28, 1997; Jackson, *Crabgrass Frontier*, p. 241.

24. Tough and MacDonald, "New York," p. 329.

25. Ibid., p. 330.

26. Ibid.

27. Ibid., p. 334.

28. Harvey Choldin, Claudine Hanson, and Robert Bohrer, "Suburban Status Instability," *American Sociological Review* 45, no. 6 (December 1980): p. 972.

29. Choldin et al., "Suburban Status."

30. Tough and MacDonald, "New York," p. 334.

31. Ibid.; Jackson, *Crabgrass Frontier*, pp. 196–202.

32. Interview with James Russo, former police chief of Hempstead Village Police Department, July 17, 2008.

33. Bruce Lambert, "Study Calls L.I. Most Segregated Suburb," *New York Times*, June 5, 2002.

34. Jackson, *Crabgrass Frontier*, p. 260.

35. McQuiston, "A&S in Hempstead."

36. Interview, James Russo and Joseph Wing, Hempstead Police Department, July 16, 2008.

37. Susan Hardwick, "Toward a Suburban Immigrant Nation," in *Twenty-first Century Gateways: Immigrant Incorporation in Suburban America*, edited by Audrey Singer, Susan Hardwick, and Caroline B. Brettell (Washington, DC: Brookings Institution Press, 2008), pp. 43, 47; Bruce Lambert, with Fernanda Santos, "'First' Suburbs Growing Older and Poorer, Report Warns," *New York Times*, February 16, 2006, p. B1.

38. Roberto Suro and Audrey Singer, *Latino Growth in Metropolitan America: Changing Patterns, New Locations*, Pew Hispanic Center, June 30, 2002.

39. Ibid.

40. U.S. Census Bureau; Bart Jones, "A Salvadoran Boom: Census: Group's L.I. Population Gaining on Puerto Ricans," *Newsday*, June 27, 2001, p. A5.

41. Doreen Carvajal, "Fresh Faces Are Making an Impact on the L.I. Landscape," *New York Times, Long Island Weekly Desk*, May 5, 1996.

42. Interview with Amory Sepulveda, Port Washington, March 2008.

43. Yolanda Rodriguez and Sidney C. Schaer, "The New Long Islanders: Wave of Immigrants Fleeing War and Poverty Finds Work on LI," *Newsday*, August 5, 1990.

44. Letta Taylor, "Melting-Pot Rage: On LI, Simmering Anger over Documented Hispanics," *Newsday*, September 17, 1993.

NOTES TO CHAPTER 4

1. Beth Verhey, *The Demobilization and Reintegration of Child Soldiers: El Salvador Case Study*, World Bank, 2001, p. 7.

2. Ibid., p. 8.

NOTES TO CHAPTER 5

1. Tommie Sue Montgomery, *Revolution in El Salvador: Origins and Evolution*, 2nd ed. (Boulder, CO: Westview Press, 1995), p. 37.

2. Ibid.

3. Ibid., p. 39.

4. Ibid., pp. 38–49.

5. Ibid., pp. 23–24.

6. Raymond Bonner, *Weakness and Deceit: U.S. Policy and El Salvador* (New York: Times Books, 1984), pp. 17–19; Montgomery, *Revolution*, pp. 23–24, 38.

7. Montgomery, *Revolution,* pp. 73–79; Bonner, *Weakness*, pp. 145–149.

8. Bonner, *Weakness*, pp. 159–163, 168–170; Montgomery, *Revolution*, pp. 106–107, 136–137.

9. Montgomery, *Revolution*, p. 139.

10. Ibid., p. 110; Bonner, *Weakness*, p. 96.

11. UN Security Council, Annex, *From Madness to Hope: The 12-Year War in El Salvador: Report of the Commission on the Truth for El Salvador,* http://www.usip.org/library/tc/doc/reports/el_salvador/tc_es_03151993_intro.html.

12. Bonner, *Weakness*, p. 134.

13. UN Security Council, *From Madness to Hope.*

14. Ibid.

15. Montgomery, *Revolution*, p. 140.

16. Mark Danner, *The Massacre at El Mozote: A Parable of the Cold War* (New York: Vintage Books, 1994), first published as "The Truth of El Mozote," *New Yorker,* December 6, 1993.

17. Danner, *Massacre*, pp. 12–13.

18. Ibid., p. 13.

19. Montgomery, *Revolution*, p. 152.

20. UN Security Council, *From Madness to Hope.*

21. Montgomery, *Revolution,* p. 152.

22. UN Security Council, *From Madness to Hope.*

23. Montgomery, *Revolution,* p. 152.

24. Bonner, *Weakness,* p. 36.

25. Ibid., pp. 74–80.

26. Ibid., pp. 44–47.

27. Ibid., p. 46.

28. Ibid., p. 47.

29. Ibid., p. 58; Montgomery, *Revolution,* p. 56.

30. Bonner, *Weakness,* p. 61.

31. Montgomery, *Revolution,* p. 133.

32. UN Security Council, *From Madness to Hope.*

33. Ibid.

34. Ibid.

35. Montgomery, *Revolution,* p. 157.

36. "El Salvador's Rising Left Wing," *Economist*, March 20, 1997.

37. Verhey, *Demobilization,* pp. 5, 7–9, 15.

38. James LeMoyne, "Salvador Troops Seize Two in Hostage Drama at School," *New York Times*, March 26, 1987.

39. Ibid.

40. Ibid.

41. Montgomery, *Revolution,* p. 219.

42. Ibid.

43. Ibid.

44. Ibid.

45. Central Intelligence Agency, *The World Factbook: El Salvador*, 2009.

NOTES TO CHAPTER 6

1. John Johnson, "Youth Gangs of Central Americans in L.A. on Rise," *Los Angeles Times*, April 24, 1990.

2. Megan Davy, "The Central American Foreign Born in the United States," Migration Policy Institute, April 2006, http://www.migrationinformation.org/USFocus/display.cfm?id=385.

3. James Diego Vigil, *A Rainbow of Gangs: Street Cultures in the Mega-City* (Austin: University of Texas Press, 2002); Sarah Grammage, "*El Salvador: Despite End to Civil War, Emigration Continues*," July 2007, Migration Policy Institute, http://www.migrationinformation.org/profiles/display.cfm?id=636.

4. Grammage, "El Salvador"; Susan Gzesh, "*Central Americans and Asylum Policy in the Reagan Era*," Migration Policy Institute, April 2006, http://www.migration information.org/Feature/display.cfm?id=384.

5. Donna Leinwand, "LAPD, Neighborhood Shaken," *Los Angeles Times*, February 25, 2000.

6. Anne-Marie O'Connor, Antonio Olivo, and Joseph Trevino, "Crime, Poverty Test Rampart Officers' Skill," *Los Angeles Times*, November 10, 1999.

7. Peter Y. Hong, "Rise in Killings May Mean Gang Truce Is Over; Violence: Surging Murder Rate in LAPD's Rampart Division Could Be an Indication the Mexican Mafia's Control Has Broken Down, Police Say," *Los Angeles Times*, October 6, 1995.

8. Vigil, *Rainbow of Gangs.*

9. Joseph Tovares, "The Zoot Suit Riots," *The American Experience*, Public Broadcasting Service, 2001.

10. Bob Baker, "Deeply Rooted in L.A.; Chicano Gangs: A History of Violence," *Los Angeles Times*, December 11, 1988.

11. Vigil, *Rainbow of Gangs*; Tovares, "The Zoot Suit Riots."

12. Tovares, "The Zoot Suit Riots."

13. Ibid.

14. Joan W. Moore, *Going Down to the Barrio: Homeboys and Homegirls in Change* (Philadelphia: Temple University Press, 1991).

15. Ibid.; Baker, "Deeply Rooted in L.A."

16. Baker, "Deeply Rooted in L.A."

17. Ibid.

18. Ibid.

19. Jesse Katz, "Latino Gang Carnage Is Part of an Invisible War; Violence: Killings in the Barrios Are Largely Ignored, Although They Claim Twice as Many Lives as in Black Areas," *Los Angeles Times*, July 12, 1992.

20. Baker, "Deeply Rooted in L.A."

21. Ibid.

22. John Johnson, "Youth Gangs of Central Americans in L.A. on Rise," *Los Angeles Times*, April 24, 1990.

23. Alex Sanchez, Homies Unidos, interview, March 3, 2004.

24. Baker, "Deeply Rooted in L.A."; Sanchez, interview, 2004.

25. Johnson, "Youth Gangs."

26. Sanchez, interview, 2004.

27. Johnson, "Youth Gangs."

28. Yvette Cabrera, "The Fall of Lafayette Park," *Los Angeles Times*, December 25, 1994.

29. Johnson, "Youth Gangs."

30. Ibid.

31. John Johnson, "War Refugees Form Deadly L.A. Gangs, Crime: Central American Refugees Immune to Violence Are a Growing Part of L.A.'s Gang Culture; 'They Laugh at Drive-By Shootings,' One Expert Says," *Los Angeles Times*, December 17, 1989.

32. Peter Y. Hong, "Violence: Surging Murder Rate in LAPD's Rampart Division Could Signify That Mexican Mafia's Control Has Broken Down, Police Say," *Los Angeles Times*, October 6. 1995.

33. Johnson, "War Refugees."

34. Beth Verhey, *The Demobilization and Reintegration of Child Soldiers: El Salvador Case Study,* World Bank, 2001.

35. Marcelo Suarez-Orozco, *Central American Refugees and U.S. High Schools: A Pscyhosocial Study of Motivation and Achievement* (Stanford, CA: Stanford University Press, 1989).

36. Linda Deutsch, "Charges Dismissed in LAPD Corruption Case That Shook Department," *Associated Press,* December 9, 2004; Richard Winton, "Former Rampart Officer Perez Is Arrested," *Los Angeles Times*, July 13, 2006; Terry McDermott, "Rafael Perez: The Road to Rampart," *Los Angeles Times*, December 31, 2000.

37. McDermott, "Rafael Perez."

38. Ann W. O'Neill, "The Rampart Verdicts: 3 Rampart Officers Convicted of Corruption," *Los Angeles Times*, November 16, 2000, p. A1.

39. Deutsch, "Charges Dismissed."

40. David Rosenzweig, "Ex-Cop Durden Gets Three Years," *Los Angeles Times*, June 12, 2002, p. 3; Don Terry, "Officers' Corruption Trial Under Way in Los Angeles," *New York Times*, October 14, 2000, p. A12.

41. Ibid.

NOTES TO CHAPTER 7

1. Constance L. Hays, "To Markets! To Markets!" *New York Times*, City Weekly Desk, November 28, 1993.

2. Tracy Wilkinson, "Gangs Find Fresh Turf in Salvador; Whether by Choice or by Force, Many L.A. Youths Have Returned to Their Homeland Bringing with Them a Violent Subculture; It's Taken Root Among Disaffected Teenagers Primed by Years of War," *Los Angeles Times,* June 16, 1994.

3. Randall Richard, "500,000 Criminal Deportees from America Wreak Havoc in Many Nations," Associated Press, October 23, 2003.

4. Scott Wallace, "You Must Go Home Again: Deported Los Angeles Gang Members Are a Crime Problem in El Salvador," *Harper's Magazine*, August 1, 2000; Office of Immigration Statistics, *Yearbook of Immigration Statistics*, Office of Management, Department of Homeland Security, 2002.

5. Douglas Engle, "San Salvador Street Gang Life Tough and Often Short," *Associated Press*, March 17, 1996; Wilkinson, "Gangs Find Fresh Turf."

NOTES TO CHAPTER 9

1. Caren Chesler, "Hempstead Schools Stuck in a Failure Rut," *New York Times*, May 30, 2004.

NOTES TO CHAPTER 10

1. Interviews with members of Salvadoran With Pride, February 2004; Evelyn Nieves, "Our Towns: Group? Gang? It's a Matter of Perspective," *New York Times*, Metro, March 8, 1998, p. 35.

2. Ibid.

3. Susan Hartman, "LI Moment: Keeping an Eye on Street Gangs, Tracking LI's Toughs," *Newsday*, January 23, 2000, p. G2.

4. Nieves, "Our Towns."

5. Interview with James Russo, former police chief of Hempstead Village Police Department, July 17, 2008.

6. Ibid.

7. John T. McQuiston, "Nassau Police Lead a Drive to Stem Growing Gang Violence," *New York Times*, May 13, 1998.

8. Robert Gearty, "Nassau Rolls a Seven as Crime Drops Again," *New York Daily News*, March 25, 1999, p. 12.

9. Shelly Feuer Domash, "Where Gangs Tread, Fear Haunts the Streets," *New York Times*, Long Island Weekly Desk, December 19, 1999, p. 1.

10. State of New York Commission of Investigation, *Combating Gang Activity in New York: Suppression, Intervention, Prevention*, May 2006, p. 38.

11. Finn-Aage Esbensen, "How Great Is G.R.E.A.T.? Results from a Longitudinal Quasi-Experimental Design," *Criminology and Public Policy* 1, no. 1 (November 2001): pp. 87–118; David B. Muhlhausen and Erica Little, *Gang Crime: Effective Constitutional Policies to Stop Violent Gangs*, Heritage Foundation, June 6, 2007; *Combating Gang Activity*, p. 38.

12. Interview with Pamela Corrente, New Jersey, November 13, 2006.

13. Pamela Corrente, "Viewpoints: In Defense of Freeport," *Newsday*, August 8, 1988, p. 53.

14. Robert Gearty, "Two Sought in Student Slay, Gang Members Tied to Freeport Shootings," *New York Daily News*, April 29, 1999.

15. Ibid.

16. Oscar Corral, "Sentenced for Helping Suspects, Man Gets Year for Aiding 2 Wanted in Death Flee," *Newsday*, August 31, 1999, p. 23.

17. Victor Manuel Ramos, "Mom Fights Back on Gang Violence," *Newsday*, November 25, 2000, p. A4.

18. Ibid.

19. Shelly Feuer Domash, "Our Gangs: Wars, and Warriors, Go Local," *New York Times*, Long Island Weekly Desk, November 22, 1998, p. 1.

20. Ibid.

21. Ibid.

22. President's Commission on Law Enforcement, *The Challenge of Crime in a Free Society* (Washington, DC: Government Printing Office, February 1967); Gerard E. Lynch, "RICO: The Crime of Being a Criminal, Parts I & II," *Columbia Law Review* 87, no. 4 (May 1987): pp. 661–764.

23. Lynch, "RICO," pp. 668, 678.

24. Lynch, "RICO."

25. Ibid., p. 694.

26. Ibid., p. 704.

27. Lynch, "RICO."

28. Ibid., pp. 704–706.

29. "Ten Men Are Indicted in a War Between Long Island Street Gangs," *New York Times*, December 22, 2000; Robert Gearty, "Hempstead Gang Nailed, Indictments Cap Year-Long Probe," *New York Daily News*, December 22, 2000.

30. Ibid.

31. Shelly Feuer Domash, "War Against Gangs Ratchets Up a Notch," *New York Times*, December 31, 2000.

NOTES TO CHAPTER 12

1. Letta Taylor, "Desperate Journeys: Kids Abused by Smugglers Bringing Them to Parents in the U.S.," *Newsday*, September 29, 2002.

2. Office of Refugee Resettlement, "Unaccompanied Children's Services," U.S. Department of Health and Human Services, Administration for Children and Families, http://www.acf.hhs.gov/programs/orr/programs/unaccompanied_alien_children.htm.

3. UNICEF, "At a Glance: El Salvador," http://www.unicef.org/infobycountry/elsalvador.html.

4. Douglas Farah, "Killing in Salvadoran Crime Wave Outpaces Deaths," *Washington Post*, March 16, 1996.

5. Ibid.

6. Ibid.; U.S. Department of Justice, "Homicide Rates Recently Declined to Levels Last Seen in the Mid-1960s," Bureau of Justice Statistics, Office of Justice Programs, http://www.ojp.usdoj.gov/bjs/glance/hmrt.htm.

7. U.S. Department of State, "Travel Advisory: El Salvador," May 1, 2008.

8. Farah, "Killing."

9. José Angel Tolentino and Edgar Lara López, *Labor Market Performance in El Salvador 2002/2003*, Global Policy Network and FUNDE (National Foundation for Development Macro Economy and Development Area), 2003.

10. Ibid.

11. *World of Information Country Report*, Quest Economics Database, 2004.

12. "El Salvador's Economy: Efforts to Tame Inflation May Not Work," *Economist*, June 13, 2008.

13. See Tolentino and López, *Labor Market*, for income gap statistics drawn from the *Statistical Yearbook for Latin America and the Caribbean* by Comisión Económica para América Latina y el Caribe (CEPAL).

14. Joaquin M. Chavez, "An Anatomy of Violence in El Salvador," *NACLA Report on the Americas* 37, no. 6 (2004): pp. 31–37.

15. Manuel Orozco, "Central American Diasporas and Hometown Associations," *Diasporas and Development*, January 1, 2007.

16. Ibid.; Kevin Sullivan, "A Salvadoran Town's Dream Rises Slowly from the Rubble; In San Agustin, Devastated by 2001 Quake, 'We Are Reborn,'" *Washington Post*, March 30, 2003; Roberto Suro, *Remittance Senders and Receivers: Tracking the Transnational Channels* (Washington, DC: Pew Hispanic Center and Multilateral Investment Fund, 2003).

17. Adam De Vasconcelos, "Transforming Labor Markets and Promoting Financial Democracy: Statistical Comparisons," Inter-American Development Bank, November 2005; Suro, *Remittance*, p. 16.

18. Taylor, "Desperate Journeys."

19. Ruth Ellen Wasem and Karma Ester, *Temporary Protected Status: Current Immigration Policy and Issues*, Congressional Research Service Report for Congress, January 27, 2006.

20. Ibid.

21. Ibid.

22. Ibid.

23. Joseph Nevins, *Operation Gatekeeper: The Rise of the "Illegal Alien" and the Making of the U.S. Mexico Boundary* (New York: Routledge, 2002), p. 4.

24. Ibid., pp. 86–92.

25. Thomas Espenshade, Jessica Baraka, and Gregory Huber, "Implications of the 1996 Welfare and Immigration Reform Acts for US Immigration," *Population and Development Review* 23, no. 4 (1997): pp. 769–801, 776.

26. United States Government Accountability Office, Report to the Honorable Bill Frist, *Illegal Immigration: Border Crossing Deaths Have Doubled Since 1995*, August 2006.

27. Arthur Rotstein, "More Border Crossers Use Sasabe Corridor," *Associated Press*, March 11, 2006; Robert Rhodes, "Few Possessions, Many Fears as Migrants Start Desert Trek," *Mennonite Weekly Review*, February 2004, http://www.menno weekly.org/.

28. Rhodes, "Few Possessions."

29. Ibid.

30. Jerry Markon, "Schools' Overspending Upsets the Community," *Newsday*, March 1, 1996; "Schools Below Standards," *Newsday*, March 28, 2002; Kim Nava-Fiorio, "Schools That Fall Below State Standards," *Newsday*, March 15, 2001.

31. Caren Chesler, "Hempstead Schools Stuck in Failure Rut," *New York Times*, May 30, 2004.

32. Jim Merritt, "Police Beat," *Newsday*, March 30, 1997; Dele Olojede and Suzanne Bilello, "For Hempstead's Teachers and Students, a Daily Lesson in Demoralization," *Newsday*, June 16, 1991.

33. New York State Education Department, School Report Card for Alverta B. Gray Schultz Middle School, 2000, 2001.

34. Michael Winerip, "After Too Many Funerals, a Priest Could Use a Blessing," *New York Times*, October 28, 2001.

NOTES TO CHAPTER 13

1. Michael Winerip, "Feeling the Aftershocks Far from Ground Zero," *New York Times*, September 23, 2001.

2. Joie Tyrrell, "The Island Reacts; A Tragedy They Will Never Forget: Across LI, Shock, Disbelief, Anger, Fear in the Aftermath," *Newsday*, September 12, 2001.

3. Jioni Palmer, "Police Charge Two After Tips Head Off Potential Violence," *Newsday*, September 17, 2001.

4. Oscar Corral, "Four Alleged Gang Members Accused of Baseball Bat Attack," *Newsday*, July 8, 2000; David Pierson, "Fifth Arrest in Bat Attack, Alleged Gang Member Charged in Slaying," *Newsday*, July 12, 2000; Ann Givens, "Gang Members Sentenced in Fatal Beating," *Newsday*, November 3, 2001.

5. Givens, "Gang Members."

6. Ginger Thompson, "Mexico President Urges U.S. to Act Soon on Migrants," *New York Times*, September 6, 2001.

7. Ibid.

8. Ibid.; David E. Sanger, "Mexico's President Rewrites the Rules," *New York Times*, September 8, 2001.

9. Sanger, "Mexico's President"; Mary Jordan and Kevin Sullivan, "Mexico Steps into Spotlight: New President Sets a Bold Course in U.S., Regional Relations," *Washington Post*, January 31, 2001.

10. Eric Schmitt, "Bush Says Plan for Immigrants Could Expand," *New York Times*, July 27, 2001.

11. "A Nation Challenged: The Immigrants; As Dragnet Continues, Citizenship Filings Rise," *New York Times*, January 1, 2002; Matthew Purdy, "A Nation Challenged: The Law; Bush's New Rules to Fight Terror Transform the Legal Landscape," *New York Times*, November 25, 2001; Tamar Lewin, "A Nation Challenged: The Detainees; Deported Immigrants with Nowhere to Go Wait in Jail," *New York Times*, December 10, 2001.

12. Linda Greenhouse, "U.S. Can Hold Immigrants Set to Be Deported," *New York Times*, April 30, 2003.

13. Susan Sachs, "Immigrants Facing Strict New Controls on Cash Sent Home," *New York Times*, November 12, 2002.

14. Tamara Audi, "Closing the Gaps: Security Has Improved, Officials Say, but There's More Work to Do," *Detroit Free Press*, September 2, 2002.

15. James Pinkerton, "Texas Border Fence on Track for Fall," *Houston Chronicle*, July 19, 2007; Stephan Dinan, "Chertoff to Hand Obama Immigration Successes," *Washington Times*, December 4, 2008.

16. Theresa Vargas and Oscar Corral, "Sending a Strong Message on Gangs; Group Appeals for Lawmakers' Help," *Newsday*, June 15, 2001; interview with Detective Richard Smith, Hempstead, July 28, 2008.

17. Theresa Vargas, "Three Arraigned in Rape Case," *Newsday*, September 11, 2001.

18. Charles Sussman and Bill Hoffmann, "Gang Duo Nabbed in Drive-By Slaying," *New York Post*, October 5, 2001.

19. Vargas, "Three Arraigned."

20. Jioni Palmer, "Hempstead Man Slain in Drive-By Shooting," *Newsday*, September 10, 2001.

21. Theresa Vargas, "Five Teens Arraigned in Stabbing Death Face First-Degree Gang Assault Charges," *Newsday*, September 18, 2001.

22. Theresa Vargas, "Hempstead Teen Dies in Shooting," *Newsday*, October 19, 2001.

23. Steven Kreytak, "Six Charged in Shooting; Tell Police in Hempstead They're Va. Members of MS-13 Gang," *Newsday*, October 16, 2001.

24. Alexandr Mondragón, "Terror pandillero en las escuelas," *La Tribuna Hispana USA*, January 2003.

25. Shelly Feuer Domash, "Nassau Police Say They're Already Strapped," *New York Times*, October 21, 2001.

26. Bruce Lambert, "Unused Computers, Unpaid 911 Bills: Nassau Tallies Waste," *New York Times*, January 2, 2003.

27. "A Double Whammy on Long Island," *New York Times*, October 5, 2002.

28. Shelly Feuer Domash, "Nassau Police Lag in Terror Training," *New York Times*, March 2, 2003.

29. Nassau County Government, "County Executive Suozzi Announces Redeployment Initiative Should Save County over $2 Million a Year and Increase Police and Public Safety," Press Release, January 15, 2002; Nassau County Government, "County Executive Suozzi Announces NASS-Stat," Press Release, March 26, 2002.

30. Robin Topping, "RICO Being Used to Fight LI Gangs," *Newsday*, May 8, 2002; Brian Harmon, "Suffolk to Use Fed Laws to Sweep Gangs from Streets," *Newsday*, April 25, 2002.

31. Samuel Bruchey, "Levy Tough on Gangs; Bill Calls for Stiffer Prison Sentences for Members," *Newsday*, February 22, 2002; Lisa Chamoff, "Stricter Anti-gang Laws Sought; Recent Arrests Worry Local, State Officials," *Newsday*, April 1, 2002; Michael Balboni, Thomas Spota, Daniel Belmont, Samantha Dias, and Sergio Argueta, "Other Voices," *Newsday*, May 5, 2002.

32. Chamoff, "Stricter Anti-gang Laws"; Sean Gardiner, "Gangbanger as 'Terrorist,'" *Village Voice*, June 19, 2007.

33. Richard Winton, "L.A. Home Turf for Hundreds of Neighborhood Criminal Groups," *Los Angeles Times*, May 13, 2005.

34. Patrick McGreevey and Sandy Banks, "On Paper, Leaving a Gang Is Difficult," *Los Angeles Times*, March 23, 2006; George Ramos, "Youths Offered Way to Get Off State Database," *Los Angeles Times*, July 25, 2000; Winton, "L.A. Home Turf."

35. Ibid.

36. Gardiner, "Gangbanger."

37. Nassau County Government, "County Executive Announces Taskforce Against Gangs (TAG)," Press Release, November 13, 2002.

38. Ibid.

39. Bruce Lambert and Elissa Gootman, "Promising End to 'Doom and Gloom,' Suozzi Unveils Plan for Nassau," *New York Times*, April 2, 2002; Bruce Lambert, "Nassau Raises Property Tax by 20 Percent in Its New Budget," *New York Times*, October 29, 2002.

40. "Budget Cuts Can Kill Kids' Choices," *Newsday*, January 9, 2000; Erik Holm, "GOP Cuts Kill Tutoring Program," *Newsday*, February 27, 2000.

41. Bruchey, "Levy Tough on Gangs."

42. David Pierson, "Fifth Arrest in Bat Attack, Alleged Gang Member Charged in Slaying," *Newsday*, July 12, 2000.

NOTES TO CHAPTER 14

1. Chau Lam, "Two Sentenced in Retaliation Death of Teen," *Newsday*, November 11, 2004.

2. Ibid.

NOTES TO CHAPTER 15

1. Brian Harmon, "Seven in Gang Admit Role in Attacks," *New York Daily News*, December 20, 2001.

NOTES TO CHAPTER 16

1. Charlie LeDuff and David M. Halbfinger, "Slums Behind Shutters; A Special Report: Wages and Squalor for Immigrant Workers," *New York Times*, May 21, 1999.

2. Charlie LeDuff, "Faded Glory on the Gold Coast; Glen Cove, Relic of the Gilded Age, Plans a Comeback," *New York Times*, February 10, 1999.

3. Linda Saslow, "Glen Cove Law Would Bar Gatherings of Illegal Aliens," *New York Times*, October 8, 1989.

4. Alvin E. Bessent and Stuart Vincent, "Ban Aimed at Aliens Criticized," *Newsday*, February 28, 1990.

5. Saslow, "Glen Cove"; Bessent and Vincent, "Ban Aimed at Aliens."

6. Ibid.

7. Ibid.

8. Bessent and Vincent, "Ban Aimed at Aliens."

9. Alison Mitchell, "Wary Recruits: Immigrants Vie for Day Jobs," *New York Times*, May 26, 1992.

10. Seth Mydans, "Los Angeles Project Aids Illegal Aliens, in Challenge to U.S.," *New York Times*, October 26, 1989.

11. Letta Taylor, "Melting Pot Rage: On LI, Simmering Anger over Undocumented Hispanics," *Newsday*, September 17, 1993.

12. Doreen Carvajal, "Out of Sight, Out of Mind, but Not Out of Work, Town Finds Space for Welcome Mat, Postage-Stamp Size, for Immigrant Laborers," *New York Times,* July 8, 1995.

13. Ibid.

14. Deborah Sontag, "Porous Deportation System Gives Criminals Little to Fear," *New York Times,* September 13, 1994.

15. Ibid.

16. Sandra Sanchez, "Heat Being Turned Up on Illegal Immigrants; Some Believe Politics Behind Increased Raids," *USA Today*, September 29, 1995.

17. Celia W. Dugger, "Raid and Release; A Special Report: A Tattered Crackdown on Illegal Workers," *New York Times*, June 3, 1996.

18. Kitty Calavita, *Inside the State: the Bracero Program, Immigration, and the I.N.S, After the Law* (New York: Routledge, 1992), p. 54; Austin T. Fragomen Jr., "The Illegal Immigration Reform and Immigrant Responsibility Act of 1996: An Overview," *International Migration Review* 31, no. 2 (Summer 1997): p. 438.

19. United States Immigration and Customs Enforcement, "Delegation of Immigration Authority Section 287(g): Immigration and Nationality Act," August 18, 2008, http://www.ice.gov/partners/287g/Section287_g.htm.

20. David Johnston, "Government Is Quickly Using Power of New Immigration Law," *New York Times*, October 22, 1996.

21. Jerry Gray, "Republicans Weaken House Bill on Combating Terrorism," *New York Times*, August 3, 1996.

22. Lena Williams, "A Law Aimed at Terrorists Hits Legal Immigrants," *New York Times*, July 17, 1996.

23. Patrick J. McDonnell, "Despite Legal Snags, Prop. 187 Reverberates," *Los Angeles Times*, November 8, 1995, p. A1.

24. Terry Sherwood, "A Search for Community: Then One Day, Suddenly, You Care," Viewpoints, *Newsday*, November 8, 1999, p. A27.

25. Ibid.

26. Vivian S. Toy, "Border Warriors," *New York Times*, October 22, 2000.

27. Paul Vitello, "Commentary: On One Island, Two Americas," *Newsday*, April 25, 2001.

28. John Moreno Gonzales, "Groups Rally for Immigrants, Protesters Denounce Weekend Meeting," *Newsday*, August 4, 2001.

29. Victor Chen, "Hard Road for Immigrant Workers, Protesters Blast Hiring on the Streets," *Newsday*, July 25, 1999.

30. Ibid.

31. Victor Chen, "Farmingville Faces Off over Immigrant Workers; Group Leads Laborers in Counter Protest Against Residents," *Newsday*, August 22, 1999.

32. Emi Endo, "Brookhaven OKs Rental Law, Critics Claim Move Is Discriminatory," *Newsday*, December 8, 1999.

33. Ibid.

34. Paul Vitello, "Melting Pot at Boiling Point," *Newsday*, October 24, 1999, p. A4.

35. Ibid.

36. Ibid.

37. Michael Cooper, "Laborers Wanted, but Not Living Next Door," *New York Times*, November 28, 1999.

38. Ibid.

39. Endo, "Brookhaven OKs Rental Law."

40. Ibid.

41. Frank Eltman, "Long Island Community Unlikely Flashpoint for Illegal Immigration Debate," *Associated Press*, August 6, 2005.

42. Juan Gonzalez, "Vote Hints of Suburban Race Issue," *New York Daily News*, April 19, 2001.

43. Elissa Gootman, "Second Man Gets 25-Year Term for Beating Mexican Laborers," *New York Times*, January 10, 2002.

44. Ibid.

45. Andrew Smith, "Victim Takes Stand; Day Laborer Tells of September Beating," *Newsday*, August 4, 2001, p. A3.

46. Smith, "Victim Takes Stand."

47. Bruce Lambert, "Next Door to Bias Crime Scene, House Is Firebombed," *New York Times*, July 8, 2003, p. B5.

48. "Second Teen Pleads Guilty to Firebombing of Hispanic Family's Home," *Associated Press*, November 24, 2003.

49. Bruce Lambert, "Advocates for Immigrants Say Suffolk Officials Foster Bias," *New York Times*, August 2, 2003, p. B5; Frank Eltman, "Arrests in Firebombing; Charges Allege 'Hate Crime,'" *Associated Press*, July 31, 2003.

50. Lambert, "Advocates for Immigrants."

51. Al Baker, "After Remarks on Migrants, An Apology," *New York Times*, August 31, 2001.

52. Lambert, "Advocates for Immigrants."

53. "Steve Levy for Suffolk County Executive," Editorial, *New York Times*, October 30, 2003.

54. Steve Levy, "A Vision for Suffolk's Future," Suffolk County Executive Steve Levy's Inaugural Address, Suffolk Community College, Selden, New York, January 1, 2004.

NOTES TO CHAPTER 17

1. Phone interview with Ellen Kelly, director of the Freeport Community Development Agency, August 11, 2008.

2. Ibid.

3. James T. Madore, "Support for Levy Worker Bill," *Newsday*, August 7, 2006.

NOTES TO CHAPTER 18

1. U.S. Government, *Human Rights Report: El Salvador, 2004*, Bureau of Democracy, Human Rights and Labor, February 28, 2005.

2. Ginger Thompson, "Gunmen Kill 28 on Bus in Honduras; Street Gangs Blamed," *New York Times*, December 25, 2004; Mary Jordan, "Central America's Gang Crisis," *Washington Post*, September 17, 2004.

3. U.S. Overseas Security Advisory Council, "El Salvador 2008 Crime and Safety Report," March 17, 2008, https://www.osac.gov/Reports/report.cfm?contentID=79615.

4. Jordan, "Central America's Gang Crisis."

5. U.S. Government, *El Salvador, 2004.*

6. U.S. Department of State, "Country Reports on Human Rights Practices: El Salvador, 2007," Bureau of Democracy, Human Rights, and Labor, March 11, 2008, http://www.state.gov/g/drl/rls/hrrpt/2007/100639.htm.

7. U.S. Government, *El Salvador, 2004.*

8. "Autoridades Hondureñas temen alianza de pandilleros y terroristas," *Agence France-Presse*, November 11, 2005; "Maras en Centroamérica: De las guerras civiles a la ultraviolencia callejera," *Agence France-Presse*, March 30, 2005.

9. "Maras en Centroamérica."

10. Intelligence Research Ltd., "Centroamerica: Ofensiva anticrimen no frena creciente violencia," *Informe latinoamericano*, December 13, 2005.

11. "Honduras: Ministro admite no existe lazo pandillas–al Qaeda," *ANSA noticiero en español*, October 7, 2004.

12. Traci Carl, "U.S., Central American Law Enforcement Unites Against Gangs; U.S. Worry Gangs Will Aid Al-Qaida," *Associated Press*, February 18, 2005.

13. Shelly Feuer Domash, "Leaders from Afar Bolstering a Gang," *New York Times*, Long Island Weekly Desk, November 7, 2004, p. 2.

14. Ibid.

15. Patrick O'Gilfoil Healy, "A Gang Sweep with a Difference," *New York Times*, Long Island Weekly Desk, March 27, 2005, p. 1.

16. John Moreno Gonzales, "Activist Fights to Stay in U.S., Tries to Reform Gang Members," *Newsday*, December 1, 2003, p. A7.

17. Ibid.

18. Ibid.

19. Ibid.

20. United States Department of Justice, "Prepared Remarks of Attorney General Alberto Gonzales," Hoover Institution Board of Overseers Conference, February 28, 2005.

21. United States Immigration and Customs Enforcement, "Operation Community Shield: Targeting Violent Transnational Street Gangs," October 1, 2008, http://www.ice.gov/pi/news/factsheets/opshieldfactsheet.htm.

22. Ibid.

23. Healy, "A Gang Sweep."

24. ICE, "Operation Community Shield."

25. Healy, "A Gang Sweep."

26. Nina Bernstein, "Officials Protest Antigang Raids Focused on Immigrants," *New York Times*, October 2, 2007, p. B3.

27. Ibid.

28. Nina Bernstein, "Citizens Caught Up in Immigration Raid," *New York Times*, October 4, 2007, p. B5.

29. Ibid.

30. Nina Bernstein, "Immigrant Workers Caught in a Net Case for Gangs," *New York Times*, November 25, 2007.

31. Ibid.

32. Ibid.

33. Nina Bernstein, "Raids Were a Shambles, Nassau Complains to U.S.," *New York Times*, October 3, 2007.

34. Ibid.

35. Bernstein, "Immigrant Workers Caught."

36. Paul Vitello, "Few Answers About Nooses, but Much Talk of Jim Crow," *New York Times*, October 21, 2007, p. 31.

37. Keith Herbert, "Hempstead Chief's Tough First Year," *Newsday*, April 14, 2008, p. A6.

38. Vitello, "Few Answers."

39. Interview with James Russo and Joseph Wing, Hempstead Village Police Department, July 17, 2008.

40. Bernstein, "Officials Protest Antigang Raids."

41. Ibid.

42. Bernstein, "Immigrant Workers Caught."

NOTES TO CHAPTER 19

1. Lauren Terrazzano, "Who's Guarding the Children? Staff at Nassau Juvenile Center Overworked, Undertrained," *Newsday*, December 31, 2000.

2. "Professor Admits Helping Prisoners Escape Because He Loved Inmate," Associated Press, June 1, 1992.

3. Lauren Terrazzano, "A System Overload, Nassau's Juvenile Detention Center Fails State Standards," *Newsday*, August 31, 2000.

4. Ibid.

5. Lauren Terrazano, "Second Ex-Guard Pleads Guilty, Faces Up to 7 Years in Jail for Shakedown of Teen's Parents," *Newsday*, May 31, 2002; Lauren Terrazzano, "Parents Allege Shakedown, Say Guards at Detention Center Took Money to 'Protect' Their Son," *Newsday*, May 2, 2000.

6. "A Secure Place," *New York Times*, September 10, 2006.

7. Howard N. Snyder and Melissa Sickmund, *Juvenile Offenders and Victims: 2006 National Report*, National Center for Juvenile Justice, March 2006, pp. 168, 200.

8. Ibid., p. 235.

9. Ibid., p. 201.

NOTES TO CHAPTER 20

1. Howard N. Snyder and Melissa Sickmund, *Juvenile Offenders and Victims: 2006 National Report,* National Center for Juvenile Justice, March 2006, p. 127.

2. David Zucchino, "Today's Violent Crime Is Old Story with a Twist: Mayhem Seems to Abound; Statistics Paint a Less Dire Picture," *Philadelphia Inquirer*, October 30, 1994.

3. Police Athletic League of New York City, "History," http://www.palnyc.org/about_us_history.asp.

4. Thomas E. Feucht and Edwin Zedlewski, "The 40th Anniversary of the Crime Report," *National Institute of Justice Journal*, No. 257, June 2007.

5. The President's Commission on Law Enforcement and Administration of Justice, *The Challenge of Crime in a Free Society* (Washington, DC: Government Printing Office, 1967), p. 50.

6. Ibid.

7. Ibid., p. 52.

8. Ibid., p. 67.

9. Ibid.

10. Ibid., p. 6.

11. Ibid., p. 57.

12. Ibid., p. 58.

13. Ibid., p. 78.

14. Ibid., p. viii.

15. Ibid., p. 85.

16. Ibid., p. 86.

17. Office of Juvenile Justice and Delinquency Prevention, "Juvenile Justice and Delinquency Prevention Act of 1974."

18. Ibid.

19. Ibid.

20. Fox Butterfield, *All God's Children: The Bosket Family and the American Tradition of Violence* (New York: Alfred A. Knopf, 1995).

21. Robert Martinson, "What Works? Questions and Answers About Prison Reform," *Public Interest*, 1974; Jerome Miller, "Criminology: Is Rehabilitation a Waste of Time?" *Washington Post*, April 23, 1989, Outlook; Jeffrey A. Butts and Daniel P. Mears, "Reviving Juvenile Justice in a Get-Tough Era," *Youth & Society* (2001): p. 181.

22. "The Crime Wave," *Time*, June 30, 1975, http://www.time.com/time/magazine/article/0,9171,917566-3,00.html.

23. Ibid.

24. Gerald Ford, "Special Message to the Congress on Crime," June 19, 1975.

25. Butterfield, *All God's Children*, p. 222.

26. Ruth Peterson, "Youthful Offender Designations and Sentencing in New York Criminal Courts," *Social Problems* 35, no. 2 (April 1988): pp. 111–130.

27. Butterfield, *All God's Children*.

28. Beth Bjerregaard, "Antigang Legislation and Its Potential Impact: The Promises and the Pitfalls," *Criminal Justice Policy Review* (2003): p. 173.

29. Andrew Stein (president of the New York City Council), "Wilding Is a Crime, Except in Law," *New York Times*, Editorial Desk, January 13, 1990; "Four Injured in Wilding Attacks," United Press International, May 25, 1989; Russell W. Baker, "Park Attack Sets New York on Edge," *Christian Science Monitor*, May 5, 1989.

30. Isabel Wilkerson, "After 2 Weeks of Mayhem, the Nation Is Asking Why," *New York Times*, December 14, 1993.

31. Ibid.

32. Michael Marriott, "Ideas and Trends: On Meaner Streets, the Violent Are More So," *New York Times*, September 13, 1992.

33. Richard E. Behrman, Carol S. Stevenson, Carol S. Larson, Lucy S. Carter, Deanna S. Gomby, and Donna L. Terman, "The Juvenile Court: Analysis and Recommendations," *Future of Children* 6, no. 3 (1996): p. 9.

34. Ibid.

35. Zucchino, "Today's Violent Crime."

36. Office of Juvenile Justice and Delinquency Prevention, *Statistical Briefing Book*, December 13, 2007.

37. Zucchino, "Today's Violent Crime."

38. Ibid.

39. Ibid.

40. James C. Frier, Deputy Assistant Director FBI, "Testimony Before the Subcommittee on Juvenile Justice," February 9, 1994.

41. Ibid.

42. David Johnston and Steven A. Holmes, "Experts Doubt Effectiveness of Crime Bill," *New York Times*, September 14, 1994, p. A16.

43. Ibid.; Fox Butterfield, "Most Efforts to Stop Crime Fall Far Short, Study Finds," *New York Times,* April 16, 1997.

44. U.S. Department of Justice, *Violent Crime Control and Law Enforcement Act of 1994* (fact sheet).

45. Ibid.

46. Johnston and Holmes, "Experts Doubt Effectiveness."

47. Department of Justice, *Violent Crime Control.*

48. Johnston and Holmes, "Experts Doubt Effectiveness."

49. Ian Fisher, "The 1994 Campaign: The Crime Issue; Cuomo Unveils His Crime Plan: Longer Terms and Treatment," *New York Times*, October 13, 1994.

50. Joseph B. Treaster, "Cuomo Seeks Sterner Laws for Juveniles," *New York Times*, June 21, 1994.

51. Fisher, "The 1994 Campaign."

52. Ibid.

53. Jennifer Warren, *One in a Hundred: Behind Bars in America 2008*, Pew Center on the States, February 2008.

54. "President Clinton's Message to Congress on the State of the Union," *New York Times*, February 5, 1997, p. A20.

55. Janet Reno, "Testimony of Janet Reno Attorney General Department of Justice," U.S. House of Representatives, Subcommittees on Crime and on Early Childhood, Youth and Families, February 26, 1997.

56. Ibid.

57. Ibid.

58. Ibid.

59. "Transcript of Remarks by President Clinton on Juvenile Justice," *Facts on File*, February 19, 1997.

60. Warren Richey, "New Approaches to Curbing Teen Crime," *Christian Science Monitor*, June 17, 1997.

61. Jerry Gray, "House Passes Bill to Combat Juvenile Crime," *New York Times*, May 9, 1997.

62. Patrick Griffin, "National Overviews," *State Juvenile Justice Profiles*, National Center for Juvenile Justice, 2008.

63. Snyder and Sickmund, *Juvenile Offenders*, p. 236.

64. Butts and Mears, "Reviving Juvenile Justice," p. 177.

65. Charles Puzzanchera, Anne L. Stahl, Nancy Tierney, and Howard N. Snyder, *Juvenile Court Statistics 2000*, National Center for Juvenile Justice, December 2004, p. 26.

66. Snyder and Sickmund, *Juvenile Offenders*, p. 199.

67. M. Sickmund, T. J. Sladky, W. Kang, and C. Puzzanchera, "Easy Access to the Census of Juveniles in Residential Placement," 2008, http://ojjdp.ncjrs.gov/ojstatbb/ezacjrp.

68. Snyder and Sickmund, *Juvenile Offenders*, p. 223.

69. J. Fagan, E. Slaughter, and E. Hartstone, "Blind Justice? The Impact of Race on the Juvenile Justice Process," *Crime and Delinquency* 33, no. 2 (April 1987); Barry Krisberg and James F. Austin, *Reinventing Juvenile Justice* (Newbury Park, CA: Sage Publications, 1993), pp. 120–134; George S. Bridges and Sara Steen, "Racial Disparities in Official Assessments of Juvenile Offenders: Attributional Stereotypes as Mediating Mechanisms," *American Sociological Review* 63, no. 4 (August 1998): pp. 554–570; Amanda Burgess-Proctor, Kendal Holtrup, and Francisco A. Villarruel, "Youth Transferred to Adult Court: Racial Disparities," Campaign for Youth Justice, http://campaign4youthjustice.org/Downloads/KeyResearch/MoreKeyResearch/AdultificationPolicyBriefVol2.pdf.

70. Bridges and Steen, "Racial Disparities."

71. Sickmund et al., "Easy Access."

72. Snyder and Sickmund, *Juvenile Offenders*, p. 65.

73. Ibid., pp. 132, 127.

74. Ibid., p. 82.

75. Steven B. Levitt, "Understanding Why Crime Fell in the 1990s: Four Factors That Explain the Decline and Six That Do Not," *Journal of Economic Perspectives* 18, no. 1 (2004): p. 23.

76. Fox Butterfield, "States Revamping Laws on Juveniles as Felonies Soar," *New York Times*, May 12, 1996.

77. Jeffrey Fagan, "The Comparative Advantage of Juvenile Versus Criminal Court Sanctions on Recidivism Among Adolescent Felony Offenders," *Law & Policy* 18, nos. 1–2 (1996): pp. 77–114.

78. Centers for Disease Control, "Effects on Violence of Laws and Policies Facilitating the Transfer of Youth from the Juvenile to the Adult Justice System: A Report

on Recommendations of the Task Force on Community Preventive Services," November 20, 2007, http://www.cdc.gov/mmwr/preview/mmwrhtml/rr5609a1.htm.

79. Bjerregaard, "Antigang Legislation," p. 178.

80. Ibid.; Malcolm Klein, *The American Street Gang: Its Nature, Prevalence, and Control* (New York: Oxford University Press, 1995).

81. Institute for Intergovernmental Research, "Frequently Asked Questions Regarding Gangs," http://www.iir.com/nygc/faq.htm; A. Egley Jr., J. C. Howell, and A. K. Major, *National Youth Gang Survey: 1999–2001* (Washington, DC: U.S. Department of Justice, Office of Juvenile Justice and Delinquency Prevention, 2006).

82. Meredith Wiley, William Christeson, and Sanford Newman, *Caught in the Crossfire: Arresting Long Island Gang Violence by Investing in Kids*, Fight Crime: Invest in Kids, October 21, 2004, http://www.fightcrime.org/ny/nygangreport.pdf, p. 4.

83. Ibid., p. 12.

84. Lauren Terrazzano, "Crackdown on Kids: Juveniles Receiving Longer Time for Less Serious Crimes," *Newsday*, November 30, 2000.

85. Ibid.

86. Wiley et al., *Caught in the Crossfire*, p. 11.

87. Ibid.

NOTES TO CHAPTER 21

1. Vivian Toy, "Stuck in Last Place," *New York Times*, Long Island Weekly Desk, May 4, 2003, p. 1.

NOTES TO CHAPTER 22

1. Carrie Melago, "Prevention Gets Push as Gang Violence Cure," *New York Daily News*, October 22, 2004.

2. State of New York Commission of Investigation, *Combating Gang Activity in New York*, May 2006, p. 9, http://www.sic.state.ny.us/Docs/Public%20Reports/pdf/gangs.PDF.

3. Ibid., p. 16.

4. Ibid.

5. Ibid., p. 31.

6. Ibid., p. 33.

7. Ibid., pp. 65–66.

8. Ibid.

9. John Moreno Gonzales, "A Call for Tougher Gang Laws: State Report Favors Increasing Penalties for the Crimes, but Some Say Rehabilitation Programs Are Ignored," *Newsday*, May 31, 2006.

10. Marie Simonetti Rosen, *A Gathering Storm: Violent Crime in America*, Police Executive Research Forum, October 2006, p. 3; Jeffrey Butts and Howard N. Snyder, *Too Soon to Tell: Deciphering Recent Trends in Youth Violence*, Chapin Hall Center for Children, University of Chicago, November 2006.

11. Rosen, *Gathering Storm*, pp. ii, 6.

12. Ibid., p. ii.

13. Butts and Snyder, *Too Soon to Tell*, p. 2.

14. Rosen, *Gathering Storm*, p. 9.

15. Sarah More McCann, "Program Helps Arizona Prisoners Get Ready for Real Life," *Christian Science Monitor*, August 1, 2008.

16. Sarah Hammond, *Adults or Kids?* National Conference of State Legislatures, April 2008.

17. Ibid.

18. Reentry Policy Council, "Spotlight Announcement: Second Chance Act Slated to Receive $45 Million in House Bill, $20 Million in Senate Bill," June 25, 2008, http://reentrypolicy.org/announcements/sca_approps.

NOTES TO CHAPTER 24

1. "Hempstead High School Burns," *New York Times*, April 6, 1919.

2. "Hempstead School Destroyed by Fire," *New York Times*, July 25, 1970.

3. "Golden Years at Hempstead High," *Life*, June 23, 1958.

4. "Racially Torn Hempstead High to Reopen with Talks on Strife," *New York Times*, March 9, 1970.

5. Ibid.

6. Ibid.

7. "Nine L.I. Students Suspended," *New York Times*, March 9, 1970.

8. "Hempstead School Destroyed."

9. Ibid.; Linda Greenhouse, "Suburban Schools Worry Over Funds but Plan New Programs," *New York Times*, September 6, 1970.

10. Suzanne Bilello, "A Poor Report Card; Anger, Doubts over Hempstead Schools," *Newsday*, August 20, 1989.

11. Ibid.

12. Ibid.

13. Ibid.

14. Ibid.

15. Ibid.

16. Dele Olojede and Suzanne Bilello, "For Hempstead's Teachers and Students, a Daily Lesson in Demoralization," *Newsday*, June 16, 1991.

17. Ibid.

18. Ibid.

19. Ibid.

20. F. Romall Smalls, "New Schools Chief Shakes Up Mt. Vernon," *New York Times*, December 20, 1998.

21. New York State Education Department, School Report Cards.

22. Alan Feuer, "Report Cites Flaws in a Hempstead School District," *New York Times*, April 13, 2005.

23. Ibid.

24. Paul Vitello, "Anxiety and Rage in Wake of Gangs," *Newsday*, November 17, 2004, p. A2.

25. Interview with Daniel, Roosevelt Fields Mall, February 1, 2008; Jennifer Blecher, "Hempstead Stabbing, Grief Tinged with Anger, Loved Ones Gather to Remember Boy, 17, as Activists Express Outrage over Scourge of Gang Violence," *Newsday*, November 21, 2004, p. A14.

26. Interview with Daniel, 2008; Nedra Rhone and Keiko Morris, "Hempstead Student's Slaying: Charged with Assault, Police Arrest Teen, a Former Gang Member, in Alleged Role in Killing but Doubt He Used Murder Weapon," *Newsday*, November 18, 2004.

27. Patrick Healy and Michelle O'Donnell, "Seventeen-Year-Old Is Stabbed to Death While Leaving L.I. School," *New York Times*, November 17, 2004, p. 6.

28. Rhone and Morris, "Hempstead Student's Slaying."

29. Ibid.

30. Vitello, "Anxiety and Rage."

31. Theresa Vargas and Jennifer Sinco Kelleher, "My Son, My Son," *Newsday*, November 17, 2004, p. A3.

32. Healy and O'Donnell, "Seventeen-Year-Old Is Stabbed."

33. Chief James Russo, "Gangs on Long Island," *New York Times*, Editorial Desk, November 24, 2004, p. 22.

34. Nassau County Government, "Suozzi Appoints Gang Czar: 30-Year Police Department Veteran to Coordinate Nassau County's Anti-gang Initiatives," Press Release, November 22, 2004, http://www.nassaucountyny.gov/agencies/County Executive/newsrelease/2004/11–22–2004.html.

35. Ibid.; Diane Ketcham, "About Long Island: The Nassau Mounties," *New York Times*, February 26, 1989.

36. Nassau County Government, "Suozzi Appoints Gang Czar."

37. Ibid.; Nassau County, "Nassau County to Award $500,000 to Local Youth Violence and Gang Prevention/Intervention Agencies," May 10, 2004, http://www.nassau countyny.gov/agencies/CountyExecutive/NewsRelease/2004/05–10–2004.html.

38. Nassau County Government, "Suozzi Appoints Gang Czar."

39. "Fighting Gangs, Fighting Fear," *New York Times*, Long Island Weekly Desk, November 28, 2004, p. 25.

40. Richard Weir, "Gang Up on Thugs! Cop Union: Unit Needs More Officers," *New York Daily News*, September 7, 2005.

41. Rhone and Morris, "Hempstead Student's Slaying"; Theresa Vargas, "Making School Safe for Students, Education Officials in Wyandanch, Hempstead, Long Beach Seek Answers After Violent Incidents," *Newsday*, December 12, 2004, p. A9; Feuer, "Report Cites Flaws."

42. Feuer, "Report Cites Flaws"; New York State Education Department, "Report on State Education Department Team Visit: Hempstead Union Free School District," Office of Elementary, Middle, Secondary and Continuing Education, December 2004.

43. Ibid.

44. "Crunch Time in Hempstead," *New York Times*, July 17, 2005.

45. New York State, "Hevesi Audit Finds Nearly $5.1 Million in Questionable, Wasteful Expenses at Hempstead School District," Office of the New York State Comptroller Alan G. Hevesi, September 19, 2005, http://www.osc.state.ny.us/press/releases/sept05/091905.htm.

46. Vivian S. Toy, "In Brief: Hempstead Removes School Board Member," *New York Times*, August 17, 2003.

47. New York State, "Hevesi Audit."

48. New York State, "Audit: State Department of Education Mismanaging School Violence Data Collection, Some Schools Underreporting Violent Incidents," Report 2005-S-38, Office of the New York State Comptroller Alan G. Hevesi, May 22, 2006.

49. New York State Education Department, "Report on State Education Department Team Visit"; Elissa Gootman, "Fewer Schools Cited for Poor Performance," *New York Times*, January 5, 2005.

NOTES TO CHAPTER 25

1. David E. Rosenbaum, "The 2000 Campaign: The Education Policies, Bush and Gore Stake Claims to Federal Role in Education," *New York Times*, August 30, 2000.

2. Anemona Hartocollis, "Racial Gap in Test Scores Found Across New York," *New York Times,* March 28, 2002.

3. The Nation's Report Card, "Long-Term Trend," National Center for Education Statistics, http://nces.ed.gov/nationsreportcard/.

4. Richard Fry and Felisa Gonzales, *One-in-Five and Growing Fast: A Profile of Hispanic Public School Students*, Pew Hispanic Center, August 26, 2008.

5. Richard Fry, *Hispanic Youth Dropping Out of U.S. Schools: Measuring the Challenge*, Pew Hispanic Center, June 12, 2003, p. iii.

6. Ibid., p. 3.

7. Richard Fry, *The Changing Racial and Ethnic Composition of U.S. Public Schools*, Pew Hispanic Center, August 30, 2007.

8. Ibid.

9. Richard Fry, *The Role of Schools in the English Language Learner Achievement Gap*, Pew Hispanic Center, June 26, 2008.

10. Amy Stuart Wells, Jennifer Jellison Holme, Anita Tijerina Revilla, and Awo Korantemaa Atanda, "How Society Failed School Desegregation Policy: Looking Past the Schools to Understand Them," *Review of Research in Education* 28 (2004): pp. 47–99.

11. James S. Coleman, *Equality of Educational Opportunity*, United States Department of Education, 1966; Wells et al., "How Society Failed."

12. Wells et al., "How Society Failed."

13. Ibid.; Juan Williams, "Nine Pioneers Showed Why School Integration Matters," *Washington Post*, September 25, 2007.

14. Wells et al., "How Society Failed"; Robert L. Crain and Rita E. Mahard, "The Effect of Research Methodology on Desegregation-Achievement Studies: A Meta Analysis," *American Journal of Sociology* 88, no. 5 (March 1983): pp. 839–854; Stephen J. Caldas and Carl Bankston III, "The Inequality of Separation: Racial Composition of Schools and Academic Achievement," *Education Administration Quarterly* 34, no. 4 (October 1998): pp. 533–557.

15. Wells et al., "How Society Failed," p. 69.

16. Peter Applebome, "Keeping Tabs on Jim Crow, John Hope Franklin," *New York Times*, April 23, 1995, and cited in Wells et al., "How Society Failed," p. 85.

17. Crain and Mahard, "The Effect of Research."

18. Wells et al., "How Society Failed," p. 56.

19. Jonathan Kozol, "Why I Am Fasting: An Explanation to My Friends," *Huffington Post,* September 10, 2007, http://huffingtonpost.com; Susan Snyder, "'No Child Left Behind' Law Bumps into Hard Reality: The Act Says Troubled Schools Can Let Students Transfer to Better Districts; It Doesn't Make Those Districts Say Yes," *Philadelphia Inquirer*, October 12, 2003.

20. Susan Hartigan, *Racism and the Opportunity Divide on Long Island*, Institute on Race and Poverty, University of Minnesota Law School, 2002.

21. New York State Education Department, "Statistics for Public School Districts, June 2002 Report to the Governor and the Legislature," Table 1.

22. New York State Education Department, "Statistics for Public School Districts," Table 2.

23. New York State Education Department, "Statistics for Public School Districts," Table 1.

24. Hartigan, *Racism*, p. 13.

25. New York State Education Department tables.

26. Jonathan Kozol, *The Shame of the Nation: The Restoration of Apartheid Schooling in America* (New York: Crown, 2005), pp. 150–160.

27. Faiza Akhtar, "Mired in Roosevelt, Albany Looks to Avoid Other School Takeovers," *New York Times*, Long Island Weekly Desk, December 25, 2005, p. 1; Patrick Healy, "L.I. Schools Show Gains Since Takeover by State, but Fears Persist," *New York Times*, Metro, May 3, 2004, p. 1.

28. Hartigan, *Racism*, p. 14

29. Ibid.

30. Hartigan, *Racism*; Michael Gormley, "State May Dissolve Long-Troubled Roosevelt School District on Long Island," Associated Press, November 9, 2001.

31. New York State Education Department, "Statistics for Public School Districts," Table 2.

32. New York State Education Department, "Statistics for Public School Districts," Table 1.

33. "Letters," *Newsday*, November 16, 2001.

34. Thomas Caramore, Keith Grubman, and Heidi Gordon, "Letters," *Newsday*, January 3, 2002.

35. Grubman, "Letters."

36. Ibid.

37. Hartigan, *Racism*, p. 15.

38. Linda Saslow, "Other School Districts Offered State Intervention," *New York Times*, Long Island Weekly Desk, February 10, 2008, p. 2.

39. Healy, "L.I. Schools."

40. Ibid.

41. Wells et al., "How Society Failed," p. 57.

42. Diana Jean Schemo, "Few Exercise Right to Leave Failing Schools," *New York Times*, August 28, 2002.

43. Kozol, "Why I Am Fasting."

44. Campbell Robertson, "Hempstead Is Flirting with Roosevelt's Fate," *New York Times*, December 12, 2004.

45. New York State Education Department, "Statistics for Public School Districts, July 2005 Report to the Governor and the Legislature," Table 1 and Table 2.

46. Institute for Student Achievement, http://studentachievement.org.

47. Michael Dobbs, "Poor Schools Sue for Funding: Higher Standards Are Basis for Seeking 'Educational Adequacy,'" *Washington Post*, June 7, 2004, p. A13.

48. Ford Fessenden, "This Is Not Your 1983 Governor's School Aid Plan," *New York Times*, Long Island Weekly Desk, February 25, 2007.

49. Nancy Swett, "Wealthy Schools Shun Fair-Aid Meet," *New York Times*, Long Island Weekly Desk, November 23, 2003, p. 2.

50. Fessenden, "This Is Not Your 1983."

51. Ibid.

52. David McKay Wilson, "Parents Demand Better Schools," *Journal News*, January 13, 2001; Martin C. Evans, "State Funds Sought for Schools Parity," *Newsday*, June 17, 1997, p. A23.

53. Raymond Hernandez, "Suit Says Minority Students Receive an Inferior Education," *Newsday*, December 4, 1998.

54. Ibid.

55. Jennifer Sinco Kelleher, "Tackling the Principal Issue: In Troubled Hempstead District, High School Stand Out," *Newsday*, May 16, 2008.

56. Sophia Chang, "Shaken, School Copes with Loss; Some Worry About Security at Hempstead High After Stabbing," *Newsday*, January 23, 2008.

57. John Hildebrand, "Hempstead School Chief Quits, Superintendent of Troubled District Tells Board Members He Will Step Down, Ending Long Tenure Full of Turmoil," *Newsday*, March 22, 2008, p. A10; Laura Rivera, "School's Lack of Security: State Report Weeks Before Fatal Stabbing at Hempstead High Said the School Needs 50% More Guards," *Newsday*, February 8, 2008.

58. Ibid.

59. Linda Saslow, "Graduation Rates Rise, and Bar Is Raised," *New York Times*, August 17, 2008.

60. Collin Nash, "Calling for Change in Hempstead," *Newsday*, February 24, 2008.

61. Ibid.

62. "Senseless, Sad, Sobering; Murder of Michael Alguera Shows the Side of Nassau Most Want to Ignore," *Newsday*, January 24, 2008.

NOTES TO THE EPILOGUE

1. Dave Marcus, "LI Hate Killing: A Good Brother, Friend," *Newsday*, November 11, 2008.

2. Henrick Karoliszyn and Mike Jaccarino, "Sue 'Lynch Mob' Kin?" *New York Daily News*, November 12, 2008.

3. Cara Buckley, "Teenagers' Violent 'Sport' Led to Killing on Long Island, Officials Say," *New York Times*, November 21, 2008; Selim Algar, Kieran Crowley, and Lukas I. Alpert, "Hate Runs Wild," *New York Post*, November 13, 2008.

4. Buckley, "Teenagers' Violent 'Sport.'"

5. Andrew Strickler, "LI Hate Killing: 'Determined' to Cause Harm," *Newsday*, November 11, 2008.

6. Reid J. Epstein, "LI Hate Killing Reaction: 'Outrage' as Pols Ponder What's Behind the Killing," *Newsday*, November 11, 2008.

7. Dave Marcus and Carl MacGowan, "Ecuadorean Leaders Call for Murder Charges," *Newsday*, November 14, 2008.

8. Anne Barnard, "Youth Charged with More Attacks on Latinos," *New York Times*, January 28, 2009.

9. Laura Rivera, "LI Killing Makes International News Story," *Newsday*, November 14, 2008.

10. *Associated Press* and Zachary Dowdy, "Gang Roundup Nabs 37 in Area," *Newsday*, October 2, 2008.

11. U.S. Government Accountability Office, "Plan Colombia: Drug Reduction Goals Were Not Fully Met, but Security Has Improved; U.S. Agencies Need More Detailed Plans for Reducing Assistance," GAO-09-71, October 6, 2008, http://www.gao.gov/products/GAO-09-71.

12. Matthew Quirk, "How to Grow a Gang," *Atlantic*, May 2008.

13. Jenifer Warren, *One in 100: Behind Bars in America 2008*, Pew Center on the States, February 2008; King's College London, "World Prison Brief: Central America," http://www.kcl.ac.uk/depsta/law/research/icps/worldbrief/?search=centrlam&x=Central%20America.

14. Timothy Hughes and Doris James Wilson, *Reentry Trends in the United States*, U.S. Department of Justice Bureau of Justice Statistics, October 25, 2002.

15. Reentry Policy Council, "Second Chance Act," Justice Center, The Council of State Governments, http://reentrypolicy.org/government_affairs/second_chance_act.

16. Hughes and Wilson, *Reentry Trends*.

17. Warren, *One in 100*.

18. Ibid.

19. New York State Office of Children and Family Services, "Empty Beds, Wasted Dollars: Transforming Juvenile Justice," March 2008.

20. Herbert Asbury, *Gangs of New York: An Informal History of the Underworld* (New York: Thunder's Mouth Press, 2001 [1928]), p. xv.

21. Gary Orfield and Chungmei Lee, *Historic Reversals, Accelerating Resegregation, and the Need for New Integration Strategies*, UCLA Civil Rights Project, August 2007.

22. Ibid.

23. The Education Trust, 2006 State NAEP (National Assessment of Educational Progress) Tables, http://www2.edtrust.org/edtrust/summaries2006/2006StateNAEP Tables.pdf.

24. Orfield and Lee, *Historic Reversals*.

25. Denise M. Bonilla and Reid J. Epstein, "LI Hate Killing: A Killing Renews Focus on Suffolk," *Newsday*, November 12, 2008.

26. Reid J. Epstein, "LI Hate Killing: Levy: It Wasn't Just a 1-day Story," *Newsday*, November 14, 2008.

27. Asbury, *Gangs*, p. xv.

INDEX